ANALECTA BIBLICA
INVESTIGATIONES SCIENTIFICAE IN RES BIBLICAS

—————————— 116 ——————————

CAROL KERN STOCKHAUSEN

MOSES' VEIL AND THE GLORY
OF THE NEW COVENANT

The Exegetical Substructure of II Cor. 3,1–4,6

EDITRICE PONTIFICIO ISTITUTO BIBLICO – ROMA 1989

ISBN 88-7653-116-5

EDITRICE PONTIFICIA UNIVERSITÀ GREGORIANA
EDITRICE PONTIFICIO ISTITUTO BIBLICO
Piazza della Pilotta, 35 - 00187 Roma

PREFACE

The aim of this study is a simple one: to understand as clearly and thoroughly as possible what the Apostle Paul has to say in a single selection taken from one of his letters. II Corinthians 3:1–4:6 has been an especially challenging text for this exercise. Like many other interpreters before me, I was first attracted to II Corinthians 3 by its very difficulty. The story of Moses' veiling is strange even in the context of the Hebrew scriptures and Paul's use of such a story in his emotional second letter to Corinth is startling and, to modern ears, bizarre. As a result of its oddity, II Corinthians 3 has often been considered a digression from the central issues of Paul's theological reflection and even the intrusion of essentially foreign material into a seriously disorganized argument. On the contrary, I have found the text to afford unusually rich opportunities for investigating the most central questions of Pauline theology and the most fundamental forms of Paul's own discourse. Analysis of this text has revealed an exegetical methodology in Paul's composition which provides structure for his argument and, I suspect, a principle of unity for larger sections of the often subdivided II Corinthians. I myself have begun to be able to see the Apostle himself at work behind his words and hear him speaking in spite of the centuries which separate us, and so my efforts in the course of this study have been amply rewarded. If the reader can say the same after turning the last page, my reward will be complete.

There are many people to thank upon the completion and publication of this work, and I would like to take the opportunity to do so now. First, I would like my husband, Peter, and my four sons, Matthew, Jeffrey, Adam and Benjamin, to know that without their belief in me I could do nothing and would have given up trying long ago. Second, my parents — Marion and Carl Kern and Agnes and Andrew Stockhausen — already know that without their help it would have been impossible for me to pursue graduate studies or complete this dissertation, and I am deeply grateful for the extended family they have unselfishly formed around our children. Third, I would like to thank my dissertation director, William Kurz, S.J., for allowing me to go my own way at my own pace, even when he knew a surer way or wished for a faster pace, and Robert Wild, S.J., whose attention to preliminary versions of the text significantly improved the quality of this final version. Fourth, I acknowledge the great debt I owe to all of my former teachers in the Theology Department of Marquette University, whose presence, wisdom and instruction I felt constantly with me as I completed this final assignment. Finally, Mr. Joel Williams, who has been my teaching assistant at Marquette University for the past two years, has provided invaluable assistance in revising and editing this manuscript for publication. I offer all of these individuals, as well as the administration of Marquette University, my profound gratitude for enabling me to see this project to a successful completion.

Carol Kern Stockhausen

All texts from the New Testament cited in this study are taken from the Revised Standard Version unless otherwise noted.

TABLE OF CONTENTS

INTRODUCTION

A Review of Scholarly Literature

II Corinthians

Paul's second letter to the Christians at Corinth is a work of distinction within the Pauline corpus. It is never considered to be a summary of Pauline theology as the Epistle to the Romans often is for its sublime expression of Christian thought in apostolic times. Yet II Corinthians 3-5 contain some of the most profound of Paul's theological statements.[1] The Letter to the Galatians, because it contains Paul's own report of his conversion to Christ and his early missionary activities,[2] is rightly used as a resource for our understanding of Paul the man. Yet II Corinthians 1:8-2:17, 6:1-13, 7:2-8:24[3] and 10-13 contain sometimes heart-breaking testimony to Paul's experiences and his emotional reaction to them.[4] The authenticity of II Corinthians has never been seriously

---

[1] Many examples of the depth of Paul's thought in II Corinthians may be adduced. Here are just a few for the sake of illustration. "God has qualified us to be ministers of a new covenant, not in a written code but in the Spirit ..." (3:6); "And we all, with unveiled face, beholding [or reflecting] the glory of the Lord, are being changed into his likeness ..." (3:18); "For it is the God who said, 'Let light shine out of darkness,' who has shone in our hearts to give the light of the knowledge of the glory of God in the face of Christ" (4:6); "For while we live we are always being given up to death for Jesus sake, so that the life of Jesus may be manifested in our mortal flesh." (4:11); "... though our outer nature is wasting away, our inner nature is being renewed every day." (4:16); "For we know that if the earthly tent we live in is destroyed, we have a building from God, a house not made with hands, eternal in the heavens." (5:1); "For the love of Christ controls us, because we are convinced that one has died for all; therefore, all have died." (5:14); "From now on, therefore, we regard no one from a human point of view; even though we once regarded Christ from a human point of view, we regard him thus no longer. Therefore, if any one is in Christ, he is a new creation ..." (5:16-17a); "... God was in Christ reconciling the world to himself, not counting their trespasses against them, and entrusting to us the message of reconciliation." (5:19); "For our sake he made him to be sin who knew no sin, so that in him we might become the righteousness of God." (5:21). All of these citations are from the Revised Standard Version of the New Testament.

[2] Gal. 1:12-2:14.

[3] I do not omit II Cor. 6:14-7:1 from this listing because of its questionable authenticity but because it is more properly to be considered a doctrinal, rather than a personal, section.

[4] The personal aspect of II Corinthians has been frequently stressed. Rudolf BULTMANN, citing JÜLICHER (*Einleitung in das Neue Testament*, 1931, p. 87), calls it the

questioned.[5] Colossians, Ephesians, Hebrews and the Pastoral Epistles have received an abundance of critical scrutiny on that score.

There is, however, one category in which II Corinthians heads the list. II Corinthians is unquestionably the most difficult of Paul's letters.[6] Its argumentation is frequently obscure to the modern reader,[7] its contents unfamiliar,[8] its construction apparently haphazard,[9] and its *Sitz im Leben* foggy.[10]

---

most personal of the letters of Paul in *Der Zweite Brief an die Korinther* (Göttingen: Vandenhoeck & Ruprecht, 1976) p. 21. For BULTMANN, however, interest in Paul as a man is overshadowed by his interest in Paul as an apostle. Alfred PLUMMER, in his commentary in the International Critical Commentary Series, *A Critical and Exegetical Commentary on the Second Epistle of St. Paul to the Corinthians* (Edinburgh: T. & T. Clark, 1915), had earlier stressed the autobiographical detail contained in the letter, but with a different emphasis. He says, "The items of autobiography, which are among the most precious details in the Epistle, ring true and are not at all like fiction. ... There is no letter which enables us to see so deeply into the working of the writer's mind and heart. Thankfulness, affection, anxiety, entreaty and indignation come to the surface in successive waves. ..." (p. xii). PLUMMER is more concerned with the man himself, but, as the first sentence shows, is using the versimilitude of detail in defense of the authenticity of the letter.

[5] PLUMMER, *Second Corinthians*, pp. xi-xiii. The question of unity overshadows that of authenticity in II Corinthians.

[6] All commentators on II Corinthians acknowledge this difficulty. For example, the recent popular New Testament Message commentary on II Corinthians begins with the words, "Paul's second epistle to the Corinthians is the most personal and also the most perplexing of his epistles." (Francis T. FALLON, *2 Corinthians* [Wilmington, Deleware: Michael Glazier Inc., 1980] p. 1). I would agree with Fallon on both counts. See also J.-F. COLLANGE in his *Enigmes de la Deuxième Epître de Paul aux Corinthiens* (Cambridge: At the University Press, 1972) p. 1, "La Deuxième aux Corinthiens est célèbre par ses obscurités." or the most lyrical comment of R. P. C. HANSON, "The document known as the Second Epistle of St. Paul to the Corinthians is certainly the most obscure and difficult of all his letters. ... It is full of dark illusions (*sic*) and unexplained references the key to which is utterly lost. As we read it, we sometimes feel as if we had turned on the wireless in the middle of an elaborate play: characters are making most lively speeches and events of great interest and importance are happening, but we do not know who exactly the speakers are and we are not sure what exactly is happening to them." *The Second Epistle to the Corinthians: Christ and Controversy*, New Edition (London: SCM Press Ltd., 1968), Original Edition (New York: Macmillan, 1954) p. 5.

[7] II Cor. 5:1-5 is a good example of this obscure argumentation, as is 5:14-18. The text with which this study is concerned is another classic locus of Paul's apparently slippery logic.

[8] For example, II Cor. 2:15-17, 6:14-7:1, or 5:1-5 as noted above.

[9] The difficult transitions in the letter are well marked in all the standard introductions and have been the subject of the bulk of the literature on the letter in modern times. They need not be rehearsed here. In English I refer the reader to the characteristically British understatement of C. K. BARRETT, "2 Corinthians contains a number of passages where the reader cannot fail to be struck by a measure of discontinuity or awkwardness in the text" in *A Commentary on the Second Epistle to the Corinthians* (New York: Harper & Row, Publishers, 1973) p. 11, where he lists and goes on to discuss them.

[10] It is the special concern and expertise of German scholarship on II Corinthians to better define this *Sitz im Leben*. It is the thesis of Mathias RISSI, for example, that "es

Understandably, therefore, II Corinthians has received somewhat less critical attention on the whole than many of the other letters in the Pauline corpus. The theological depth of the early chapters has remained unsounded for the most part. The line of argument followed there in Chapters 3 to 6 has not been discovered and its connection with the topical material in Chapters 1-2 and 8-13 is still blurry. The only area in which understanding of II Corinthians has significantly advanced to the present time is in the area of historical research into the social milieu of the Graeco-Roman environment into which the letter was sent. This clarification of the unclear *Sitz im Leben* of II Corinthians is due, as I have noted, to the special expertise of German scholarship.

Commentators have, of course, been somewhat fascinated with the very difficulty of the text of II Corinthians. This fascination has been manifest very recently in two ways. First, interpreters have given repeated and intense scrutiny to several isolated passages within the letter. Chapter Five, especially verses 1-10 and verses 16-21, has been one such locus.[11] Chapter Twelve, verses 1-10, has been another.[12] These specific texts

---

unmöglich ist, den Brief zu verstehen ohne den Charakter der Gegnerschaft des Apostels in Korinth zu kennen," *Studien zum zweiten Korintherbrief* (Zürich: Zwingli Verlag, 1969) p. 7. This is the premise of most German scholars presently dealing with II Corinthians, under the influence of the work of the great German historians, Walter BAUER and Adolf VON HARNACK especially. This thesis that if we could know about events in Corinth we could *better* understand II Corinthians cannot be gainsaid. Therefore, commentaries and articles appearing in German are less inclined to stress the "enigmes" of Paul's argument in 2:14-7:2 à la COLLANGE than they are to point out historical inconsistencies in Chapters 1,8-9 and 10-13 and to solve them on an historical basis.

[11] For example, in the last twenty-five years alone, the following articles have appeared focused on the problems of II Corinthians, Chapter 5. L. SABOURIN, "Note sur 2 Cor. 5,21: Le Christ fait peché," *Sci Eccl* 11 (1959) pp. 419-424; E. E. ELLIS, "II Corinthians v. 1-10 in Pauline Eschatology," *NTS* 6 (1959-1960) pp. 211-224; K. HANHART, "Paul's Hope in the Face of Death," *JBL* 88 (1969) pp. 445-457; J. W. FRASER, "Paul's Knowledge of Jesus: II Corinthians v. 16 Once More," *NTS* 17 (1971) pp. 293-313; U. BORSE, "Zur Todes- und Jenseitserwartung Pauli nach 2 Kor. 5,1-10," *Bib Leb* 13 (1972) pp. 129-138; F. HAHN, "'Siehe, jetzt ist der Tag des Heils' Neuschöpfung und Versöhnung nach 2. Korinther 5:14-6:2," *Evang Theol* 33 (1973) pp. 224-253; J. I. VINCENTINI, "'Dejense reconciliar con Dios' Lectura de 2 Corintios 5:14-21," *Revist Bib* 36 (1974) pp. 97-104; A. STÖGER, "Die Paulinische Versöhnungstheologie," *Theol Prakt Quart* 122 (1974) pp. 118-131; N. M. WATSON, "2 Cor. 5:1-10 in Recent Research," *Aus Bib Rev* 23 (1975) pp. 33-36; R. J. RAJA, "Be Reconciled," *Biblebhashyam* 1 (1975) pp. 152-157; W. LILLIE, "An Approach to II Corinthians 5:1-10," *Scot Journ Theol* 30 (1977) pp. 59-70; O. HOFIUS, "Erwägungen zur Gestalt und Herkunft des paulinischen Versöhnungsgedankens," *Zeit Theol Kirch* 77 (1980) pp. 186-199.

[12] For example, the reader may refer to P. BONNARD, "Faiblesse et puissance du Chrétien selon St. Paul," *Etud Théol Rel* 33 (1958) pp. 61-70; J. CAMBIER, "Le critère paulinien de l'apostolat en 2 Cor. 12,6s," *Biblica* 43 (1962) pp. 481-518; H. D. BETZ, "Eine Christus-Aretalogie bei Paulus (2 Kor. 12,7-10)," *Zeit Theol Kirch* 66 (1969) pp. 288-305; G. G. O'COLLINS, "Power Made Perfect in Weakness: 2 Cor. 12:9-10," *CBQ* 33 (1971)

have been paid so much attention either because their content is especially puzzling or because the theological topics which they treat are of particular interest to the interpreter himself. Questions about the meaning of death and life after death with which Paul deals in II Cor. 5:1-5 are always of vital importance in Christian reflection, as is the theological issue of Christ's reconciliation of the world to God, so unexpectedly mentioned and then as suddenly dropped in II Cor. 5:18-19. With regard to these texts, however, interpretation has frequently been reduced to a theological mining operation, with ideas being taken out of the text without regard for their form or function within II Corinthians itself. The use of scripture to provide theological material and guidance for the contemporary Christian community is of course not open to criticism. However, the insights so obtained could only be enriched by a renewed investigation into their place within Paul's thought as it is expressed more fully in the context of II Corinthians. Moreover, a critical appreciation of Paul's argument in II Corinthians as a whole and of the structure of the text could be built up if context were more fully dealt with in the investigation of particular passages.

Similarly, modern curiosity about Paul's "thorn in the flesh" has occasioned a considerable number of articles on II Cor. 12:7 during the 1950's and 1960's with solutions which sometimes discover a particular physical ailment as the referent of Paul's ambiguous phrase.[13] As interest

---

pp. 528-537; W. KERN, "Die Kirche—Gottes Kraft in menschlicher Schwäche," *Geist Leb* 50 (1977) pp. 321-326; J. ZMIJEWSKI, "Kontextbezug und Deutung von 2 Kor. 12,7a. Stilistische und strukturale Erwägungen zur Lösung eines alten Problems," *Bib Zeit* 21 (1977) pp. 265-272.

[13] There are three main solutions to the mysterious "thorn in the flesh" which have been offered in the course of interpretation of the passage: 1) that Paul refers to a physical ailment; 2) that he refers to temptations of the flesh or to a devil sent to try him and 3) that Paul means the persecution that he encountered from his opponents. Of these, number 3 is both the oldest and the most recent, as well as the most realistic. Commonly referred to John Chrysostom, the theory mentioned has recently become the dominant view. See T. Y. MULLINS, "Paul's Thorn in the Flesh," *JBL* 76 (1957) pp. 299-303; P. ANDRIESSEN, "L'impuissance de Paul en face de l'ange de Satan," *Nouv Rev Theol* 81 (1959) pp. 462-468 (a good summary as well); J. J. THIERRY, "Der Dorn im Fleische (2 Kor. xii 7-9)," *Nov Test* 5 (1962) pp. 301-310; N. CAPODICASA, "Gli avversari di Paolo e la 'spina nella carne' (2 Cor. 12,7)," *Stud Pat* 20 (1973) pp. 570-589 (*NTA* 18 [1974] p. 332 for summary); H. BINDER, "Die angebliche Krankheit des Paulus," *Theol Zeit* 32 (1976) pp. 1-13; M. L. BARRE, "Qumran and the 'Weakness' of Paul," *CBQ* 42 (1980) pp. 216-227. Among those who have defended the second theory are M. KOMASA, "Znaczenie metafory 'skolops te sarki' (2 Kor. 12,7)," *Ruch Bib Lit* 11 (1958) pp. 211-230 (*NTA* 3 [1959] p. 267 for summary) and R. M. PRICE, "Punished in Paradise (An Exegetical Theory on II Corinthians 12:1-10)," *Journ Stud NT* 7 (1980) pp. 33-40, while N. G. SMITH in "The Thorn that Stayed. An Exposition of II Corinthians 12:7-9," *Interp* 13 (1959) pp. 409-416 has decided that we shouldn't try to guess. The physical ailments determined to be Paul's "thorn" include a "subarachnoid hemorrhage in the occipital

in finding plausible medical information about Paul's condition has declined in recent years, interest in manifestations of the spirit and in ecstasy has increased with the rise of new Christian charismatic groups. The 1970's, accordingly, produced a number of articles on the identity of the "man in Christ" of II Cor. 12:2 who was caught up to the third heaven to receive otherwordly communications.[14] Once again, this attention to II Corinthians was prompted more by the circumstances and attitudes of the contemporary scene than by a consideration of the major issues for the epistle itself.

The second way in which the recent interest in the difficulty of II Corinthians has been manifested is in the avenues which more general treatments of II Corinthians as a whole have taken in approaching the text. These avenues are once again two in number, a pair of mutually dependent inquiries. The first question has to do with the unity of II Corinthians as a single letter. This unity has been very seriously questioned. Numerous theories of the composition and compilation of letter segments of varying lengths have been developed, particularly in German scholarly circles.[15]

---

region" resulting in "epilepsy of hallucinogenic origin" (A. Hisey, "A Paragnostic View of Paul the Apostle" in *Unitarian Universalist Christian* 33 (1978) pp. 12-19; cf. A. Hisey and J.S.P. Beck, "Paul's 'Thorn in the Flesh': A Paragnosis," *Journ Bib Rel* 29 (1961) pp. 125-129; intermittent blindness (P. Nisbet, "The Thorn in the Flesh," *Exp Times* 80 [1969] pp. 126ff.) and recurring attacks of fever (J. Bernard, "Lorsque je suis faible, c'est alors que je suis fort. 2 Cor. 12:7-10," *Assemb Seign* 45 [1974] pp. 34-39). Most recently, on this side of the continuing debate over the single phrase, D.M. Park calls it an unidentified physical ailment involving extreme pain ("Paul's skolops te sarki: Thorn or Stake? 2 Cor. xii 7," *Nov Test* 22 [1980] pp. 179-183).

[14] H. Saake, "Paulus als Ekstatiker. Pneumatologische Beobachtungen zu 2 Kor. 12,1-10," *Biblica* 53 (1972) pp. 404-410; L. Hermann, "Apollos," *RSR* 50 (1976) pp. 330-336; A.T. Lincoln, "Paul the Visionary: The Setting and Significance of the Rapture to Paradise in II Corinthians xii, 1-10," *NTS* 25 (1979) pp. 204-220.

[15] The number of critics who assume the original disunity of the epistle has now become legion. Even so cautious an exegete as Alfred Plummer wrote in 1915 that "There is considerable probability that it is composite ..." concerning II Corinthians and went on to give a summary of the historical and structural difficulties against the unity of the document as it now stands and an index to the authors who stood on both sides of the question to that date (*Second Corinthians*, pp. xxii-xxxvi). The unity of II Corinthians was first questioned by Semler (*Paraphrasis secundae epistulae ad Corinthios*, 1776) who separated 12:14-13:13 as a later addition. It was first seriously challenged by Hausrath in *Der Vierkapitelbrief des Paulus an die Korinther* (Heidelberg, 1870) who maintained that Chapters 10-13 were a separate letter. See J. Héring, *La Seconde Epître de Saint Paul aux Corinthiens* (London: Epworth Press, 1958), English translation by A.W. Heathcote, 1967, p. xi. At the present time, the preference for disunity is based upon the more recent work of Rudolf Bultmann in *Der zweite Brief an die Korinther*, which, while published only in 1976, embodies his work on the letter over a long period of time beginning in 1940, and on that of Günther Bornkamm, "Die Vorgeschichte des sogenannten Zweiten Korintherbriefs" in *Sitzungsberichte der Heidelberger Akademie der Wissenschaften*, Phil-Hist Klasse, 1961:2; also in English translation in *NTS* 8 (1962) pp. 258-264 and

It will not be the purpose of this study to resolve this question concerning the unity of II Corinthians, nor even to enter into it. However, I would like to point out that the origin of this approach to II Corinthians lies not only in the fact that the travel details and circumstances described in the letter do not match up well, but also in the serious difficulties presented by the rough, repetitive and apparently unconnected structure of the letter as it comes to us. Commentators have frequently thought that these structural difficulties can best be solved by recourse to theories of multiple letters and letter-fragments less than perfectly joined. However, II Corinthians is unanimously attested in the manuscript tradition as a unity and has been so treated in the tradition of the churches. This fact recommends considerable caution in arguing against the received traditional unity.

Moreover, although historical difficulties may appear to be resolved by these theories of multiple letters, the structural difficulties are not solved by them. They are ignored. It is still necessary to explain how II Corinthians got to be the way it is, so quickly and so uniformly that it is unanimously attested in the tradition. The interpreter is thus thrown back upon the same structural problems with which he began.

The section of II Corinthians with which this study will be most concerned, II Cor. 3:1-4:6, lies in the central section of the epistle which is regarded as its doctrinal heart. The unity of II Cor. 2:14-6:10 is the least questioned in the letter. Therefore, the treatment of my passage and its immediate context will not involve most of the compositional theories regarding II Corinthians, since these theories deal in the main with the relationships of the earliest chapters of the letter, 1:1-2:13, to the final chapters, 10-13, and with the double structure of chapters 8 and 9 and their possible relationship to the former question. Nevertheless, an analysis of the structure of the central doctrinal section could provide evidence for further study of the problem of unity, since any correspondences discovered between the content of that central section and information or

---

Walter Schmithals, "Die Korintherbriefe als Briefsammlung," *ZNTW* 64 (1973) pp. 263-288 and his major work, *Die Gnosis in Korinth* (Gottingen: Vandenhoeck & Ruprecht, 1965) and that of their students. See also N. Hyldahl, "Die Frage nach der literarischen Einheit des Zweiten Korintherbriefes," *ZNTW* 64 (1973) pp. 289-306 and, in English, W. H. Bates, "The Integrity of II Corinthians," *NTS* 12 (1965) pp. 56-69. All commentaries offer summaries of the current divisions made in the text, since it has now become obligatory to acknowledge the challenge against unity and has even become professionally embarrassing to defend it. The most recent scholarly commentary to appear in English, Victor P. Furnish, *II Corinthians* (Garden City, New York: Doubleday & Company, Inc., 1984) in the Anchor Bible Series adopts a cautious "two letter hypothesis," while acknowledging the desire of some scholars to defend the unity of the letter as it stands, pp. 29-41.

events reported in other sections argues for the unity of the parts in spite of historical difficulties and factual discrepancies. At the least it may offer some clues as to the redactional plan of the letter if composite.

The second approach to II Corinthians often taken in general treatments of the letter cannot be conceptually separated from the first. The second question most frequently asked concerns the nature and identity of the opponents against which the letter itself and, in particular, Paul's numerous critical remarks and accusations within it are directed.[16] Since these accusations and indirect reports of opposing viewpoints seem contradictory in some cases, theories about the identity of Paul's various opponents are often inextricably bound up with theories concerning the original disunity of the letter, posited upon just such discrepancies.

As I said with reference to the question of unity itself, it is not my purpose to solve the vexing problem of the identity of the opposition to Paul. In my opinion, there is already a large enough variety of theories regarding the proper picture of Paul's opponents. These have recently been presented in summary form by John Gunther.[17] The fact that Paul did deal with some who opposed him is certain, but to decide definitively between the various pictures offered of them is impossible. What is important to realize, however, is this: such studies as those cited and

---

[16] Dieter GEORGI's work, *Die Gegner des Paulus im 2. Korintherbrief*. Wissenschaftliche Monographien zum Alten und Neuen Testament 11 (Vluyn: Neukirchener Verlag, 1964) has of course become the classic example of this approach. Of the many other treatments of the opponent question, I will cite only a few key articles. G. FRIEDRICH, "Die Gegner des Paulus im 2. Korintherbrief," in *Abraham unser Vater Festschrift für Otto Michel*, O. BETZ, M. HENGEL and P. SCHMIDT, eds. (Leiden: E. J. Brill, 1963) pp. 181-215; D. GEORGI, "Der Kampf um die reine Lehre im Urchristentum als Auseinandersetzung um das rechte Verständnis der an Israel ergangenen Offenbarung Gottes," in *Antijudaismus im Neuen Testament?*, P. ECKERT, P. LEVISON and M. STÖHR, eds. (1967) pp. 83-87; D. W. OOSTENDORP, *Another Jesus: A Gospel of Jewish-Christian Superiority in II Corinthians* (Kampen, 1967); C. K. BARRETT, "Paul's Opponents in II Corinthians," *NTS* 17 (1970-1971) 233-254; E. E. ELLIS, "Paul's Opponents: Trends in Research," in *Christianity, Judaism and Other Graeco-Roman Cults* (Leiden: E. J. Brill, 1975) pp. 264-298; and most recently G. BARTH, "Die Eignung des Verkündigers im 2 Kor. 2,14-3,6," in *Kirche: Festschrift für Günther Bornkamm*, D. LÜHRMANN and G. STRECKER, eds. (Tübingen: Mohr [Siebeck], 1980) pp. 257-270.

[17] *St. Paul's Opponents and Their Background* (Leiden: E. J. Brill, 1973) pp. 1-2. It is interesting to notice that there are nearly as many theories about the identity of Paul's opponents as there are books and articles on the subject. They do, however, fall into two main divisions: Jewish or Gnostic. Although the theory of gnostic opponents was very popular some time ago, the theory of Jewish opponents is carrying the day at the moment. This inability to finally resolve the critical issue also plagues those who deal with the question of the unity of the letter. The consequent proliferation of theories on both questions indicates to me that we have exhausted the insufficient evidence on which to work in these areas and should make a new start in another direction. That is what this study proposes to do, not to deny the historical and structural problems of II Corinthians, just to suggest another possible approach to the letter.

many others as well have responded to one of the major difficulties of II
Corinthians, that is, its ill-defined *Sitz im Leben*. Paul's historical remarks
in II Corinthians are obscure, disorganized and contradictory to an
unusual degree. The effort to better define his opponents is a critical
response to this particular difficulty which Paul's own text presents.

II Corinthians 3

The passage from II Corinthians with which this study itself is concerned is among those whose difficulty has always captured the interest of
biblical scholars. II Corinthians 3:1-18 is the most written about text in
the entire letter. Within that section, verses 6, 17 and 18 have most often
been the subject of critical attention.[18]

II Cor. 3:6 contains the famous Pauline antithesis between the letter
and the spirit. From the Patristic age there have been two basic ways of
understanding this antithesis. Origen is credited with the view that Paul
refers to two alternate levels of meaning within the Old Testament
scripture and two corresponding methods of reading and understanding
it.[19] Such a position is completely compatible with Origen's own
exegetical technique and assumptions and I hope to show, while not
accepting this reading without reservation, that it does grasp one of the
dimensions of Paul's intention. On the other hand, since Chrysostom
commentators have held that the πνεῦμα of II Cor. 3:6 refers to the holy
spirit understood personally as representative of the new covenant just as
the stone tablets of the law are representative of the old covenant. Paul

---

[18] For example, see most recently Jacob KREMER, "'Denn der Buchstabe tötet, der
Geist aber macht lebendig:' Methodologische und Hermeneutische Erwägungen zu 2 Kor.
3,6b," in *Begegnung mit dem Wort, Festschrift for H. Zimmermann*, J. ZMIJEWSKI, ed.
(Bonn: Peter Hanskin Verlag, 1980) pp. 219-246 and "Neueste Methoden der Exegese,
dargelegt an 2 Kor. 3.6b," *Theol Prakt Quart* 128 (March, 1980) pp. 246-259. Kremer
applies modern hermeneutical theories in his exegesis while ascribing to the Origenist
position described below. A selection of the previous literature on this verse alone includes
C. H. DODD, "New Testament Translation Problems II, *Bible Translator* 28 (1977)
pp. 110-112 (among those who would oppose Kremer); P. RICHARDSON, "Spirit and Letter:
A Foundation for Hermeneutics," *Evang Quart* 45 (1973) pp. 208-218; E. KÄSEMANN,
"The Spirit and the Letter" in *Perspectives on Paul*, translated by Margaret Kohl
(London: SCM Press Ltd., 1971) pp. 138-166; Boaz COHEN, "Note on Letter and Spirit in
the New Testament," *HTR* 47 (1954) pp. 197-203; Bernardin SCHNEIDER "The Meaning of
St. Paul's Thesis 'The Letter and the Spirit,'" *CBQ* 15 (1953) pp. 163-207 (which contains
a most helpful survey of the interpretation of II Cor. 3:6 in the Fathers); K. PRÜMM, "Der
Abschnitt über die Doxa des Apostolats 2 Kor. 3,1-4,6 in der Deutung des hl.
Chrysostomus: Eine Untersuchung zur Auslegungsgeschichte des paulinischen Pneumas,"
Biblica 30 (1949) pp. 161-196, 377-400; H. LIESE, "De Spiritu et Littera (2 Cor. 3:4-11),"
VD 11 (1931) pp. 225-229.

[19] See B. SCHNEIDER, "Letter/Spirit," p. 166. This position is not the dominant one
today.

therefore is understood to refer in his letter/spirit antithesis to two covenants, as typified by their specific benefits.[20] Leaving aside the important question of how Paul himself might have understood the concept of "holy spirit" in this context and at such an early stage of Christian theological development, this position too represents a real appreciation of Paul's argument. I hope to show, however, that when II Cor. 3:6 is viewed in its proper context in II Cor. 3:1-18 these two historically adverse positions are not necessarily mutually exclusive alternatives.

Like verse 6, II Cor. 3:17 also has to do with the spirit and has been the subject of even more extensive debate than the previous verse.[21] Paul's puzzling statement that "the Lord is the spirit" has led many interpreters to say that Paul has here identified Jesus Christ and the spirit. This conclusion is based upon Paul's customary use of the *Kyrios* title to refer to the exalted Christ, but ignores the context in which this particular use of the title is set. Such an identification has been especially upsetting to Karl Prümm, who has argued convincingly against it in the articles noted, because it appears to deny the personal nature of the Holy Spirit and in so doing fails to support the Catholic Church's trinitarian doctrine.

Already in the 1950's, apart from Prümm's massive historical argument, the seeds of an effective challenge to this identification of Jesus Christ and the Spirit in II Cor. 3:16 were sown on exegetical grounds. Lucien Cerfaux has shown that in the context of Old Testament

---

[20] See K. PRÜMM, "Der Abschnitt," passim and B. SCHNEIDER, "Letter/Spirit," pp. 172-175.

[21] On this verse in particular see most recently D. GREENWOOD, "The Lord is the Spirit: Some Consideration of 2 Cor. 3:17," *CBQ* 34 (1972) pp. 467-472 and A. GIGLIOLI, "Il Signore e lo Spirito," *Revist Bib* 20 (1972) pp. 263-276; J. D. G. DUNN, "2 Corinthians III, 17—'The Lord is the Spirit,'" *JThSt* 21 (1970) pp. 309-320; W. S. VORSTER, "2 Kor. 3:17: Eksegese en Toeligting," *Neotestamentica* 3 (1969) pp. 37-44; J. SCHILDENBERGER, "'Der Herr aber ist der Geist,' 2 Kor. 3,17a im Zusammenhang des Textes und der Theologie des hl. Paulus," *Studiorum Paulinorum Congressus* I (Rome, 1961) pp. 451-460; Ingo HERMANN, *Kyrios und Pneuma* (Munich: Kösel, 1961); W. SCHMITHALS, "Zwei gnostische Stellen im zweiten Korintherbrief," *Ev Th* 18 (1958) pp. 552-573, English translation in *Gnosticism in Corinth*, translated by J. Steely (New York: Abingdon Press, 1971) pp. 302-325; P. GALLETTO, "'Dominus autem spiritus est' II Cor. 3,17," *Revist Bib* 5 (1957) pp. 245-281; P. GRECH, "2 Cor. III, 17 and the Pauline Doctrine of Conversion to the Holy Spirit," *CBQ* 17 (1955) pp. 420-437; S. LYONNET, "S. Cyrille d'Alexandrie et 2 Cor. III, 17," *Biblica* 32 (1951) pp. 25-31; B. SCHNEIDER, *Dominus autem Spiritus est: II Cor. 3,17a* (Rome: Officium Libri Catholici, 1951); K. PRÜMM, "Die katholische Auslegung von 2 Kor. 3,17a in den letzten vier Jahrzehnten nach ihren Hauptrichtungen," *Biblica* 31 (1950) pp. 316-345, 459-482, *Biblica* 32 (1951) pp. 1-24, and "Israels Kehr zum Geist—2 Kor. 3,17a im Verständnis der Erstleser," *ZKT* 72 (1950) pp. 385-442; U. S. HOLZMEISTER, *2 Cor. 3,17: "Dominus autem Spiritus est." Eine exegetische Untersuchung mit einer übersicht über die Geschichte der Erklärung dieser Stelle* (Innsbruck: 1908); L. KRUMMEL, "Exegetische und dogmatische Erörterung der Stelle 2 Kor. 3,17: 'der Herr ist der Geist,'" *St Kr* 32 (1859) pp. 39-100.

quotations Paul's ordinary use of the title "*Kyrios*" for Christ is suspended and *Kyrios* in fact then always refers to the God of the Old Testament as it does in the Septuagint.[22] It has been argued since then that Paul's phrase should be so understood since it follows a quotation of Exodus 34:34 there. Furthermore, the fact that verse 17 does not begin a new thought,[23] but refers to verse 16 indicates also that the *Kyrios* of verse 17 must be the same as the *Kyrios* of verse 16, where the referent clearly cannot be Christ.[24] The question should now be laid to rest. It seems to me that it has been effectively closed by the work of Prümm, Schneider and Dunn, and I will base my argument in this study on their conclusion that the *Kyrios* of II Cor. 3:17 is primarily the Lord of the Old Testament. This text of II Corinthians should no longer be used to draw conclusions for or against the modern trinitarian dogma, since its original purpose was to make an exegetical statement.

Finally, II Corinthians 3:18 has received some attention as one of the great "mystical" passages of the Pauline corpus. Paul says there that he and all Christians are being transformed into Christ. Reitzenstein saw this as a unique Pauline instance of transformation by vision parallel to that commonly associated with the Greek mystery religions.[25] Other authors have argued for the Jewish background of Paul's thought here.[26] It is possible, however, to admit a real parallel with the Graeco-Roman religious milieu while still affirming the intimate connection of the verse with the preceding argument which has Exodus 34 as its basis. The interpretation of Hellenism and Judaism has been masterfully established by Martin Hengel in *Judaism and Hellenism*. This study will make use of his insight.[27]

---

[22] L. CERFAUX, "Kyrios dans les citations pauliniennes de l'Ancien Testament," in *Recueil L. Cerfaux* I (Gemblaux: 1954) pp. 173-188.

[23] Witness the double "δέ" of v. 17 used to refer back to the immediately preceding material.

[24] P. GRECH, "2 Cor. III, 17," argued this way in 1955 as does J. D. G. DUNN, "2 Corinthians III, 17," in a more expanded form in 1970. Dunn's work is a specific rebuttal of Ingo Hermann's *Kyrios und Pneuma*. The arguments were summarized earlier as well in SCHNEIDER's *Dominus autem Spiritus est*, pp. 159-160.

[25] R. REITZENSTEIN, *Historia Monachorum und Historia Lausiaca, eine Studie zur Geschichte des Mönchtums und der frühchristlichen Begriffe Gnostiker und Pneumatiker* (Göttingen: Vandenhoeck & Ruprecht, 1916) pp. 242ff., and through him much of German scholarship. For example, S. SCHULZ, "Die Decke des Moses," *ZNTW* 49 (1958) pp. 1-30 accepts this "history of religions" approach to II Cor. 3:18 and it becomes an important component of his argument regarding the extraneous nature of the verse.

[26] P. CORSSEN, "Paulus und Porphyrios zur Erklärung von 2 Kor. 3,18," ZNTW 19-20 (1919-1921) pp. 2-10; A. FEUILLET, *Le Christ Sagesse de Dieu d'après les Epîtres pauliniennes*. Etudes Bibliques (Paris: Librairie Le Coffre, 1966) pp. 137-155.

[27] Martin HENGEL, *Judentum und Hellenismus: Studien zu ihrer Begegnung unter besonderer Berücksichtigung Palästinas bis zur Mitte des 2 Jhrs. v. Chr.* (Tübingen: J. C. B. Mohr [Paul Siebeck], 1973), translated by John Bowden as *Judaism and Hellenism*, 2 vols. (Philadelphia: Fortress Press, 1974).

Very recently, Jan Lambrecht has investigated the idea of the transformation of the Christian in II Cor. 3:18 from such a balanced perspective, taking into consideration the linguistic data discussed in the two studies mentioned below as well as the context of the passage, providing an excellent review of scholarship on this particular facet of Paul's theology. Lambrecht concludes that Paul intended in II Cor 3:18 "to explain the essence of Christian life," making use of a Hellenistic motif as well as a parallel with Moses to express his own more profound idea of unity with Christ.[28]

Two more narrowly focused studies on II Cor. 3:18 have been devoted to only one word in that verse: κατοπτριζόμενοι. In 1949 J. Dupont did a fairly brief but thorough study[29] in which he concluded that the verb must mean "to reflect as a mirror," on the basis of a lack of linguistic evidence to forbid such a conclusion and the force of the context in which the verb is used by Paul against the history of religious concentration on the vision aspect of the verse. Nearly a decade later, Norbert Hugede published a lengthy study[30] of I Corinthians 13:12 and II Corinthians 3:18, the two passages in the Pauline corpus in which Paul uses the metaphor of a mirror, in which he concludes the opposite. He says that κατοπτριζόμενοι in II Cor. 3:18 must mean "to see in a mirror" on the strength of a small amount of linguistic evidence supporting that meaning and on the basis of the clear meaning of I Cor. 13:12, in spite of the admitted force of the context in the opposite direction. I can only conclude that both of these experts are correct and try to show through a renewed analysis of the context in which this rare verb is used in II Corinthians that it both supports and indicates a deliberate word-play on both possible meanings.

Evaluation of Scholarly Resources

II Corinthians as a whole has, of course, been the subject of numerous commentaries, ancient and modern. Among the modern works, the International Critical Commentary done by Alfred Plummer in 1915, although somewhat dated, remains the most valuable commentary in English.[31] Similarly, although it too is quite old, Windisch's volume in the Kritischexegetischer Kommentar series done

---

[28] J. LAMBRECHT, "Transformation in 2 Cor 3,18," *Biblica* 64 (1983) pp. 243-254.

[29] J. DUPONT, "Le Chrétien, miroir de la gloire divine d'après II Cor. III, 18," *RB* 56 (1949) pp. 392-411.

[30] N. HUGEDE, *La métaphore du miroir dans les épîtres de saint Paul aux Corinthiens* (Neuchâtel-Paris: Delachaux et Niestlé, 1957).

[31] Alfred PLUMMER, *A Critical and Exegetical Commentary on the Second Epistle of St. Paul to the Corinthians,* International Critical Commentary (Edinburgh: T. & T. Clark, 1915).

[32] H. WINDISCH, *Der zweite Korintherbrief* (Göttingen: Vandenhoeck & Ruprecht, 1924).

in 1924[32] is still the bulwark of German scholarship on the letter. Resting as it does on the overwhelming historical scholarship of Karl Prümm, *Diakonia Pneumatos* is also extremely valuable in German.[33] In French, the commentary in *Etudes Bibliques* by Allo[34] and the exegetical studies on II Corinthians 2:14-7:4 by J. F. Collange[35] are the most important works done on a large scale.

In his 1924 commentary, Windisch recognized the need to call II Corinthians 3:7-18 a midrashic text, closely tied to the text of Exodus 34:29-35 for the purpose of interpreting it.[36] Of course, Paul's reference to the scene of Moses' descent from the mountain with the second tablets of the law had not been missed by earlier attentive reading of the text. But, the most influential study devoted to an analysis of the operation of II Cor. 3:7-18 as midrash was done only in 1958 by Siegfried Schulz.[37] His article affected the subsequent interpretation of the passage profoundly. Schulz concluded that in II Cor. 3:7-18 Paul had incorporated and corrected a midrash on Exodus 34 composed by his opponents in Corinth. He draws this conclusion on the basis of the unusual amount of unique vocabulary present in this short segment of text and from the logical inconsistencies apparent in its argumentation.[38]

Schulz's reconstruction of an opposing exegesis from the Pauline text has had far-reaching consequences. First, it has deprived the argument Paul does present of any originality and so of most of its force. Second, and more important, it called a halt for a considerable time to further efforts to understand Paul's text in itself. With the acceptance of Schulz's position all difficulties may henceforth be solved with recourse to the opposing position's uneasy entry into the Pauline text. Third, Schulz's selection of the section comprised by verses 7-18 as reflecting the opposing source document has tended to sever those verses from their context and in so doing has severely limited understanding of them.

In 1964 Dieter Georgi published his dissertation on the opponents whom Paul faced in Corinth positing and using a reconstruction of an opponent's midrash as a source incorporated into II Corinthians 3:7-18

---

[33] Karl PRÜMM, *Diakonia Pneumatos, I, Theologische Auslegung des Zweiten Korintherbriefes* (Freiburg: Herder, 1967).

[34] E.-B. ALLO, *Saint Paul: Seconde Epître aux Corinthiens, Second Edition (Paris: Librairie Le Coffre, 1956)*.

[35] J. F. COLLANGE, *Enigmes de la deuxième Epître aux Corinthiens*, Society for New Testament Studies Monograph Series 18 (Cambridge: At the University Press, 1972).

[36] H. WINDISCH, *Der zweite Korintherbrief*, p. 112.

[37] S. SCHULZ, "Die Decke des Moses—Untersuchungen zu einer vorpaulinischen Überlieferung in 2 Cor. III 7-18," *ZNTW* 49 (1958) pp. 1-30.

[38] SCHULZ, "Die Decke," pp. 1-2. He is indebted for these insights to Windisch.

as one important link in his reconstruction of the opponents' identity.[39] Georgi's work was very well received in scholarly circles and is certainly the major work on II Corinthians to appear in the last quarter century. Although I can only applaud Georgi's command of Graeco-Roman literature and his knowledge of the ancient Hellenistic social milieu, I must regret the popularity achieved for Schulz's treatment of II Cor. 3:7-18 by Georgi's work on the opponents question.

In fact, the reconstruction of a hostile literary source standing behind II Cor. 3:7-18 has been seriously questioned recently[40] and is frequently rejected.[41] Nevertheless, the effects of this tangent in the history of the interpretation of the passage must be overcome, even in treatments of the text which do not presuppose it. II Corinthians 3:7-18 must be understood in itself, on its own terms and in its own literary context. Recently Earl Richard has pointed out that it is just this task which has not been resolutely undertaken to date.[42] In fact, however, in

---

[39] Dieter GEORGI, *Die Gegner des Paulus im 2. Korintherbrief: Studien zur Religiösen Propaganda in der Spätantike*. Wissenschaftliche Monographien zum Alten und Neuen Testament 11 (Vluyn: Neukirchener Verlag, 1964) pp. 274-282.

[40] For example, by C.J.A. HICKLING in "Is the Second Epistle to the Corinthians a Source for Early Church History?," *ZNTW* 66 (1975) pp. 284-287 and "The Sequence of Thought in II Corinthians, Chapter Three," *NTS* 21 (1975) pp. 380-395.

[41] Among those who reject the Schulz/Georgi reconstruction of an opponents' midrash from the text of II Cor. 3:7-18 are the following: W.C. VAN UNNIK, "'With Unveiled Face,' An Exegesis of 2 Corinthians iii 12-18," *Nov Test* 6 (1963) p. 156; A. FEUILLET, *Le Christ Sagesse de Dieu*, pp. 116-117; W. SCHMITHALS, *Gnosticism in Corinth*, pp. 287-288; J.F. COLLANGE, *Enigmes*, p. 68; C.K. BARRETT, *Second Corinthians*, p. 114; C.J.A. HICKLING, "Is the Second Epistle?," p. 284 and "The Sequence of Thought," p. 389; Earl RICHARD, "Polemics, Old Testament and Theology. A Study of II Cor. III, I-IV, 6," *RB* 88 (1981) pp. 343-344; Thomas E. PROVENCE, "Who is Sufficient for These Things?," *Nov Test* 24 (1982) pp. 54-55, 68; LAMBRECHT, "Structure and Line of Thought in 2 Cor 2,14-4,6," *Biblica* 64 (1983), pp. 344-380. These authors are unanimous in rejecting the reconstruction for lack of evidence. W.C. van Unnik's comments are particularly amusing. He says, "In the end he [Schulz] solves no riddles, but only creates new ones. Presumably because a veil is over my mind, I fail to see what he wants us to see. There is not a shred of evidence that the apostle is commenting upon a previously existing document or teaching, nor is it clear why Paul himself should have been unable to make this application of the Exodus story. Before setting out on hypothetical reconstructions behind the given text, we should first try to understand the text as it stands." (p. 156). In his recent article, "Glory Reflected in the Face of Christ (2 Cor. 3:7-4:6) and a Palestinian Jewish Motif" *Theo Stud* 72 (1981) pp. 630-644, J.A. FITZMYER has opted, following H. LIETZMANN in *An die Korinther I/II*, Fifth edition, revised by W.G. Kummel (Tübingen: Mohr [Siebeck], 1969) p. 111, to reject an anti-Pauline origin of the midrash in favor of its composition by Paul himself previously for another occasion and its subsequent insertion into 2 Corinthians 3 (p. 632). This is no real improvement.

[42] Earl RICHARD, "Polemics," p. 343. Professor Richard was kind enough to allow me to see his article in manuscript form after my own work on this aspect of the text for the present study was completed. I wish to express my gratitude to him and happily acknowledge the help that his work has provided in sharpening the focus of the final version of my own.

England and the United States in the past decade several studies have been done which have made a start.[43] All of these treatments except the unpublished dissertation of Peter Jones, however, necessarily suffer from the limitations imposed by the brevity of their format. Furthermore, all but the most recent studies by Earl Richard and Jan Lambrecht limit themselves to a discussion of II Cor. 3:7-18 alone and so lack a necessary reference to context. It is among these recent scholarly efforts, therefore, that I feel my own study will be able to take its place and make its own contribution.

Outline, Intentions and Presuppositions of The Present Inquiry

The Goal of This Study

As I have mentioned before now, the focus of the present exegetical exercise is on II Corinthians 3:1-18 and its conclusion, 4:1-6. The purpose of an exercise in critical biblical interpretation such as this must always be to appropriate for the modern reader as much of the meaning originally intended by its author as possible. As the writer of this selected bit of ancient literature, Paul meant to convey something to those who originally received and read his letter. However, those original readers lived and thought within an historical and conceptual world very different in many respects from our own, just as Paul himself did. Therefore, writer and readers originally shared a mental and experiential space from which the present day interpreter may be excluded by historical distance. This hermeneutical problem is commonplace to all modern exegetes. Indeed, it is the particular task of historical-critical exegesis to bridge this temporal gap by providing information about the writer's world in order to reinstate the original writer-to-reader relationship.

This exegetical task may be performed in a number of ways, however, according to which aspect of the lost world of the writer is being reconstructed. For example, the recent studies mentioned above which have to do with identifying and describing the opponents against

---

[43] To mention only the best of these—J. D. G. Dunn, "2 Corinthians III, 17" has a lenghty discussion of 3:7-18 as a whole; A. T. Hanson, "The Midrash in II Corinthians 3: A Reconsideration," *JSNT* (1980) pp. 2-28; Morna D. Hooker, "Beyond the Things that are Written? St. Paul's Use of Scripture," *NTS* 27 (1981) pp. 295-309; E. Richard, "Polemics, Old Testament and Theology. A Study of II Cor. III, I-IV, 6," *RB* (1981) pp. 340-367; Lambrecht, "Structure and Line of Thought in 2 Cor 2,14-4,6," *Biblica* 64 (1983), pp. 344-380; and an unpublished dissertation from Princeton done in 1973 by Peter Jones, entitled The Apostle Paul: A Second Moses According to II Corinthians 2:14-4:7.

whom Paul fought in Corinth are really attempts to recapture the experiential aspect of the reader/writer relationship for the modern reader. They are efforts to reconstruct Paul's social or historical setting in order to better understand a document produced out of and presumably influenced by it. In exegetical terminology, they seek to establish its determinative *Sitz im Leben*. Furthermore, such studies also seek to clarify aspects of the text itself which appear meaningless or unconnected, and in doing so explain not only *Sitz im Leben* but text. They do so primarily, as I have said, by supplying historical information from outside of the document in question, or by inferring such historical data on the basis of the document itself.[44]

There are, however, other approaches to the text and to the re-creation of the author's world. In this study I have chosen to investigate the conceptual, rather than the social, world of Paul as author.

I have chosen as well to do a literary analysis of II Cor. 3:1-4:6 rather than an historical one. My focus is therefore on the content and structure of II Cor. 3:1-4:6 itself, on argument rather than on *Sitz im Leben*.[45] Every author uses particular words to express his thought and uses those words in specific combinations to structure and communicate his thought. In addition he may use standard forms of argument, common in his intellectual environment and therefore easily understood by his contemporaries. In this way the author produces an argument on the conscious level through which he intends to convey meaning to his readers and convince them of its truth or value.

Furthermore, the author may also use words or combinations of words, consciously or unconsciously, which suggest or bring into play the underlying notions which are the common coin of his intellectual milieu, those ideas which are the presuppositions which support his deliberately formulated argument. The awareness of the presence of intellectual and cultural presuppositions in everyone has today become an axiom in the science of biblical criticism. Just as we must be alert to them in ourselves as readers if we are to properly interpret a text from another age, rather than misinterpreting it in conformity to our own expectations, so we must be aware of the author's own presupposed intellectual world and its influence on his text in order to properly understand it.

---

[44] The methodology is most vulnerable to criticism at this point. The accusation of circularity is most fully discussed by HICKLING in "Is the Second Epistle to the Corinthians a Source for Early Church History?."

[45] A similar methodology is used by Wilhelm WUELLNER in "Paul's Rhetoric of Argumentation in Romans: An Alternative to the Donfried-Karris Debate Over Romans," *CBQ* (1976) pp. 330-351, also in *The Romans Debate*, Karl P. DONFRIED, ed. (Minneapolis, Minnesota: Augsburg Publishing House, 1977) pp. 152-174. He too tries to understand Paul's argument via analysis of the forms he uses to pursue it. Wuellner emphasizes Greek rhetorical forms, while I use Jewish exegetical forms because of the subject matter of my text.

These two levels of meaning in II Corinthians 3:1-4:6, that of deliberate argument on the one hand and that of his larger presupposed conceptual world on the other, will be the objects under investigation in the following pages. One uses the evidence of the literary product as it stands to discover both of these levels of meaning. A renewed, thorough and careful scrutiny of the words that Paul uses and the combinations and forms in which he uses them will allow us to better understand both what he wanted to say to his reader consciously and what his less deliberate adoption of thematic or conceptual patterns says to us about him and his world. As the preceding review of scholarly literature on II Corinthians, and especially II Corinthians 3 has shown, in the past the re-creation of the historical world of the text and the author has been more frequently and more successfully attempted than has such a literary analysis of his text. In this inquiry I am concerned to show more fully than has been done in the past the coherent logical structure of II Corinthians 3:1-4:6 as it has been dictated by the conceptual and cultural world which provided both the raw materials and the blueprints for its construction.

The Structure of this Study

The present exegetical study, then, will be divided into two chapters following the natural divisions of the text itself and the direction of the literary analysis as just defined. II Corinthians 3:1-18 contains a consciously constructed argument centered around the concept of covenant and directed toward the definition of the Pauline covenant ministry.[46] This

---

[46] It is universally agreed that II Corinthians 3-6 has to do with a defense and definition of Paul's apostolic ministry. The relevance and importance of the concept of covenant to this defense is a matter of some disagreement, however. An allusion to the Sinai covenant in II Cor. 3:7ff, is, of course, never missed. Many authors also note an allusion to the new covenant promised by Jeremiah in II Cor. 3:6. However, the theme of covenant is rarely fully integrated into the argument of the chapter as a whole, much less seen as the basis for the ensuing lengthy discussion of ministry. This is, at least in part, the result of the splitting off of 3:7-18 from its context which stems from the work of Windisch and Schulz. For the majority of modern commentators (WINDISCH; LIETZMANN; SICKENBERGER, *Die Briefe des Heiligen Paulus an die Korinther und Römer* (Bonn: Peter Hanstein, 1932); ALLO; THRALL, *The First and Second Letters of Paul to the Corinthians* (Cambridge: At the University Press, 1965); HUGHES, *Paul's Second Epistle to the Corinthians* (Grand Rapids, Michigan: Wm. B. Eerdmans Publishing Co., 1962); PRÜMM; J. J. O'ROURKE, "The Second Letter to the Corinthians," *Jerome Biblical Commentary*, R. BROWN, J. FITZMYER and R. MURPHY, eds. (Englewood Cliffs, N.J.: Prentice-Hall, Inc., 1968); F. F. BRUCE, *1 and 2 Corinthians* (London: Oliphants, 1971); COLLANGE; BARRETT and FALLON, Paul's discussion of covenant in II Cor. 3:6-17 is a digression in response to a specific challenge to his apostolate on the basis of the Mosaic covenant and ministry. When this challenge has been answered, the argument concerning ministry resumes from a completely different point of view. I, on the other hand, wish to argue that the concept of

argument is customarily and easily divided into two sections, 3:1-6 and 3:7-18, consciously or unconsciously, on the basis of the Old Testament background supporting each section. Chapter One will deal with the first of these sections and Chapter Two with the last. The focus of my study, then, will rest on Paul's explicit argumentation and its explanation via its presupposed exegetical substructure.

II Corinthians 3:1-18, however, is part of an extended literary unit and not an isolated fragment. Paul himself has provided a concluding statement for his argument in II Cor. 4:1-6.[47] Furthermore, 3:1-4:6 stands at the head of a lengthy exposition which is usually judged to run to the middle of Chapter 6 without serious structural disruption.[48] No unit within this whole, therefore, can be well understood standing alone without regard for the direct conclusions which the author himself draws from it or for the context in which his argument stands, the purposes of which it may be expected to serve. Therefore, a brief concluding chapter will be devoted to II Cor. 4:1-6 as it completes the argument of Chapter 3

---

covenant is significant for Paul himself, even when it is not explicitly mentioned. I wish to explore the notion of covenant and its implications more deeply than is usually done with reference to II Corinthians and in a different way. In support of this attempt I may cite the commentaries of PLUMMER and BULTMANN, who do the most thorough analyses of this theme in II Cor. 3 and the essays of Mathias RISSI; Karol GABRIS, "Neuer Bund zum Dienst am Leben," *Communio Viatorum* 7 (1964) pp. 57-72; W. C. VAN UNNIK, "La conception paulinienne de la nouvelle alliance," in *Litterature et Theologie Pauliniennes* (Brussels: Desclée De Brouwer, 1960) pp. 109-126; and Earl RICHARD, all of whom emphasize the importance of covenant in Paul's argument.

[47] In 1915 PLUMMER, in *Second Corinthians*, noted on p. 109 that "Here again (4:1), as between i, and ii.', the division of chapters is unintelligently made. The first six verses of this chapter belong to the preceding one, and the close connexion between the two paragraphs is obvious. ..." Several recent commentators have followed his lead in connecting 4:1-6 to the preceding verses. See Earl RICHARD, "Polemics;" J. A. FITZMYER, "Glory Reflected;" P. JONES, "The Apostle Paul; " H. A. KENT, "The Glory of Christian Ministry: An Analysis of 2 Corinthians 2:14-4:18," *Grace Theological Journal* 2 (1980) pp. 171-189.

[48] In spite of the vehement debates regarding the unity of II Corinthians, no serious critics question the coherence of II Cor. 2:14-7:4, with the single exception of II Cor. 6:14-7:1. On the dubious authorship and poor structural connections of that section, see the literature cited in note 15 above, the standard commentaries on II Corinthians and the following selected bibliography. J. A. FITZMYER, "Qumran and the Interpolated Paragraph in 2 Cor. 6,14-7,1," *CBQ* 23 (1961) pp. 271-280 and H. D. BETZ, "2 Cor. 6:14-7:1: An Anti-Pauline Fragment?," *JBL* 92 (1973) pp. 88-108. Both reject the passage as interpolated. M. E. THRALL, "The Problem of II Cor. vi 14-vii 1 in Some Recent Discussion," *NTS* 24 (1977) pp. 132-148 surveys some earlier material and herself decides that the discussion has so far proved inconclusive. Both G. D. FEE, "II Corinthians vi,14-vii,1 and Food Offered to Idols," *NTS* 23 (1977) pp. 140-161 and J. D. M. DERRETT, "2 Cor. 6,14ff. A Midrash on Dt. 22,10," *Biblica* 59 (1978) pp. 231-250 defend the authenticity and integrity of the section in its present context. I regard the problem of II Cor. 6:14-7:1 as unsolved and so will neither reject that section from the context of II Cor. 3:1-4:6 nor lean upon it in the course of my own argument.

and to the literary context of 3:1-4:6, especially the large "apostolic defense" which runs from 2:14-6:10. The conclusion of this study will discuss the presuppositions with which Paul has approached the Old Testament texts with which his explicit argument in 3:1-18 deals and suggest ways in which those presuppositions are illuminative of the larger unit as well. Finally, we will see numerous avenues for further study of II Corinthians, and of Paul's letters in general, opened up by the methodological approach of the present work and the awareness of Paul's own methodological and theological presuppositions it reveals.

Presuppositions of this Study

No absolute disjunction can ever be made, of course, between literary and historical investigation. Therefore, even though the emphasis in this study will be on explaining II Corinthians 3:1-4:6 as a literary product, a certain amount of historical data concerning Paul and his probable milieu is presupposed and brought to bear on the investigation from the beginning and then tested out by its results. Similarly, limited conclusions in the historical sphere may legitimately be drawn on the basis of the literary analysis upon its completion.

Paul and Early Christianity

On the evidence of his own letters and of the Acts of the Apostles as well, the Apostle Paul was a Jew, well travelled and well educated, aware of and influenced by the prevailing Hellenism of his day but trained by the Pharisaical school at that time struggling for, and eventually winning, dominance in Palestine.[49] It has long since become an unfortunate cliché

---

[49] Rom. 9:1-3; 11:1-2; I Cor. 15:8-9; II Cor. 11:22; Gal. 1:13-24; Acts 9:1-2, 14, 20-22, 28-29; 13:14-16ff.; 16:37-38; 17:1-4, 10-12; 21:39; 22:3-5, 25-28; 23:6-8; 26:4-11, 19-23; 28:23. It is hardly a new insight to view Paul as a Jew and try to reappropriate the Jewish heritage which he brought to Christianity. Modern understanding of the Judaism of the first century has not always led to a realistic conception of his background, however. I refer the reader to the excellent little essay, "Paul and Judaism Since Schweitzer"by W. D. DAVIES which serves as the Introduction to the Fourth Edition of his classic work, *Paul and Rabbinic Judaism* (Philadelphia: Fortress Press, 1980) pp. vii-xv. The essay was first read as a paper at the annual meeting of the Society of Biblical Literature in 1964, while *Paul and Rabbinic Judaism* was first published in 1948. In that major work, Davies amply illustrates the elements which Paul and Pharisaic, or Rabbinic, Judaism share, whereas his contact with apocalyptic Judaism had been exclusively emphasized earlier. Another major work in the same genre, *Paul and Palestinian Judaism* by E. P. SANDERS, appeared in 1977 (Philadelphia: Fortress Press). Since the publication of these and other studies noted therein, the interpreter can feel comfortable in exploring the full spectrum of Judaism in Paul's time in order to better understand his thought. Nevertheless, the available awareness of Paul's Jewish traditions and his training within Judaism has only very recently begun to seep into exegetical analyses of his letters

that the specialty of the Pharisee was a meticulously applied skill in the interpretation of scripture. Disregarding the pejorative connotations that this characterization of the movement has come to bear, we can recognize that careful scriptural exegesis assumed an increasing importance in that group.[50] The gospels themselves bear witness to disputes between Jesus and various Jewish groups regarding the correct interpretation of both laws and prophecies.[51] Whether these stories stem from events in the life of Jesus or reflect disputes in the formative years of his church, they nevertheless show that the interpretation of the scriptures of the Jewish community was of vital interest to first-century Jews and Christians. It has, indeed, become nearly axiomatic, on the basis of the works of C. H. Dodd for example, that the earliest Christian preaching was based upon the emerging sect's application to Jesus of key prophetic texts.[52]

---

themselves. Or course, there have been studies devoted to Paul's use of the Old Testament. For example, H. VOLLMER, *Die Alttestamentlichen Citate bei Paulus* (1895); W. WINDFUHR, "D. Ap. Paulus als Haggadist," *ZAW* 44 (1926) pp. 327ff.; A. VON HARNACK, *Das Alte Testament in den Paulinischen Briefen und in den Paulinischen Gemeinden,* SAB Phil.-Hist. Kl. 12 (1928); Otto MICHEL, *Paulus und Seine Bibel* (1929); J. BONSIRVEN, *Exégèse Rabbinique et Exégèse Paulinienne* (Paris: Beauchesne et ses Fils, 1938); S. LYONNET, "S. Paul et l'exégèse juive de son temps," *Melanges Robert* (Paris, 1957) pp. 494-506; P. VIELHAUER, "Paulus und das Alte Testament," *Studien zur Geschichte und Theologie der Reformation, Festschrift for E. Bizer* (1969) pp. 33-62; E. Earle ELLIS, *Paul's Use of the Old Testament* (London: Oliver and Boyd, 1957); A. T. HANSON, *Studies in Paul's Technique and Theology* (London: SPCK, 1974), chapters 7-10; Hans-Jürgen VAN DER MINDE, *Schrift und Tradition bei Paulus* (Munich: Verlag Ferdinand Schöningh, 1976). These are, however, general works and are interested primarily in Old Testament quotations and Paul's textual tradition as illustrated by those quotations. Only very recently have articles begun to appear which try to grapple in depth with specific texts in the Pauline letters as exegetical argument. For example, Nils DAHL, "Contradictions in Scripture" in *Studies in Paul* (Minneapolis, Minnesota: Augsburg Publishing House, 1977) pp. 159-177; Terrance CALLAN, "Pauline Midrash: The Exegetical Background of Gal. 3:19b," *JBL* 99 (1980) pp. 549-567. In this study I will look at II Cor. 3:1-4:6 in depth as a document produced by a Pharisaically trained Hellenistic Jew of the first century, taking advantage of all of this previous development.

[50] It is to the heirs of the first-century Pharisee that we owe the invaluable preservation of Jewish exegesis in the Talmud and Midrash.

[51] Mt. 12:2-14 par.; 15:1-6 par.; 19:3-12 par.; 21:23-27 par.; 22:15-46 par.

[52] C. H. DODD, *The Apostolic Preaching and its Developments* (New York: Harper & Brothers, Publishers, 1935) and *According to the Scriptures* (London: Nisbet & Co., Ltd., 1952); Barnabas LINDARS, *New Testament Apologetic* (Philadelphia: The Westminster Press, 1961). On the basis of such early works there has been an explosion of interest in the use of the Old Testament in the New at the literary level, especially in the Gospels and Acts of the Apostles. The bibliography is far too extensive to note here, so I have included a section in the general Bibliography under separate heading devoted to this topic in order to indicate the importance of this branch of current New Testament studies.

Actualization of Prophecy

Such a process is not unique to the early Christian group, nor to the coalescing rabbinical schools. During the two centuries before the birth of Jesus as well as the two centuries which followed, numerous other groups within Judaism turned to the scriptures for their inspiration and also applied prophecies directly to explain their own perception of the present and future action of God.[53] This is equally true of the apocalyptic circles that produced the Book of Daniel[54] and the Baruch[55] and Enoch literary cycles,[56] of the sages who produced

---

[53] I do not mean to imply that such an interpretative process existed *only* at this period. During the time of classical prophecy, for example, it was from the Pentateuch that Jeremiah, Isaiah and Ezekiel drew much of their material. To verify this it is only necessary to search their works for creation or exodus imagery. I merely wish to assert here that such a process was alive and even burgeoning around the beginning of the Christian era as well, with the prophecies themselves added as fuel for such interpretation.

[54] The origin of and parallels to Daniel 12:1-3 have been discussed by G. W. Nicklesburg in *Resurrection, Immortality and Eternal Life in Intertestamental Judaism*, HTS 26 (Cambridge: Harvard University Press, 1972). Its relationship to Jeremiah 25:11-12 in Chapter 9 is explained by Emil Schürer in *The Literature of the Jewish People in the Time of Jesus* (New York: Schocken Books, 1972) pp. 53-54 and by Nicklesburg in *Jewish Literature Between the Bible and the Mishnah* (Philadelphia: Fortress Press, 1981) p. 86. The work of Schürer cited here is a reprint of Volume III of his 1874 German work translated in 1924 as *History of the Jewish People in the Time of Jesus Christ*. It retains its importance for the study of Jewish intertestamental literature in spite of its age and its somewhat hostile stance.

[55] On the dependence of I Baruch on Isaiah, Jeremiah, Ezekiel and Daniel as well as the Pentateuchal narratives, see the introduction and notes by O. C. Whitehouse in R. H. Charles, *The Apocrypha of the Old Testament* (Oxford: Clarendon Press, 1913), "I Baruch," pp. 569-595 and Nicklesburg, *Jewish Literature*, pp. 110-111. On II and III Baruch, see the introduction and notes by Charles himself for II Baruch and by H. M. Hughes for III Baruch in R. H. Charles, *The Pseudepigrapha of the Old Testament* (Oxford: Clarendon Press, 1913), "II Baruch," pp. 470-526, "III Baruch," pp. 527-541. The preoccupation of II Baruch with the figure of Adam and the biblical Jeremiah traditions is well known. Biblical material is continually interlaced in both apocalypses. See Nicklesburg, *Jewish Literature*, pp. 281-287, 299-303. This intertestamental Jewish literature also shows extensive parallelism within itself (see the parallels with Daniel and IV Ezra cited by Charles and Nicklesburg). This is due to the reworking of similar biblical materials as much as to the recurrence of similar contemporary concerns.

[56] The books of Enoch take their point of departure from the biblical figure of Enoch and also show a special interest in the figure of Noah and the narrative accounts concerning them in the early chapters of Genesis. See R. H. Charles, *Pseudepigrapha*, pp. 163-281 for I Enoch and pp. 425-469 for II Enoch. I do not wish to minimize the structural difficulties in the books by mentioning Enoch and Noah together here, although the presence of these figures does indicate roughly the presence of various sources within the present I Enoch. I only wish to indicate the primary scriptural referent of this cycle of literature. See Nicklesburg, *Jewish Literature*, pp. 46-55, 185-188, 214-223.

the Wisdom of Solomon,[57] and of the ascetic group which demonstrated its critique of the contemporary religious authority in Judaism by withdrawing into the desert at Qumran.[58]

Interest in the Fathers

It was certainly not only to the prophetic texts that the interpreters of scripture looked at this period. The immediate pre- and post-Christian centuries also show a dramatic increase in pseudepigraphical books ascribed to the great figures from the earliest period of Israel's history, as the mention above of the books of Enoch has already indicated. A great interest in and a literature ascribed to Adam,[59] Enoch and Noah,[60] the

---

There is considerably more scholarly interest in the use of Enoch literature by the New Testament authors and at Qumran, than in the use of the Old Testament in the books of Enoch. See James H. CHARLESWORTH, *The Pseudepigrapha and Modern Research.* Septuagint and Cognate Studies 7S (Chico, California: Scholars Press, 1981) pp. 100-105. Therefore, the introduction and notes to Charles' edition of these works, although quite old, remain the best resource for tracing its biblical referents along with the new critical edition of *The Old Testament Pseudepigrapha* edited by James CHARLESWORTH, 2 Volumes (Garden City, New York: Doubleday & Company, Inc., 1983-1985).

[57] Aside from its use of Proverbs 1 and 8, M.J. SUGGS has suggested Deutero-Isaiah as the basis for text on the suffering righteous man of Wisdom 2-5 ("Wisdom of Solomon 2;10-5: A Homily Based on the Fourth Servant Song," *JBL* 76 [1957] pp. 26-33). See also Addison WRIGHT, *The Literary Genre Midrash* (Staten Island, New York: Alba House, 1967) p. 126 and his earlier articles, "The Structure of Wisdom 11-19," *CBQ* 27 (1965) pp. 28-34 and "The Structure of the Book of Wisdom," *Biblica* 48 (1967) pp. 165-184.

[58] In the literature of the Qumran sect, we possess a Community Rule, modeled in many ways after Pentateuchal legislation, an expansion of the Abraham narrative of Genesis 15, a book of psalms modeled after the canonical Psalms and parts of contemporizing commentaries on the books of Habakkuk and Isaiah, to indicate only the scope of the covenanters relationship to and use of scriptural traditions.

[59] *The Life of Adam and Eve*, first century A.D., a haggadic midrash on Genesis 1-4 (CHARLES, *Pseudepigrapha*, S.A. WELLS, ed., pp. 123-154). Among intertestamental books otherwise ascribed, Adam is of paramount importance in *II Baruch* and *IV Ezra* especially. Both of these works date from the first century A.D. Interest in Adam continued in and beyond the early Christian period. The Nag Hammadi library contained an *Apocalypse of Adam*, also dating from the first or second century A.D., and a *Testament of Adam* exists as appended to the *Cave of Treasures*, although scholars feel that the Adam fragment dates from the late second century A.D. (see CHARLESWORTH, *Pseudepigrapha and Modern Research*, pp. 91-92).

[60] *I* and *II Enoch* have already been noted above, as has the incorporation of the Noahic literature into *I Enoch*. A third book of Enoch dates between the first century and the third century A.D. A separate *Book of Noah* circulated independently in the second century B.C., on the evidence of *Jubilees* and the *Testament of Levi*, but is now preserved only in fragments within *Jubilees* itself and *I Enoch*, and in some fragments found in Qumran Cave 1 (see CHARLESWORTH, *Pseudepigrapha and Modern Research*, pp. 166-167).

Patriarchs, especially Joseph,[61] and Moses[62] emerges in this particular period.

The fathers are typically understood to be the recipients of privileged information in extra-terrestrial revelations which they are instructed to pass on to Israel or to a special group within Israel in the pseudepigraphical books.[63] These heroic figures from the past were at the same time frequently taken as models for the proper religious attitudes and ethical behavior for contemporary Jews, since they had been judged worthy of such special favor.[64] It is from the historical narratives of the Pentateuchal books that the original inspiration for these apocryphal expansions are drawn. Biblical narratives are repeated but amplified by current religious experience and prophetic insight.[65]

Although the imagery of the apocalyptic books may strike the modern reader as bizarre and the detail of the elaborations on the bare

---

[61] Abraham, Jacob and Joseph are the patriarchal figures of primary interest around the first century A.D. Works concerning these figures include: *Apocalypse of Abraham* (first century A.D., a haggadic midrash on Genesis 15:9-17); *Testament of Abraham* (first century A.D., concerning events preceding the death of Abraham); *The Ladder of Jacob* (date uncertain, a haggadic midrash of Genesis 28:10-17); *Testament of Jacob* (date uncertain, a midrashic expansion of Genesis 47:29-50:26); *Testament of the Twelve Patriarchs* (second century B.C., with later Christian redaction, a recounting of the deeds of the sons of Jacob in testament form); *Joseph and Asenath* (late first century A.D., a haggadic midrash on Genesis 41:45); *Prayer of Joseph* (lost, possibly a midrash on Genesis 32:24-31, date uncertain but possibly second century A.D.). For editions and critical and bibliographical data, consult CHARLESWORTH, *Pseudepigrapha*, pp. 70-211, passim. This recent work of Charlesworth, along with the older bibliographical volume edited by Gerhard DELLING, *Bibliographie zur Jüdisch-Hellenistischen und Intertestamentarischen Literatur 1900-1965* (Berlin: Akademie-Verlag, 1969) are the major resource volumes on the non-canonical literature of this period.

[62] Moses is also among the most important figures of this period, but rather more important for the early rabbis than for the apocalyptic sects. Nevertheless, he has his share of pseudepigraphical works attributed to him. These include: *Apocalypse of Moses* (the Greek recension of *The Life of Adam and Eve*, see above note 59); *Assumption of Moses* (first century A.D., including an originally distinct *Testament of Moses*, midrashic expansion of Deuteronomy 34); *Prayer of Moses* (from *Liber Antiquitatum Biblicarum* 19:14-16, circa A.D. 100, an expansion of the biblical narratives from Genesis through 2 Samuel). See L. GINZBERG, *Legends of the Jews*, 8 vols. trans. Henrietta Szold (Philadelphia: The Jewish Publication Society of America, 1909), vols. 2 and 3 for the rabbinic material concerning Moses. Other volumes contain information regarding the other figures mentioned above, arranged according to the order of the biblical narrative.

[63] I Enoch 1:2; II Enoch 1:1-10; 3:1-3; 7:1; 8:1, etc.; III Baruch 1:8-2:1ff.; see D. S. RUSSELL, *Between The Testaments* (Philadelphia: Fortress Press, 1960) pp. 95-96.

[64] This is true especially of Enoch, Abraham, Joseph and Moses. See, for example, I Enoch 104:10-13; 105:1-2; *Joseph and Asenath* in its entirety; Paul's use of Abraham in Romans 4 and Galatians 3, and *Assumption of Moses* 11:16; also RUSSELL, *Between the Testaments*, p. 97.

[65] The information provided in note 61 above clearly indicates the nature of this literature as rewritten biblical narrative.

bones of the biblical narratives unwarranted, in fact this literature was not produced in a cavalier or even in an undisciplined way. If a Pentateuchal narrative is used as the basis for a later expansion, it is very likely that some detail in the original story invites an explanation, or at least leaves room for one.[66] Research on the compositional methodologies of the Jewish intertestamental literature is still in its childhood, if not its infancy, and it is not the purpose of this brief introduction to fully illustrate the point. Perhaps one pertinent example will suffice to indicate my reasons for making this statement.

In the apocryphal book, *The Assumption of Moses* as in other later pseudepigraphical and rabbinic texts, Moses is credited with a divine vision of the heavenly realms and with a privileged prophetic revelation of the future of Israel and the world.[67] It is extremely likely that the development of this legend is an explanation of the events which might have taken place on the basis of Exodus 24:18, "Then Moses entered the cloud as he went on up the mountain. And he stayed on the mountain forty days and forty nights." Forty days and forty nights is a long time, and although Exodus 25-31 does provide some information about what the Lord and Moses were conferring about all that time, even the wilderness generation began to wonder about Moses' long absence (Exod. 32:1). That generation did not know what was happening to Moses, but the groups which produced the later pseudepigraphical and midrashic works felt that they did.

Certainly, this is partly the result of a lively religious imagination and the natural development of legend. It is also, however, a response to the prophetic heritage by then available to Israel, to an authentic religious impulse to honor Moses with visions resembling those granted to the later prophets, and to the religious environment of the times for which divine visions were an accepted part of the life of a "man of God."[68] It must be remembered, too, that although the books of Moses

---

[66] With regard to the Enoch literature, NICKLESBURG cites Gen. 5:24, "Enoch walked with God; and he was not, for God took him," and comments that "The two halves of this cryptic passage suggest *in nuce* the two principal elements of a sizable amount of Jewish revelatory literature that is attached to the name of this ancient patriarch: (1) Enoch was righteous in an unrighteous age. (2) Therefore God saw fit to remove him from this earth in order to transmit to him esoteric revelation about the nature of the universe and about the end-time; he wrote down this revelation so that it could be transmitted to the righteous who would live in the last days" (*Jewish Literature*, p. 46).

[67] *Assumption of Moses* 2-10:10; see GINZBERG, *Legends* III, pp. 110-142 and notes for the rabbinic material on Moses' sojourn in heaven.

[68] I do not wish to enter here into the debate over the precise portrait which should be drawn of the *theios aner* in the first century and to what degree such a designation is applicable to Jesus, Moses or Paul. I refer the reader to two recent books devoted to the question and to the extensive literature cited therein, D. L. TIEDE, *The Charismatic Figure as Miracle Worker*, SBL Dissertation Series 1 (Missoula, Montana: Scholars Press, 1972)

were highly revered, there was not quite the same concept of a closed canon of scripture that exists in both Judaism and Christianity today.[69] Therefore, the biblical interpreter who produced an apocryphal or pseudepigraphical expansion of a biblical narrative may well have justifiably felt that, far from doing violence to a sacred text, he was providing a completely legitimate explanation of it. In my investigation of II Cor. 3:1-4:6 we will see Paul both providing a similar expansion of an event in the life of Moses described in Exodus 34 and using Moses as a model for contemporary Christian Jews like himself.

Methods of Biblical Interpretation

In studying rabbinic literature too, one finds that the use of scripture is not haphazard at all, but is carried on very carefully according to a set of rules designed to preserve and honor the text interpreted and to control the scope of possible interpretations to be drawn from it. The famous rules or *middoth* of Hillel and Ishmael are familiar to all students of early Jewish literature and are becoming increasingly well known to

---

and C.H. HOLLADAY, *Theios Aner in Hellenistic Judaism*, SBL Dissertation Series 40 (Missoula, Montana: Scholars Press, 1977). It is the thesis of Dieter GEORGI that Paul's opponents in Corinth, and specifically in II Cor. 3:7ff. saw Moses as a *theios aner* and modelled themselves after him. (*Die Gegner*, pp. 258-265). He selects as the outstanding evidence for this view Philo's description of Moses in Vit. Mos. II, 69f. (*Die Gegner*, p. 259). Philo's presentation of Moses does indeed provide good evidence for a *theios aner* picture and for the validity of the category at that time. I would prefer, in distinction to Georgi, a picture of Moses, and of Paul on his model, as the humble and suffering prophet. This is not to deny that Paul's opponents may well have held the *theios aner* view. It is only to assert and, in a future work, explain how Paul did not. No one will deny, at any rate, the relevance of ecstasy and vision for either the *theios aner* or the prophet in this period.

[69] This is not to deny the sacred nature of the Torah at a much earlier period (at least 200 B.C.) or of the Prophets shortly thereafter. But in Christian times, debates regarding several of the Writings were still going on. This indicates that the body of scripture was not as rigid as it is today and that books, now non-canonical, could be very influential, such as *I Enoch*, *IV Ezra*, and the *Wisdom of Solomon*. See RUSSELL, *Between the Testaments*, pp. 59-62. He disagrees with himself, however, when he says on p. 61 that "... by New Testament times at least the Canon of Scripture was virtually closed." and then on p. 62 that "the matter of the Canon was still a point of debate in the second and third centuries A.D." On the formation of the Old Testament Canon, see also Otto EISSFELDT, *The Old Testament, an Introduction;* translated by P. R. Ackroyd (Oxford: Basil Blackwell for Harper and Row, 1965) pp. 559-571 and the literature cited there. For more recent work on canon, see J. A. SANDERS, *Torah and Canon* (Philadelphia: Fortress Press, 1972); "Adaptable for Life; The Nature and Function of Canon," in *Magnalia Dei*, F. M. CROSS et al., eds. (Garden City: Doubleday, 1976) pp. 531-560, and "Text and Canon: Concepts and Method," *JBL* 98 (1979) pp. 5-29; Brevard CHILDS, *Biblical Theology in Crisis* (Philadelphia: Westminster, 1970) and *Introduction to the Old Testament as Scripture* (Philadelphia: Fortress Press, 1979); Joseph BLENKINSOPP, *Prophecy and Canon* (Notre Dame: University of Notre Dame Press, 1977).

students of early Christian literature as well.[70] It must be admitted that the work of the rabbis as it is preserved was assembled too late to be directly applicable in a discussion of the literature surrounding the very beginning of the Common Era. Nevertheless, an increasing number of scholars realize that certain of these rabbinic exegetical techniques pre-existed their incorporation into the lists of rules as they now exist and can be helpful in understanding biblical interpretation as carried on at an earlier period, just as the contents of certain Talmudic and Targumic texts are sometimes helpful parallels to first-century Jewish and Christian texts.[71] In this study two of the most basic rabbinic exegetical rules, the *kal va-homer* inference and the *gezera shava* analogy will be used to explain Paul's handling of the scripture texts that his argument in II Cor. 3:1-18 interprets.

---

[70] These are conveniently presented and briefly explained in the article "Hermeneutics" in the *Encyclopedia Judaica* 8, pp. 366-371 with a small bibliography. The author feels that "The indications are that the rules are earlier than Hillel," who lived in the first century B.C.

[71] Geza VERMES is the current champion of this cause. In a very recent article he says "Few serious scholars would deny today that rabbinic writings, though compiled between A.D. 200 and 500, include a large quantity of traditions traceable to the first century A.D. and that with a minimum amount of critical skill, it is often possible to distinguish among them between the old and the more recent. ... In short, it has become obvious to many — in theory at least! — that expertise in the Jewish background to the New Testament is not an optional extra, but that, on the contrary, no adequate understanding of Christian sources is conceivable without it." "Jewish Studies and New Testament Interpretation," *JJS* 31 (1980) pp. 1-17. In his conviction that the earliest layers may be discerned within later rabbinic collections, Vermes is the direct heir of Renée BLOCH, who outlined a method for doing just that in her article "Note méthodologique pour l'étude de la littérature rabbinique," *RSR* 43 (1955) pp. 194-227, translated in *Approaches to Ancient Judaism* I, W. S. GREEN, ed. (Missoula, Montana: Scholars Press, 1978) pp. 51-76. Vermes tried out her method in his book *Scripture and Tradition in Judaism* (Leiden: Brill, 1961). An increasing number of scholars agree with them, including Merrill MILLER in "Targum, Midrash, and the Use of the OT in the NT," *JSJ* 2 (1971) p. 49; P. BORGEN in *Bread from Heaven* (Leiden: Brill, 1965); E. Earle ELLIS in numerous works on Pauline hermeneutics including *Paul's Use of the Old Testament* and *Prophecy and Hermeneutic in Early Christianity* (Tübingen: J. C. B. Mohr [Paul Siebeck], 1978); Richard LONGENECKER in *Biblical Exegesis in the Apostolic Period* (Minneapolis, Minnesota: Wm. B. Eerdmans, 1975); R. LE DÉAUT in "A propos a Definition of Midrash," *Int* 25 (1971) pp. 259-282 and Daniel PATTE in *Early Jewish Hermeneutic in Palestine*, SBL Dissertation Series 22 (Missoula, Montana: Scholars Press, 1975) to name only a few key representatives. The acceptance of rabbinic parallels to the New Testament is not always admitted explicitly; sometimes it is simply done without remark. For example, in his *Interpreters Dictionary of the Bible* article, "Shekinah," (4, pp. 317-319), D. MOODY cites a number of New Testament contacts with the use of the term in Judaism without noting what would be for others a difficult time discrepancy, since "Shekinah" is a targumic and talmudic word, but not a biblical one.

Gezera Shava

The *gezera shava* in rabbinic legal texts is an analogy which rests on a similarity of *verbal expression* in two separate texts, which on the basis of this verbal similarity are linked and used to explain, clarify or amplify one another.[72] Therefore, on the basis of a word or words which the two texts share, they are perceived to be in fact similar and related. Such linking through hook words is basic to the mnemonics of most folk literature and to the educational system of many ancient cultures.[73] Items in a series are linked in verbal expression for the sake of memorization. A good example contemporary to II Corinthians is offered by the words of Jesus in the Synoptic Gospels, which are frequently linked through a hook-word structure.[74] While these synoptic sayings or similitude catenae are a good analogy to the form of such verbal text linkage and while the effort to memorize may lie at the root of more sophisticated uses of the form, the impulse to interpret such linked texts on the basis of each other requires something else as well. In order to regard such verbally linked texts as mutually interpreting, the biblical interpreter must perceive the field from which the texts are selected as unified in some way. It is easy to understand why the Jesus sayings were thus linked. They were understood to stem from a single speaker, Jesus.[75]

Something analogous to this "single speaker" idea also exists with regard to non-legal scriptural texts verbally linked and used to interpret each other. The Jewish scriptures were, already in the first century and long before, regarded as a unity as the word of God for Israel and its

---

[72] H. L. STRACK, *Introduction to the Talmud and Midrash* (New York: The Jewish Publication Society of America, 1959) p. 94; Moses MIELZINER, *Introduction to the Talmud*, fourth edition (New York: Bloch Publishing Company, 1968) pp. 142-155 (The fourth edition cited contains a new bibliography including works from 1925-1967, thus nearly bridging the gap between the third edition, appearing in 1925, and the present day and greatly increasing the value of the work); Richard Longenecker, *Biblical Exegesis, p. 34*.

[73] See Rudolf BULTMANN, *History of the Synoptic Tradition*, revised edition. Translated by John Marsh (New York: Harper & Row, 1963) p. 325 with regard to the gospels and E. Earle ELLIS, *Paul's Use* p. 50 for the Pauline letters; D. PATTE, *Early Jewish Hermeneutic* pp. 13-14; and W. S. TOWNER, *The Rabbinic Enumeration of Scriptural Examples* (Leiden: Brill, 1973) pp. 154-181 for later rabbinic uses of the hook-word technique.

[74] BULTMANN, *History*, pp. 325-326 cites Mk. 4:21ff.; 9:33ff. and Lk. 11:7-24, 33-36 as New Testament examples of hook-word linkage. There are many more, for example, the "kingdom of heaven" parables in Mt. 13:44-52.

[75] Or, they were *presented* as stemming from him, even if they in fact arose within the early church from prophets or were provided by the cultural milieu and selected for their appropriateness.

heirs.[76] In Exodus, Leviticus, Numbers and Deuteronomy Moses is constantly depicted as receiving the word of God and communicating it.[77] The prophets most of all enunciate a message directly from God to the people, as the standard form of the prophetic oracle indicates.[78] Particularly in the Pentateuch and the prophetic corpus, then, the verbal expression of the biblical text itself was perceived as a direct communication through Moses or the prophet from God himself, in virtue of which that verbal expression was both valuable and unified. The unity of the word of God as preserved in the books of Moses and the prophets, in content and so also in verbal expression, based on their divine authorship, is the necessary presupposition of the *gezera shava* as an exegetical technique. Though the rabbinic standardization of that technique is known to us from post-Christian times, the New Testament itself provides the evidence for similar mutual interpretation of verbally linked non-legal texts in the first century.[79] This study will show that this simplest of exegetical methods was known and used by Paul in the construction of II Corinthians 3:1-4:6.

---

[76] The fact that this is true *in theory* hardly needs proof. It is assumed by everyone who works with rabbinic materials as the guiding principle of rabbinic exegesis and is so obvious in the New Testament itself that it is rarely mentioned. See D. PATTE, *Early Jewish Hermeneutic*, pp. 19-27; M. MILLER, "Targum Midrash, Etc.," p. 58; R. BLOCH, "Midrash" in *Dictionnaire de la Bible*, Supplément 5, 1263-1281, English translation in *Approaches to Ancient Judaism* I, pp. 29-50, esp. pp. 32f.; Ragnar BRING, "Paul and the Old Testament," *Studia Theologica* 25 (1971) p. 2; D.S. RUSSELL, *Between the Testaments*, p. 64. *In practice*, however, it is always true, as C.H. DODD is correct in pointing out for early Christian use of the Old Testament, that certain sections of the scriptures as a whole are selected and much used because they are felt to respond particularly well to the current needs of the religious community using them (*According to the Scriptures*, pp. 60, 126).

[77] The Exodus text with which Paul works in II Cor. 3:7-18 is a good example of this general pattern. In Ex. 34:32 and 34 Moses is depicted as receiving words from the Lord which he transmits to Israel. It is clearly implied that he transmits only what the Lord commanded and *all* that the Lord commanded. It is true that in later Judaism the idea arose that Moses did not write down all that was commanded, but taught some things only orally (GINSBERG, *Legends* III, p. 142). This is clearly an apologetic for the oral Torah. But nowhere in Judaism is it ever asserted that Moses taught of himself, rather than transmitting a divine message.

[78] The frequent "messenger" form of the prophetic oracle — "Thus says the Lord," followed by direct quotation — indicates the consciousness of delivering a divine message. See EISSFELDT, *The Old Testament*, pp. 148-150, 561; G. VON RAD, *Old Testament Theology* II (New York: Harper & Row, 1965) pp. 36-38; J. LINDBLOM, *Prophecy in Ancient Israel* (Philadelphia: Fortress Press, 1962) pp. 108-114.

[79] In Rom. 9:32-33, Isa. 8:14 and 28:16 are obviously linked through λίθος and are interpreted as referring to the same reality. In I Peter 2:4-8, Isa. 8:14, 28:16 and Ps. 118:22 are linked and used in the same way. A different combination appears in Heb. 1:5, where Ps. 2:7 and 2 Sam. 7:14 are linked through υἱός and referred to the person.

Kal Va-Homer

The inference *kal va-homer*, on the other hand, does not necessarily rest on the verbal unity of scripture, but on any perceived correspondence between two statements or events and the presumed superiority of one. The argument asserts that what is true of the inferior member of a similar pair must be true also of the superior, and to a superior degree.[80] This is simply an example of reasoning *a fortiori*. This rule of syllogism is familiar in Greek rhetoric of the New Testament period as an argument *a minore ad maius*. Both the similarity which is the ground of comparison and the dissimilarity on the basis of which the argument functions are presupposed and not proven by the inference. The purpose of the inference itself is only to indicate the presence of a characteristic in the superior on the basis of its known presence in the inferior. It requires no special argument to assert that Paul has used such reasoning in the interpretation of scriptural texts in II Corinthians 3:7-18. His use of this form is clear in verses 7-9 and 11 and is recognized by many commentators.[81] It is obvious in the Epistle to the Romans as well.[82]

Pesher

Since the Judaism of the first century of the Common Era was as varied as historians now agree that it was,[83] it is no surprise that such a

---

[80] H. L. Strack, *Introduction*, p. 94; M. Mielziner, *Introduction*, pp. 130-136; R. Longenecker, *Biblical Exegesis*, p. 34.

[81] Windisch, *Der zweite Korintherbrief*, p. 112; Allo, *Seconde Epître*, p. 87; Bultmann, *Der zweite Brief*, p. 82; Bonsirven, *Exégèse Rabbinique*, p. 317; S. Schulz, "Die Decke," p. 5; H. Mueller, "Die Auslegung alttestamentlichen Geschichtsstoffs bei Paulus," *Theologische Literaturzeitung* 10 (1961), col. 789; Georgi, *Die Gegner*, p. 279; H. Ulonska, "Die Doxa des Mose," *EvTh* 26 (1966) p. 384; Prümm, *Diakonia Pneumatos*, p. 125; Isaac I. Friesen, *The Glory of the Ministry of Jesus Christ* (Basel: Friedrich Reinhardt Kommissionsverlag, 1971) p. 48; Collange, *Enigmes*, pp. 76-82; Martin H. Scharlemann, "Of Surpassing Splendor. An Exegetical Study of 2 Corinthians 3:4-18," *Concordia Journal* 4 (1978) p. 116; Richard, "Polemics," p. 353; Thomas E. Provence, "Who is Sufficient for These Things? An Exegesis of 2 Corinthians 2:15-3:18," *Nov Test* 24 (1982) p. 73; J. Lambrecht, "Structure and Line of Thought," pp. 355-356. Not all of these authors note the Jewish background of the form, and none fully explore its function and implications.

[82] Such a *kal va-homer* argument is the basic structure of Rom. 5:9-20. Interestingly, Windisch cites Rom. 5:15,17 and Rom. 11:12,24 in order to explicate the form in II Cor. 3:7-11 (*Der zweite Korintherbrief*, p. 112). The argument of Rom. 5:15-17 has most recently been superbly analyzed by Jack Levison at the annual meeting of the Society of Biblical Literature in December, 1982 in his paper entitled "New Pseudepigraphical Adam Data and Their Relation to Paul's Theology."

[83] The abandonment of any harsh antithesis between Palestinian and Hellenistic or between Pharisaic and Apocalyptic Judaism at this period has now reached the level of consensus. See W. D. Davies, *Paul and Rabbinic Judaism*, p. viii and Martin Hengel,

variety of ways existed at that time in which the scriptures were handled
by different groups within Judaism. This brief review has mentioned the
production of pseudepigraphical works in the names of biblical heroes of
the past as a means of continuing, interpreting and appropriating their
traditions. We have also seen the roots of and parallels to the meticulous
and logical scriptural exegesis of later centuries in evidence in the
Synoptic Gospels and the letters of the New Testament. Lastly, I would
like to point to a particular aspect of the biblical exegesis of the Qumran
sect as a parallel to the methodology of the Pauline text with which this
study will shortly begin to deal.

The monks of Qumran are a good example of the tendency to adopt
and identify with biblical models in ethics and life style in their withdrawal
from mainstream society in Palestine to a life of conscious asceticism in the
desert. Many scholars have pointed out this phenomenon as a deliberate
imitation of the wilderness period under Moses common also to several
political messianic leaders in the first century.[84] They also, however,
undertook more scholarly biblical commentary in which they interpreted
prophetic books in particular by applying them verse by verse to the
current circumstances of the social, religious and political life of the sect,
and its expectations for the future. Although only a small portion of this
exegesis remains, it is enough to indicate both its method, called *pesher* in
imitation of the introductory formula used, and the intention which guided
it.[85] The impulse of the Qumran interpreter was to show how the biblical
text was directly relevant to the community's life and to draw from the text
hope and instruction for the community's future. The prophet who wrote
long before was understood to have been speaking directly to the
interpreter's own day, so that his message could only be understood
completely from that standpoint.[86] In the following study we will see Paul

---

Judaism and Hellenism I, pp. 1, 104. Any radical division between earliest Christianity and
Judaism itself is likewise untenable. As it emerged, Christianity was a sect *within* Judaism.
(DAVIES, *Paul and Rabbinic Judaism*, pp. xxxv-xxxvi).

[84] W. R. STEGNER, "The Self-Understanding of the Qumran Community Compared
with the Self-Understanding of the Early Church," unpublished Ph.D. dissertation, Drew
University, 1960; Howard M. TEEPLE, *The Mosaic Eschatological Prophet*, SBL
Monographs 10 (Philadelphia: Society of Biblical Literature, 1957) pp. 30-31, 64-66;
Wayne A. MEEKS, *The Prophet-King* (Leiden: Brill, 1967) pp. 171-173; Peter JONES, "The
Apostle Paul: A Second Moses," pp. 232-236.

[85] The monks of Qumran commented on at least Habakkuk (the best preserved of
their commentaries), Hosea, Micah, Isaiah, Zephaniah, Nahum, and also some of the
Psalms. All of these works, however, are preserved only in fragmentary form.

[86] For background discussion of the term "pesher" and of *pesher exegesis*, the reader
may refer to E. Earle ELLIS, *Paul's Use*, pp. 139-147; R. LONGENECKER, *Biblical Exegesis*,
pp. 38-45; D. PATTE, *Early Jewish Hermeneutic*, pp. 299-308; William H. BROWNLEE, *The
Midrash Pesher of Habakkuk*, Society of Biblical Literature Monograph Series 24
(Missoula, Montana: Scholars Press, 1979) pp. 23-36; and Maurya HORGAN, *Pesharim:*

adopting such a viewpoint, and even using a form similar to that which the Qumran pesher frequently took, when he deals with scriptural texts in II Cor. 3:14-17.

Summary

Despite the great variety which existed in Judaism at the beginning of our era, however, there is at least one point on which all of the segments of society and all of its literary remnants agree. For all of these groups and for all of these literary forms, biblical traditions and the scriptural texts themselves were the stuff out of which and through which these various groups sought and found self-identification and through which they assimilated their own religious experience.[87] This is in evidence in the increased importance of the great men of the biblical narratives, in the production of pseudepigraphical works containing rewritten biblical narratives, and in the production of verse-by-verse applications of scriptural texts at Qumran. Even the Wisdom literature of the period, although not all pseudepigraphical, begins to contain recitals of the deeds of the fathers, as Sirach and the Wisdom of Solomon do.[88] In the New Testament the Epistle to the Hebrews contains a recitation of the deeds of faith performed by the great men of old,[89] and so also bears witness to the continuing importance of the older biblical hero as role model in the Christian group.[90] For the Christian, however, Jesus Christ had become the single pivot toward which all of this variety was turned, for Paul in II Corinthians 3 no less than for others.

Qumran Interpretations of Biblical Books, The Catholic Biblical Quarterly Monograph Series 8 (Washington, D.C.: The Catholic Biblical Association of America, 1979) pp. 229-259.

[87] Even Philo, who may seem to have been neglected here, felt it necessary to ground, or apply, his philosophical system within his received scriptural tradition. A catalogue of his works easily illustrates the importance for him of the Pentateuch and of various biblical figures, especially Moses. I have not dealt with his works here, and I shall not deal with them extensively in this study, for two reasons. First, I believe that Philo's treatment of Moses has been amply discussed in the works of GEORGI, MEEKS, TIEDE and HOLLADAY cited above, and its relationship to II Cor. 3:7-18 sufficiently investigated. I wish to elaborate on a different aspect of the first-century picture of Moses which is better illustrated by the literature I have emphasized. Second, I feel that the relationship between the thought of Philo and that of Paul, while sometimes interesting and illuminating, is basically tangential and secondary. Therefore, the works of Philo are not a major focus of this study. Cf. E. Earle ELLIS, *Paul's Use*, pp. 52-54.

[88] Sirach 44:1-49:16; Wisdom 10:1-11:1, although this recital is cast as a hymn to Wisdom itself.

[89] Hebrews 11:2-12:1.

[90] As Heb. 12:2 clearly indicates, however, Jesus is first set in the company of these biblical figures and then becomes the central model around which all the others coalesce.

The historical presupposition of this essay is that the foregoing brief description of the Judaism of the beginning of the Common Era describes the primary intellectual and religious world in which Paul lived, thought and wrote. I assume that the now canonical scriptures and the intertestamental literature of the Jews were for him, as for his contemporaries, a primary source of religious reflection and a primary vehicle for the expression of religious experience and theological insight. I assume, further, that it is probable that the particular methods of biblical interpretation which were in use among his contemporaries in this milieu will also be in evidence in his own treatment of biblical passages. The focus text for this study is one in which Paul is in fact quite obviously dealing with at least one scriptural text, Exodus 34:27-35, and at least one biblical figure, Moses.

Statement of Thesis

My thesis regarding II Corinthians 3:1-4:6 is then as follows. The argument and content of II Cor. 3:1-4:6 can best be understood with reference to an exegetical background or substructure which informs and supports it. The task of the two central chapters will be to discover this substructure, analyze it according to analogous contemporary exegetical models and methods, and describe its effect on the surface argument of the text itself. This exegetical substructure is in turn supported by interpretive presuppositions drawn from and shared with the Judaism of the day and nascent Christianity. The conclusion of this study will indicate traces of these presuppositions and the questions they raise, as an anticipation of work to appear in a subsequent volume.

The major differences between this and other treatments of II Corinthians, and in particular of II Corinthians 3, should be obvious from the brief review of scholarly literature undertaken at the beginning of this Introduction and will be further elaborated in the course of this study. One of the most important differences is in my focus on the background to the text as a literary and exegetical document rather than on the historical circumstances which gave rise to it. Very little really new "Pauline theology" is likely to emerge at this late date, and none was expected here. The effort throughout is rather to look at Paul's argument for its own sake, through the window of the biblical texts with which he dealt and of the multiform Judaism of his time and to see if that vantage point will yield some fresh insight into how his argument originally worked and into the conceptual world out of which it emerged. I see Paul as a Jew of his own time, converted to Jesus Christ and committed to preaching the gospel, but committed as well to explaining this new religious experience in terms of the biblical traditions of the past. With these presuppositions and goals stated as openly and clearly as possible at the outset, I can undertake once again to better understand what A. T. Hanson has recently called "the Mount Everest of Pauline texts as far as difficulty is concerned ...." [91]

---

[91] Although Professor HANSON's reference was to II Cor. 3:18 alone ("The Midrash in II Corinthians 3," p. 19), I feel justified in extending it to include the whole passage. Hardly a commentator fails to note the extreme difficulty of II Corinthians 3 as he or she begins, and I am no exception. See W. C. VAN UNNIK, "With Unveiled Face," pp. 153-154, who also regards it as one of the most interesting and important of all Pauline texts; Morna HOOKER, "Beyond the Things that are Written?," p. 296 and J. A. FITZMYER, "Glory Reflected on the Face of Christ," p. 630.

Chapter One

II CORINTHIANS 3:1-6

Introduction

The Text[1] and its Boundaries

Do we begin again to recommend ourselves? Or do we make use, as some do, of letters of recommendation to you or from you.[2] You are our

---

[1] The following is my own translation of II Corinthians 3:1-6 from the Greek. It is presented for your convenience here, and a similar personal translation will appear at the beginning of Chapter Two. Reference to the notes on these translations will acquaint the reader with my decisions regarding the textual problems and syntactic difficulties that I consider significant in each section. Since any translation already involves interpretation, my deliberate choice of English expression will indicate in advance my viewpoint on Paul's meaning as well. My own outline of the Greek text of II Cor. 3:1-4:6 is appended to this study. The preceding *caveat* applies there as well.

[2] As is generally recognized, the μὴ of II Cor. 3:1b expects the answer "no." With its use, the tone and direction of the ensuing discussion are set. Paul rejects at the start the use of letters of recommendation on his behalf either to or from the Corinthian Christian community. It is the introduction of the topic of these letters that marks this section off from its preceding context. The ideas of competence and commission had already been introduced in II Cor. 1:21-22 and 2:16-17. The thematic importance of *written recommendation* in the text which follows is thereby emphasized. Another small point should also be noticed concerning the vocabulary and syntax of this introductory verse. The sentence begins with the verb, "ἄρχω—to begin." It is this verb which should receive the strongest stress when Paul's sentence is read because of its emphatic position, and the "πάλιν" which follows should be read with it. Paul is disputing the need to *begin again* with the Corinthians. Why should he make a new start? I do not think that ἄρχω is superfluous here, as it could be in late Jewish usage, *A Greek-English Lexicon of the New Testament and other Early Christian Literature*, Translated and edited by W. F. ARNDT and F. W. GINGRICH (Chicago: The University of Chicago Press, 1957) p. 113. On the contrary, I think it indicates Paul's most serious objection to recommending himself: he does not need to go back to the beginning with the Corinthians. The πάλιν which follows indicates that he has already recommended himself to them. It is, therefore, not the case that Paul rejects recommendation. It is not even necessarily true that Paul did not possess some written recommendation on his *first* visit to Corinth, although the ensuing argument indicates that he probably did not. The dispute concerns the *timing* of such recommendation, as well as its form. Contra PLUMMER, *II Corinthians*, pp. 76-77. The literature on this verse is in general directed toward the accusations which gave rise to Paul's rhetorical questions rather than the form of the questions themselves. See COLLANGE, *Enigmes*, p. 43; PRÜMM, *Diakonia Pneumatos*, p. 100; WINDISCH, *Der zweite Korintherbrief*, pp. 102-103 as examples of that approach.

letter, engraved on our hearts,[3] known and read by all men:[4] you are displayed as a letter from Christ,[5] delivered by us,[6] inscribed not with ink but with the spirit of the living God, not in tablets of stone but in tablets which are hearts of flesh. And such great confidence we have through Christ towards God! Not that we are competent in ourselves, so as to reckon anything as coming from ourselves, rather our competence is from God, who has also made us competent to be ministers of a new covenant, not a written covenant but a spiritual covenant: for what is written kills, but the spirit gives life.

II Corinthians 3:1-6 can be distinguished from the material which precedes it primarily through its introduction of a new topic, letters, both epistolary letters and alphabetic letters. It can similarly be distinguished from the material immediately following because of the obvious concen-

---

[3] The textual variant "ὑμῶν" is certainly secondary. The external evidence for "ἡμῶν" is overwhelming (p⁴⁶, A, B, C, D, G, K, P, Ψ, 0243, 81, 104, 181, 326, 330, 451, 614, 629, 630, 1241, 1739, 1877, 1962, 1984, 1985, 2127, 2492, 2495ᵛⁱᵈ, Byz Lect, itᵃʳ,ᵈ,ᵈᵉᵐ,ᵉ,ᶠ,ᵍ,ˣ,ᶻ, vg, syrᵖ,ʰ, copˢᵃ,ᵇᵒ, goth, arm). Moreover, "ἐγγεγραμμένη ἐν ταῖς καρδίαις ἡμῶν" is a good correlative for II Cor. 7:3, "προείρηκα γάρ ὅτι ταῖς καρδίαις ἡμῶν ἐστε..." See Bruce M. Metzger, A Textual Commentary on the Greek New Testament (The United Bible Societies, 1971) p. 577. Surprisingly, the Revised Standard Version and the New American Bible have both adopted the poorly attested "ὑμῶν." In response to this remarkable lapse in the RSV translation, William Baird argued persuasively in favor of ἡμῶν in his article entitled "Letters of Recommendation: A Study of II Cor. 3:1-3" JBL 80 (1961) pp. 166-172 on the basis of its place in the argument of verses 1-3, and not only on the strength of its attestation.

[4] The verb "ἐγγράφω" in contrast to the simple form "γράφω" has "public" connotations. While it can be a synonym for the simple form, ἐγγράφω is frequently used for public enrollment or registration, inscriptions, and writs of execution or indictments. See A Greek-English Lexicon, ed. H. G. Liddell and R. Scott (Oxford: Clarendon Press, 1968) p. 468 and Arndt-Gingrich, Lexicon, p. 212. As such it is a word very well suited to Paul's purposes here. He is concerned with the sort of engraving or inscription which can be "known and read by all men."

[5] I take the genitive "Χριστοῦ" to be subjective with the majority of commentators. See Barrett, Second Corinthians, p. 108; Collange, Enigmes, pp. 48-49, but also Prümm, Diakonia Pneumatos, pp. 102-103. The sense is that the Corinthian Christians are a letter written by Christ and delivered by Paul on his own behalf. Cf. Baird, "Letters of Recommendation," p. 170. Windisch, as well as many other German commentators following him, introduces the idea of the Himmelsbrief to explain Paul's metaphor here. See Windisch, Der zweite Korintherbrief, p. 105; Georgi, Die Gegner, p. 166 and the literature cited there on the origin and attestation of this concept.

[6] The verb here is διακονέω, the common word for Christian service or ministry, and not a term ordinarily reserved for mail delivery. It is at home in this section of II Corinthians, however, where διακονία/διακονέω in various forms are used seven times throughout 3:1-4:6 and where the theme of ministry is of paramount importance. It is not inappropriately translated as "delivered" in 3:3, on the other hand, since its basic sense is "to discharge a commission for." In the context of letters of recommendation, the proper term in English is "deliver," or "carry."

tration of that section, 3:7-18, on a specific event of the Exodus tradition. The first six verses of Chapter 3, therefore, form a discrete section within II Cor. 3:1-4:6 which may profitably be discussed separately before it is treated in context.[7]

Recognition of its Problems

Although these six verses do show a certain unity around the twin poles of competence (a theme continued from 1:12-14, 21-22; 2:16-17) and letter, neither their meaning nor their reference is at all clear at first reading. On the one hand, Paul is not being specific enough. He gives very little information about the background events which gave rise to his outright refusal to supply letters of recommendation (3:1) or his lyric expression of confidence (3:4).[8] On the other hand, he is not completely coherent. His metaphors are mixed. He slides from one topic to another with no explanation and no apparent pattern. Everyone acknowledges these difficulties.[9]

Several examples of the text's ambiguities will illustrate these general problems. It may be inferred from verse 1 that at the time of writing Paul refuses to use letters of introduction, at least to or from Corinth. It is equally clear that there are others who do possess and use such letters. The existence and use of letters of recommendation among Jews and in Pauline churches is known to us. We possess at least one, written by Paul

---

[7] Many commentators put a break between verses 3 and 4, rather than viewing verses 1-6 as a unit. They often see verses 1-3 as more closely connected with 2:14-17. BARRETT, *Second Corinthians*; BRUCE, *1 and 2 Corinthians*; FALLON, *2 Corinthians*; WINDISCH, *Der zweite Korintherbrief*; PRÜMM, *Diakonia Penumatos* and COLLANGE, *Enigmes* all divide the text in this way. PLUMMER, although admitting that the first three verses are transitional, does not. He decides that "there is more pause between the chapters (II Cor. 2 and II Cor. 3) than between vv. 3 and 4." He views them as introductory to Paul's argument in II Cor. 3:1-6:10 as a whole (*II Corinthians*, p. 75). I agree. The argument of the present chapter will illustrate the close connection between 3:3 and 3:6 in particular. See also LAMBRECHT, "Structure and Line of Thought," especially pp. 350-353 and his very interesting study of the concentric structure of II Cor. 2:14-4:6.

[8] Unless such passages as II Cor. 1:3-5, 9-10, 12, 15, 20-21 and 2:14-16 are sufficient explanation.

[9] Very recently, Morna HOOKER's description of the state of this text is a good example. After stating that the chapter begins with "a brilliant metaphor," she goes on to say that "Paul's metaphor—typically becomes a mixed one. ... Paul has jumped from one image to another; put them together, and he is clearly in a mess ..." ("Beyond the Things That are Written?" p. 296). Later Paul is accused of a series of *non sequiturs* (pp. 296, 299) and HOOKER asks, "Why *should* anyone expect Paul to apply the image consistently, after beginning the whole section with a glorious mixed metaphor? It is typical of Paul to explore an idea in this confusing but very rich way." (p. 298). On the contrary, what is typical is for Paul's interpreters to be confused by his method of argumentation. Paul is not in a mess in II Corinthians 3, although an exegete easily might be.

himself on behalf of Phoebe, in Romans 16:1-2 and the following to verse
16.[10] But no further information about those who do use letters is offered
here. No previous argument explains Paul's abrupt rejection of such an
ordinary means of social legitimation. And, finally, no information seems
to be offered here about the differences between those who do use such
letters and Paul, who does not, although an important distinction is
surely implied in the first verse.

Verse 2 seems at first glance to relieve some of this difficulty, but, in
fact, it only deepens the confusion. In saying, "You are our letter," Paul,
according to many interpreters, refers to his status as founder and father
of the Corinthian Christian community as an argument against his need
for letters of recommendation with regard to it.[11] As founder of the
community, it is argued, Paul sarcastically denies his need for
recommendation to it or from it. I would agree. But does Paul's reference
to the Corinthians' conversion really answer the implied objection? A
reproach against Paul for not possessing a legitimating letter on his first
visit to them would not be answered by his subsequent work among them
if the nature and results of that work were under attack or in question —
that is, if the Corinthians had come to feel that they were not the right
sort of "Christians" because Paul was not the right sort of "apostle."

In his major work, *Die Gegner des Paulus im Zweiten Korintherbrief*,
Dieter Georgi has provided valuable information concerning the function
of letters of recommendation in Hellenistic Judaism and the Greco-
Roman milieu in general, as well as an interesting hypothesis regarding
the content and use of such letters in the case of Paul's opponents in II
Corinthians. For Georgi, Paul's opponents possessed letters which
attested to their works in the spirit as apostles who conformed to the
model of Moses as θεῖος ἀνήρ, who worked "signs and wonders" for
Israel in Egypt and the wilderness, and to the model of Christ as θεῖος
ἀνήρ, who performed miraculous and powerful deeds during his earthly
life.[12] Accordingly, for Georgi, behind II Cor. 3:1-2 lies the reproach that
Paul not only lacked such letters, but had failed to conform to this
apostolic model. He had not sufficiently displayed the power and
miracle-working ability of the man of God. He did not preach a Jesus
who had done so. Therefore, his work in Corinth was cast in doubt by
the appearance of other apostles with such credentials, who laid greater

---

[10] BAIRD, "Letters of recommendation," p. 169.

[11] Paul's statement here should be compared with the very similar I Cor. 9:2, "If to
others I am not an apostle, at least I am to you; for you are the seal of my apostleship in
the Lord." So BARRETT, *Second Corinthians*, p. 107 and E.-B. ALLO, *Saint Paul Seconde
Epître aux Corinthiens*, Etudes Bibliques (Paris: Librairie Lecoffre, 1956) pp. 81-82.

[12] GEORGI, *Die Gegner* pp. 38, 127, 131-138, 147-148, 213-218, 243-244, 264-266, in
particular. This is the general thesis of the book and so is to be found throughout.

emphasis on pneumatic manifestations and opposed his gospel on Christological grounds.

There is ample evidence in I Corinthians 1:10-17; 3:4-9, II Corinthians 10-13 and Galatians 1:6-9; 3:1-5; 4:12-20; 5:7-12 of the arrival in Pauline communities of rival apostles or missionaries with a different message. I agree with Georgi that in the case of II Corinthians the attack may have begun on the level of charismatic ability and activity in conformance to a θεῖος ἀνήρ pattern. I do not think, however, that this answer alone solves all of the difficulties of II Corinthians 3:1-6, because it does not fully plumb the depths of Paul's response to this challenge, nor was it intended to do so.[13] Professor Georgi has supplied a great deal of the historical specificity that Paul's own letter lacks. Even against the sociological backdrop which he has provided, however, the argument of II Cor. 3:1-6 remains obscure.

The statement in II Cor. 3:2 that a group of people is a letter, in fact, removes the discussion which ensues from the level of straightforward discourse regarding acceptable social credentials and behavior to the level of metaphor. The metaphor, "You are our letter," works well enough, but only if one accepts Paul's premise. The existence of the Corinthian Christian community is a witness to Paul's effective apostleship *if* Paul's life and their lives are seen as authentically Christian. It is obviously this premise that the opponents decline to grant. So Paul's argument goes on. But questions about the validity and function of his metaphor immediately appear as he does so. What kind of letter is engraved on a heart? How can the Corinthians be engraved on Paul's heart, and why? How can anything engraved on a heart be read by all men?

Matters get no better in verse 3. What have tablets of stone got to do with the letters of recommendation with which Paul began? The section closes without mentioning letters of recommendation again. By verse 6, the discussion is centered on covenants — a new, spiritual one versus a written one. How have we come the distance between verse 1 and verse 6, between letters of recommendation and a spiritual covenant? Has Paul "begun to recommend himself" in answer to the question posed in the first verse by the time he gets to the sixth? If he has, how has he done it?

It is plainly the case that in II Corinthians 3:1-6, we are faced with a text that cannot stand on its own. It lacks both sufficient content and adequate argument. This is not a new idea. All commentaries on II Corinthians 3 acknowledge its obscurity and admit the difficulty of adequately describing its *Sitz im Leben*. And, as I have noted, most interpreters of II Cor. 3:1-6 in particular agree that Paul confuses his metaphors, or that his argument slips from one level to another, or that it

---

[13] GEORGI, *Die Gegner*, p. 274.

functions through an almost unconscious process of free association.[14] But this state of affairs is then accepted too easily. To date, the obscurities of Paul's self-recommendation have not been squarely faced or satisfactorily analyzed. The real question is this: how does Paul argue for the validity of his premise, that his life and apostleship are authentically "Christian" and that therefore the Corinthians are truly "in Christ" as the result of his work?

Definition of the Starting Point

The starting point of my answer is, on the basis of the foregoing brief analysis, that in II Corinthians 3:1-6 we are presented with a text that is inexplicable as it stands. This fact is taken seriously. It therefore requires something from outside the text in itself to fully explain its meaning because its argument is incompletely expressed. No amount of analysis done on these six verses alone will completely clarify them because of insufficient data and an inarticulated logical structure. Presuming an intelligent author, even if not a perfect one, we are, I think, entitled to assume that II Cor. 3:1-6 is the way it is because Paul has allowed it and not entirely by mistake. If this is the case, there are two possible explanations, both of which seem to apply. Either information is lacking because Paul did not wish to convey it, or a background is assumed as familiar to the reader. In II Corinthians 3:1-6, Paul has intended to draw focus away from a negative situation by declining to discuss it directly. So he has omitted the historical information about opponents, their accusations and the unpleasant situation in Corinth which the modern reader so earnestly desires. He has chosen instead to argue on another level, the background for which he apparently feels entitled to assume.

I have already noted that the text appears upon initial reading to function on two levels. It presents and presumably seeks to answer a difficulty encountered by Paul in the course of his ministry. Paul may have been reproached by someone for a lack of credentials.[15] On this account he may have been accused of self-recommendation in the sense of carrying on a ministry without foundation. His ability and his authority seem to have been put into question. Because of this, the Corinthians themselves may have turned against him, wavered, or been seriously

---

[14] RICHARD, "Polemics," pp. 344-345 in dependence on KÄSEMANN; FITZMYER, "Glory Reflected on the Face of Christ," p. 634 with regard to II Cor. 3:7-4:6. See LAMBRECHT, "Structure and Line of Thought," pp. 365-369 for an interesting overview of scholarly interpretations emphasizing this aspect of the text.

[15] I tend to take this literally. Paul is not being sarcastic. Both the Corinthians and his opponents in Corinth were demanding written legitimation of Paul's ministry.

confused.[16] With Georgi I agree that it was against a particular view of Christ derived from Moses as the model for Christology and so for apostleship that Paul was measured and found wanting.[17] Hints of all this may be gathered from verses 1, 2a, 4 and 5.

However, the answer to the accusations directed at Paul from within his social and religious milieu, whatever precise form they took, is not given on that same level. This is the first real difficulty of the text that we possess. As I have said, in verse 2 with the phrase "You are our letter," Paul lifts his argument out of its origin in the life situation of the Corinthian church and into the realm of metaphor. He proceeds in verses 2, 3 and 6 to climb from one image to another, from letter to covenant, until at the end the accusation regarding letters of recommendation and lack of competence may be disregarded entirely. Yet it must be presumed that his argument, though apparently somewhat removed from its hostile *Sitz im Leben* does answer its objections.

Since the text functions on these two levels, called here the social level, or the level of *Sitz im Leben*, and the metaphorical level, or the level of argument, and since neither level provides an immediate explanation

---

[16] HICKLING, "The Sequence of Thought," p. 382.

[17] GEORGI finds the particular view of Moses which supported the opponents' Christology and self-image expressed in Philo's *Vit. Mos. II*, 69-70, for example (*Die Gegner*, p. 259). This text reads "This last [intercourse with women] he had disdained for many a day, almost from the time when, possessed by the spirit, he entered on his work as a prophet, since he held it fitting to hold himself always in readiness to receive the oracular messages. As for eating and drinking, he had no thought of them for forty successive days, doubtless because he had the better food of contemplation, through whose inspiration, sent from heaven above, he grew in grace, first of mind, then of body also through the soul, and in both so advanced in strength and well-being that those who saw him afterwards could not believe their eyes. For we read that by God's command he ascended an inaccessible and pathless mountain, the highest and most sacred in the region, and remained for the period named, taking nothing that is needed to satisfy the requirements of bare sustenance. Then, after the said forty days had passed, he descended with a countenance far more beautiful than when he ascended, so that those who saw him were filled with awe and amazement; nor even could their eyes continue to stand the dazzling brightness that flashed from him like the rays of the sun." This translation is taken from the Loeb Classical Library edition of Philo's works, Volume VI, ed. F. H. COLSON (Cambridge: Harvard University Press, 1935, reprinted in 1950) pp. 483-485. The scriptural sources of the passage are obviously Ex. 24:18 and 34:28-35. It is difficult to say with assurance that this is indeed how Paul's opponents in Corinth viewed Moses. Georgi's assertion is based on the earlier premise of STRACHAN and others (GEORGI, *Die Gegner*, pp. 13-14) that Ex. 34:28-35 was a very important text for Paul's opponents. In *Vit. Mos. II*, 69-70 Philo deals with this text, as Paul does in II Cor. 3:7-18, but it does not necessarily follow that Philo's treatment corresponds to that of Paul's opposition nor that its importance for Paul stems from that opposition. It is interesting, however, that Philo, like Paul, asserts that those who saw Moses' glorified face could not continue (ἀντέκειν) to look at it, although he does not explicitly mention the veil which is so important for Paul in II Cor. 3.

for the logical structure of the text, the interpreter has two avenues down which to go in order to find explanatory material. He may seek to augment his knowledge of either the *Sitz im Leben* of the text or of the metaphors and images used in the course of its argument. Recent interpretation has frequently chosen to elucidate the *Sitz im Leben*. The work of Dieter Georgi has been cited here as the best example of this approach. However, even if this *Sitz im Leben* has been adequately reconstructed, the ambiguities of Paul's own argument would not thereby necessarily be completely clarified. This is especially true of the multi-level argument of II Corinthians 3:1-6.

Since this is the case, and since so very much work has already been done on the *Sitz im Leben* questions,[18] I choose to pursue the other route in seeking material to explain this obscure Pauline text. I will investigate the background of the images and concepts used in the passage, in the hope that in this way the structure of the argument will also be illuminated. In this approach, it is the verbal and conceptual world of the text which is sought rather than Paul's social world. This interpretative route is available because the exegete is in possession of a written text, a literary composition directly susceptible to analysis of its vocabulary, grammar and structure. This is the procedure with which the remainder of this chapter, and indeed the rest of this study, will be involved.

Proposed Solution

Since I have illustrated that a major source of confusion in II Corinthians 3:1-6 is the mixture of two levels of argument, the first step in interpreting the passage must be to un-mix Paul's mixture. I will therefore concentrate on the argument of the text, prescinding from its *Sitz im Leben*, having once acknowledged it there. Any interpreter of II Corinthians 3:1-6 must recognize the implied accusation with which it begins. But, to continue to explain the text on that level, when Paul has not chosen to so compose it, cannot result in an explanation with sufficient relevance to the text which we actually possess. On the other hand, any interpreter who seeks to explain the passage on both levels at once, as we possess it, will inevitably end with an explanation which is as confused as the Pauline text itself. This chapter will, therefore, investigate II Cor. 3:1-6 single-mindedly on the level of metaphor or conceptual content in order to elicit the background which will explain its argumentation.

I have described the second major source of confusion in II Corinthians 3:1-6 as its inexplicit argumentation, or more simply, its

---

[18] See my Introduction, pp. 11-12.

mixed metaphors. It is the thesis of this chapter that there is discoverable from the vocabulary of the section a text-complex from the Old Testament centered around Jeremiah 31 (LXX 38):31-34 constituted by hook-word connections. This background text-complex determines its metaphors, explains the confusing shifts or slips in Paul's imagery, and in this way clarifies the logic of his argument. This text-complex thus forms an indispensable background apart from which II Corinthians 3:1-6 is not coherent or meaningful. Unless this background is made specific, Paul's metaphors will remain hopelessly mixed. This is the case because those metaphors are dependent upon, and are in fact pointers to, the vocabulary of the scriptural texts which undergird his argument. Paul, therefore, must have presumed knowledge of it on the part of his audience. It is to the loss of awareness of this Old Testament background material that the apparent confusion of the text can be traced.[19]

Once this scriptural background has been rediscovered and the workings of Paul's argument revealed, his answer to whatever criticisms he received becomes clear. In the course of II Corinthians 3:1-6, Paul begins to describe himself as a true Christian apostle on the model of Moses. He is the bringer of a covenant just as Moses was. Paul's covenant, however, is radically different from that which Moses brought,

---

[19] The article by Earl RICHARD, "Polemics, Old Testament, and Theology. A Study of II Cor. III, 1-IV, 6," cited previously is the only attempt of which I am aware to deal seriously and in depth with the structure of Paul's argument in II Cor. 3:1-6. There are numerous points of agreement between Richard's treatment of the passage and my own, particularly in the use of the hermeneutical technique of *gezerah shavah* as the principle of the association of the texts from Jeremiah and Ezekiel which are in evidence in II Cor. 3:1-3 ("Polemics," p. 347). However, there are two significant points of disagreement. First, RICHARD sees Paul's argument in II Cor. 3 itself as structured by the hook-words which link Jeremiah 38 (LXX) and Ezekiel 11 (36). As the argument which follows here will show, I see these hook-word links as part of a coherent exegetical background standing behind II Cor. 3:1-6. This exegetical background informs Paul's own argument, which contains pointers to it, but does not structure it. Second, RICHARD understands the larger section, II Cor. 3:1-4:6, to be an exegesis of Jeremiah 38 (LXX). This exegesis is carried on through the application of related scriptural texts, including Ex. 34:29-35, to Jer. 38 (LXX) via verbal links ("Polemics," pp. 352, 362). I agree that Jeremiah 38:31-34 (LXX) is the most important biblical text for the understanding of II Cor. 3:1-4:6, but I cannot agree that the Pentateuchal text, Ex. 34:29-35, is used to interpret a text from the Prophets. It should be the other way around. As far as we are aware of exegetical practice in Judaism at this time, the expected procedure would be to use a text from a prophet to interpret a text from the books of Moses. Surely, the Torah was always primary, even if its interpretation was derived increasingly from the words of the prophets. See John BOWKER, *The Targums and Rabbinic Literature* (Cambridge: University Press, 1969) pp. 9-12 and Ben Zion WACHOLDER, "Prolegomenon" to *The Bible as Read and Preached in the Old Synagogue*, Vol. I (New York: KTAV Publishing House, 1971) pp. xiv-xv. In distinction to RICHARD and in agreement with the majority of commentators, I see Paul using Jeremiah 38 (LXX) to interpret Ex. 34:29-35.

and so his apostleship is also significantly different from its Mosaic pattern.[20] The differences between Paul's covenant and the covenant of Moses are the fulcrum of his argument and the basis of the reproaches of his opponents. Nevertheless, like that of Moses, Paul's competence stems directly from God. Therefore, letters of recommendation are superfluous for him. Only his actions can prove whether or not he comes from God. Paul argues from verse 2 on that his life and the life of the Christians in Corinth as Christian does show that he has indeed been the minister of a new, spiritual covenant that gives life to a new people of God comparable to, but also different from, the old people led out of Egypt by Moses and given life in the wilderness through him. This comparison with and contrast to Moses continues in II Cor. 3:7-4:6, and occasionally reappears throughout the letter. It is the way that Paul has chosen, not to recommend himself, but to give his Corinthians a reason to be proud of him in the face of his accusers (II Cor. 5:12).

Reconstruction of the Exegetical Background of II Corinthians 3:1-6

Vocabulary Analysis

II Corinthians 3:1-6 contains several very unusual expressions, some unusual for Paul, some unusual in themselves. The vocabulary of any written document is the first key to its meaning.[21] Moreover, scriptural interpretation within Judaism which has its roots in this period shows a particular preoccupation with the words of scripture.[22] In imitation of such exegetical procedure, the first step in my own investigation of the conceptual world of Paul's text will be a careful search for the background of his unusual terminology.

All of the words of the text are potentially significant, as we shall see in the course of this chapter.[23] Some are important primarily for the

---

[20] This is also the thesis of Peter JONES in his unpublished dissertation, "The Apostle Paul: A Second Moses According to II Corinthians 2:14-4:7" and in an article based on it, "L'Apôtre Paul: Un second Moïse pour la Communauté de la nouvelle Alliance: Une Etude sur l'Autorité apostolique paulinienne," *Foi et Vie* 75 (1976) pp. 36-58.

[21] The second key is, of course, the structure into which this vocabulary is set.

[22] Daniel PATTE, *Early Jewish Hermeneutic*, pp. 13-14; Richard LONGENECKER, *Biblical Exegesis*, p. 48.

[23] The word "ἱκανός" in II Cor. 3:5-6 provides a clue to a significant segment of Paul's scriptural background. As a common word, however, its importance can only be assessed after other references to the scriptures, located through more unusual words and phrases, have established Paul's primary frame of reference.

structure they provide or indicate.[24] Many, however, occur frequently in common speech and in the New Testament. These do not provide an easy entry into the particular world of a specific text. So, the interpreter must turn first to the unusual or unique words and phrases used by the author in order to focus and narrow the scope of research.

In the case of II Corinthians 3:1-6, I have chosen several key expressions, which lead quickly into the background sought. These are 1) new covenant (καινῆς διαθήκης, v. 6); 2) hearts of flesh (καρδίαις σαρκίναις, v. 3); 3) stone tablets (ἐν πλαξιν λιθίναις, v. 3); and 4) engraved on the heart (ἐγγεγραμμένη ἐν ταῖς καρδίαις, v. 2). Each of these phrases has its source in the Septuagint version of the Old Testament.[25] The exact texts which form the background for Paul's use of these biblical phrases in II Cor. 3:1-6, therefore, can be easily pinpointed due to the infrequency of the expressions.

New Covenant

The use of the idea of covenant to express the relationship between God and his people was one of the most basic religious insights inherited within Judaism. The covenant concept is a foundational theme of the Old Testament as a whole, which provides the expected field of reference for the term "διαθήκη" at this time. The expression "καινὴ διαθήκη," however, occurs only once in the Old Testament. A single prophetic text, Jeremiah 31 (LXX 38), is the classic locus for the promise of a new covenant within the Old Testament and the only text in which the phrase "καινὴ διαθήκη" occurs.[26]

---

[24] Connectives, prepositions, pronouns and simple verbs are primarily structural indicators. However, the καὶ of II Cor. 3:6 is also a significant clue to the intended content of the verse as well, as we shall see in the discussion of ἱκανός and Exodus 3-4 which follows at the end of this chapter.

[25] As I begin my own analysis, I will apologize for the use of this term once and for all. I am aware that it is sometimes offensive to modern Judaism to have its scripture relegated to the past as though the faith and community of Judaism no longer existed. But for a modern Christian the term "Old Testament" is so familiar that the possible insult is lost on the ear. There is simply no other convenient term to use in this study. The term "Hebrew Scriptures" would imply an inappropriate language distinction. "Jewish Scriptures" seems to deny the importance for the Christian community that is precisely what I am trying to illustrate. So, since the term "Old Testament" itself occurs for the first time in the course of the text under investigation in this study, I feel that I must use it. It is appropriate here if nowhere else.

[26] W. C. van Unnik, "La conception de la nouvelle alliance," *Recherches Biblique* V (Louvain: Desclée De Brouwer, 1960) p. 114; "On sait que, pour l'étude de l'expression 'nouvelle alliance' dans l'A.T., le texte classique—et même le seul où se recontre la formule—est Jr 31,31ss." The entire article, which is a survey of Paul's general understanding of the new covenant and its importance for his thought, has much which augments the present study of II Cor. 3:1-4:6. It is particularly important for mentioning,

The phrase is similarly scarce in later Jewish and Christian literature. The phrase "new covenant" is used frequently only in the Qumran literature. Indeed, it seems to have been a favorite self-description of the Dead Sea community to style itself as "the men of the new covenant." [27] The Qumran documents, however, rarely cite Jeremiah 31 (38 LXX) explicitly as the source of this concept and so give little evidence about exegesis of that text in the period. [28] The best that they do provide, therefore, is evidence of the popularity of the concept in at least one other group nearly contemporaneous with the Christian community to which Paul was addressing himself in II Cor. 3:1-6. Like Paul, the "covenanters" of Qumran did not feel the need to specify Jeremiah as their source of inspiration. Outside of Qumran, the promise of the new covenant is almost never mentioned in Jewish literature, wherein attention remains focused on the original covenant mediated through Moses. [29] Even in Qumran, moreover, the "new covenant" remains essentially only a radical renewal of the Mosaic covenant. On the contrary, for Paul, there is significant disjunction between the new covenant promised by the prophets and its Mosaic prototype.

In the New Testament, the phrase "καινὴ διαθήκη," appears only here in II Corinthians 3:6, in the Eucharistic words of Jesus as they are reported in the Synoptic Gospels and in I Corinthians 11:25, [30] and within

---

if not elaborating, vast areas of classically "Pauline" theology which are in fact outgrowths of the "new covenant" idea, but not commonly recognized as such, righteousness (p. 121) and the mission to the Gentiles (p. 117) for example.

[27] Annie JAUBERT, *La notion d'alliance dans le Judaisme*, Patristica Sorbonensia 6 (Paris: Editions du Seuil, 1963) pp. 209-249; Frank Moore CROSS, Jr., *The Ancient Library of Qumran* (London: Gerald Duckworth & Co., 1958) pp. 56, 58, 164; Geza VERMES, *Discovery in the Judean Desert* (New York: Desclee Company, 1956) pp. 44-61 passim; Peter JONES, "The Apostle Paul," pp. 202, 223, 229, 236, 249, 352 (where II Cor. 3 and 1 QH 4 are compared and 1 QH 4 appears to contain a reference to Jer. 31 parallel to Paul's references in II Cor. 3:2 and 3).

[28] With one notable exception: 1 QH 4 not only mentions a covenant with a law "engraved on my heart" reminiscent of Jer. 31:33, but appears to evidence further the combination of this theme with that of illumination and /or covering of the face similar to the theme of the glorification and veiling of Moses' face as related to the theme of "new covenant" by Paul in II Cor. 3. See Jones, "The Apostle Paul," pp. 351-373 for a full discussion of parallels between the Qumran documents and II Cor. 3-4. The expression *berit ḥdašah* is used in CD 6:19 and 1 Qp Hab 2:3. It also surely stems from Jer. 31; FITZMYER, "Glory Reflected on the Face of Christ," p. 642.

[29] Hermann L. STRACK and Paul BILLERBECK, *Kommentar zum Neuen Testament aus Talmud und Midrash*, Vol. III (München: C. H. Beck'sche Verlagsbuchhandlung, 1954), pp. 89-91, 501, 704; Johannes BEHM, "διαθήκη," in the *Theological Dictionary of the New Testament*, Vol. II, ed. Gerhard KITTEL, trans. G. W. Bromiley (Grand Rapids: Wm. B. Eerdmans, 1964) p. 129.

[30] Actually καινή appears before διαθήκη only in the Pauline and the Lukan (22:20) Eucharistic Texts, and is a variant reading in Matthew and Mark.

quotations of Jeremiah 38:31-34 (LXX) itself in Hebrews 8:8ff. and 12:24. The Hebrews texts, although certainly later than II Corinthians and therefore possibly dependent upon it, indicate clearly the source of the phrase, "καινὴ διαθήκη," in the promise of Jeremiah by quoting that text at length in its Septuagint form. The Eucharistic words, although certainly earlier than II Corinthians, can hardly themselves have been the source of the intricate argument pursued by Paul in II Cor. 3:1-6. Instead, my analysis will indicate that variations in the Eucharistic words themselves, according to their several attestations, may bear witness to an exegetical process such as I will shortly outline for II Cor. 3:1-6, a process with its ultimate source in Jeremiah 31 (38 LXX) itself.

In the absence of another adequate source, then, and because of the single appearance of the phrase "καινὴ διαθήκη" in the Old Testament, Jeremiah 31 (38 LXX) must stand behind the appearance of its key phrase in II Corinthians 3:6. For the convenience of the reader, I will display this and the other background texts in the Greek of the Septuagint and in English translation.[31] For the sake of conclusions later to be drawn in this and the subsequent chapter from the contents surrounding the specific verse in which a key word occurs, and so as not to have to display the same texts again in larger segments, I will include here a somewhat longer section than may seem relevant at this time.

Jeremiah 38:29-34 [32]

29) ἐν ταῖς ἡμέραις ἐκείναις οὐ μὴ εἴπωσιν Οἱ πατέρες ἔφαγον ὄμφακα, καὶ οἱ ὀδόντες τῶν τέκνων ἡμωδίασαν· 30) ἀλλ' ἢ ἕκαστος ἐν τῇ ἁμαρτίᾳ

[31] The Greek texts of Jeremiah 38:29-34; 39:37-42 and Ezekiel 11:16-23; 36:24-32; 37:1-14 to follow are taken from the best critical texts available: *Septuaginta. Vetus Testamentum Graecum*, ed. Societatis Litterarum Gottingensis (Göttingen: Vandenhoeck & Ruprecht) Vol. XV (Jeremiah) 1957; Vol. XVI (Ezekiel) 1952, both edited by Joseph Ziegler. The texts from Exodus (34:1-4, 27-28; 4:10-12) are taken from *The Old Testament in Greek*, ed. A. BROOKE and N. MCLEAN (Cambridge: University Press, 1909), a supplemented text of the Codex Vaticanus with critical apparatus. Psalm 50:1-12 in Greek is also from the Göttingen edition, *Septuaginta. Psalmicum Odis*, ed. Alfred RAHLFS (Göttingen: Vandenhoeck & Ruprecht, 1967). In all cases the English translation which follows is taken from *The Septuagint Version of the Old Testament and Apocrypha with an English Translation*, ed. C. L. BRENTON (Zondervan, 1978), originally published by Samuel Bagster & Sons, London, in 1851.

[32] Since it is the Septuagint text which I am citing, I will use the Septuagint numbering of the chapters from Jeremiah whenever the reference is to the text which Paul has used and to which he refers. This procedure will be followed also with regard to numbering variations which occur in other texts quoted from the Septuagint in the course of this study. In the absence of the quotation of a large enough section of the Old Testament text by which to judge, a Greek word or expression must be assumed to stem from a Greek version of the Old Testament. I find arguments based upon which Hebrew word a given Greek word would probably translate much less convincing than an exact correspondence of Greek expression.

αὐτοῦ ἀποθανεῖται, καὶ τοῦ φαγόντος τὸν ὄμφακα αἱμωδιάσουσιν οἱ ὀδόντες αὐτοῦ. 31) Ἰσοὺ ἡμέραι ἔρχονται, φησὶ κύριος, καὶ διαθήσομαι τῷ οἴκῳ Ισραηλ καὶ τῷ οἴκῳ Ιουδα διαθήκην καινήν, 32) οὐ κατὰ τὴν διαθήκην, ἣν διεθέμην τοῖς πατράσιν αὐτῶν ἐν ἡμέρᾳ ἐπιλαβομένου μου τῆς χειρὸς αὐτῶν ἐξαγαγεῖν αὐτοὺς ἐκ γῆς Αἰγύπτου, ὅτι αὐτοὶ οὐκ ἐνέμειναν ἐν τῇ διαθήκῃ μου, και· ἐγὼ ἠμέλησα αὐτῶν, φησὶ κύριος· 33) ὅτι αὕτη ἡ διαθήκη, ἣν διαθήσομαι τῷ οἴκῳ Ισραηλ μετὰ τὰς ἡμέρας ἐκείνας, φησὶ κύριος Διδοὺς δώσω νόμους μου εἰς τὴν διάνοιαν αὐτῶν καὶ ἐπὶ καρδίας αὐτῶν γράφω αὐτούς· καὶ ἔσομαι αὐτοῖς εἰς θεόν, καὶ αὐτοὶ ἔσονταί μοι εἰς λαόν· 34) καὶ οὐ μὴ διδάξωσιν ἕκαστος τὸν πολίτην αὐτοῦ καὶ ἕκαστος τὸν ἀδελφὸν αὐτοῦ λέγων Γνῶθι τὸν κύριον· ὅτι πάντες εἰδήσουσί με ἀπὸ μικροῦ αὐτῶν καὶ ἕως μεγάλου αὐτῶν, ὅτι ἵλεως ἔσομαι ταῖς ἀδικίαις αὐτῶν καὶ τῶν ἁμαρτιῶν αὐτῶν οὐ μὴ μνησθῶ ἔτι.

29) In those days they shall certainly not say, The fathers ate a sour grape and the children's teeth were set on edge. 30) But every one shall die in his own sin; and the teeth of him that eats the sour grape shall be set on edge. 31) Behold the days come, saith the Lord, when I will make a new covenant with the house of Israel, and with the house of Juda: 32) not according to the covenant which I made with their fathers in the day when I took hold of their hand to bring them out of the land of Egypt; for they abode not in my covenant, and I disregarded them, saith the Lord. 33) For this is my covenant which I will make with the house of Israel; after those days, saith the Lord, I will surely put my laws into their mind, and write them on their hearts; and I will be to them a God and they shall be to me a people. 34) And they shall not at all teach every one his fellow citizen, and every one his brother, saying, Know the Lord; for all shall know me, from the least of them to the greatest of them: for I will be merciful to their iniquities, and their sins I will remember no more.

The context of Jeremiah 38:31-34 (LXX) contains another reference to the promised covenant, although without containing the phrase "καινὴ διαθήκη" itself. This second covenant promise describes instead several additional features of the covenant to come, not included in the promise of Jeremiah 38. The intervening material is not immediately relevant, so I will provide here only the text of the promise itself in Jeremiah 39:37-42 (LXX).

37) Ἰδοὺ ἐγὼ συνάγω αὐτοὺς ἐκ πάσης τῆς γῆς, οὗ διέσπειρα αὐτοὺς ἐκεῖ ἐν ὀργῇ μου καὶ ἐν θυμῷ μου καὶ ἐν παροξυσμῷ μεγάλῳ, καὶ ἐπιστρέψω αὐτούς εἰς τὸν τόπον τοῦτον καὶ καθιῶ αὐτοὺς πεποιθότας, 38) καὶ ἔσονταί μοι εἰς λαόν, καὶ ἐγὼ ἔσομαι αὐτοῖς εἰς θεόν. 39) καὶ δώσω αὐτοῖς ὁδὸν ἑτέραν καὶ καρδίαν ἑτέραν φοβηθῆναί με πάσας τὰς ἡμέρας καὶ εἰς ἀγαθὸν αὐτοῖς καὶ τοῖς τέκνοις αὐτῶν μετ' αὐτούς. 40) καὶ διαθήσομαι αὐτοῖς διαθήκην αἰώνιον, ἣν οὐ μὴ ἀποστρέψω ὄπισθεν αὐτῶν· καὶ τὸν φόβον μου δώσω εἰς τὴν καρδίαν αὐτῶν πρὸς τὸ μὴ ἀποστῆναι αὐτοὺς ἀπ' ἐμοῦ. 41) καὶ ἐπισκέψομαι αὐτοὺς τοῦ ἀγαθῶσαι

αὐτοὺς καὶ φυτεύσω αὐτοὺς ἐν τῇ γῇ ταύτῃ ἐν πίστει καὶ ἐν πάσῃ καρδίᾳ καὶ ἐν πάσῃ ψυχῇ. 42) ὅτι οὕτως εἶπε κύριος Καθὰ ἐπήγαγον ἐπὶ τὸν λαὸν τοῦτον πάντα τὰ κακὰ τὰ μεγάλα ταῦτα, οὕτως ἐγὼ ἐπάξω ἐπ'αὐτοὺς πάντα τὰ ἀγαθά, ἃ ἐλάλησα ἐπ' αὐτούς.

37) Behold, I will gather them out of every land, where I have scattered them in my anger, and my wrath, and great fury; and I will bring them back into this place and will cause them to dwell safely: 38) and they shall be to me a people, and I will be to them a God. 39) And I will give them another way, and another heart, to fear me continually, and that for good to them and their children after them. 40) And I will make with them an everlasting covenant, which I will by no means turn away from them, and I will put my fear into their heart that they may not depart from me. 41) And I will visit them to do them good, and I will plant them in this land in faithfulness, and with all my heart, and with all my soul. 42) For thus saith the Lord; as I have brought upon this people all these great evils, so will I bring upon them all the good things which I pronounced upon them.

This text is not immediately relevant to II Corinthians 3:1-6, but does become important to the following section, 3:7-18, and to the larger context in II Corinthians. I will have more to say about Paul's use of this text later, but it is best displayed here as a part of the emerging group.

Hearts of flesh

The expression "καρδία σαρκίνη" occurs in the Septuagint in only two places: Ezekiel 11:19 and 36:26. It does not occur in the New Testament outside of II Cor. 3:3. In fact, the phrase is so unmistakably tied to these Ezekiel passages that once again Paul's unusual expression leads directly to the Old Testament itself as its source. Ezekiel 11:19 and 36:26 are quite similar and certainly parallel one another. Solely on the basis of the expression "heart of flesh" it is impossible to decide to which one Paul is referring. The larger contexts in which these specific verses appear in Ezekiel are different, however, and are each relevant in quite distinct ways to Paul's argument in II Corinthians 3:1-4:6. I will therefore display both texts here for the sake of later discussions. In the case of Ezekiel 36, a very large portion of the following context as well must be cited later in the chapter.

Ezekiel 11:16-23

16) διὰ τοῦτο εἶπον Τάδε λέγει κύριος ὅτι 'Απώσομαι αὐτοὺς εἰς τὰ ἔθνη καὶ διασκορπιῶ αὐτοὺς εἰς πᾶσαν τὴν γῆν, καὶ ἔσομαι αὐτοῖς εἰς ἁγίασμα μικρόν ἐν ταῖς χώραις, οὗ ἂν εἰσέλθωσιν ἐκεῖ. 17) διὰ τοῦτο εἶπον Τάδε λέγει κύριος Καὶ εἰσδέξομαι αὐτοὺς ἐκ τῶν ἐθνῶν καὶ συνάξω αὐτοὺς ἐκ τῶν χωρῶν, οὗ διέσπειρα αὐτοὺς ἐν αὐταῖς, καὶ δῶσω αὐτοῖς τὴν γῆν τοῦ Ἰσραηλ. 18) καὶ εἰσελεύσονται ἐκεῖ καὶ ἐξαροῦσι πάντα τὰ βδελύγματα

αὐτῆς καὶ πάσας τὰς ἀνομίας αὐτῆς ἐξ αὐτῆς. 19) καὶ δώσω αὐτοῖς καρδίαν ἑτέραν καὶ πνεῦμα καινὸν δώσω ἐν αὐτοῖς καὶ ἐκσπάσω τὴν καρδίαν τὴν λιθίνην ἐκ τῆς σαρκὸς αὐτῶν καὶ δώσω αὐτοῖς καρδίαν σαρκίνην, 20) ὅπως ἐν τοῖς προστάγμασί μου πορεύωνται καὶ τὰ δικαιώματά μου φυλάσσωνται καὶ ποιῶσιν αὐτά· καὶ ἔσονταί μοι εἰς λαόν, καὶ ἐγὼ ἔσομαι αὐτοῖς εἰς θεόν. 21) καὶ εἰς τὴν καρδίαν τῶν βδελυγμάτων αὐτῶν καὶ τῶν ἀνομιῶν αὐτῶν, ὡς ἡ καρδία αὐτῶν ἐπορεύετο, τὰς ὁδοὺς αὐτῶν εἰς κεφαλὰς αὐτῶν δέδωκα, λέγει κύριος. 22) Καὶ ἐξῆραν τὰ χερουβιν τὰς πτέρυγας αὐτῶν, καὶ οἱ τροχοὶ ἐχόμενοι αὐτῶν, καὶ ἡ δόξα θεοῦ Ισραηλ ἐπ' αὐτὰ ὑπεράνω αὐτῶν· 23) καὶ ἀνέβη δόξα κυρίου ἐκ μέσης τῆς πόλεως καὶ ἔστη ἐπὶ τοῦ ὄρους, ὃ ἦν ἀπέναντι τῆς πόλεως.

16) Therefore say thou, Thus saith the Lord: I will cast them off among the nations and will disperse them into every land, yet will I be to them for a little sanctuary in the countries which they shall enter. 17) Therefore say thou, Thus saith the Lord; I will also take them from the heathen, and gather them out of the lands wherein I have scattered them, and will give them the land of Israel. 18) And they shall enter in there and shall remove all the abominations of it, and all its iniquities from it. 19) And I will give them another heart, and will put a new spirit within them; and will extract the heart of stone from their flesh, and give them a heart of flesh: 20) that they may walk in my commandments, and keep mine ordinances and do them: and they shall be to me a people, and I will be to them a God. 21) And as for the heart set upon their abominations and their iniquities, as their heart went after them, I have recompensed their ways on their heads, saith the Lord. 22) Then the cherubs lifted up their wings, and the wheels beside them; and the glory of the God of Israel was over them above. 23) And the glory of the Lord went up from the midst of the city, and stood on the mountain which was in front of the city.

And Ezekiel 36:24-32

24) καὶ λήμψομαι ὑμᾶς ἐκ τῶν ἐθνῶν καὶ ἀθροίσω ὑμᾶς ἐκ πασῶν τῶν γεῶν καὶ εἰσάξω ὕμᾶς εἰς τὴν γῆν ὑμῶν. 25) καὶ ρανῶ ἐφ' ὑμᾶς ὕδωρ καθαρόν, καὶ καθαρισθήσεσθε ἀπὸ πασῶν τῶν ἀκαθαρσιῶν ὑμῶν καὶ ἀπὸ πάντων τῶν εἰδώλων ὑμῶν, καὶ καθαριῶ ὑμᾶς. 26) καὶ δώσω ὑμῖν καρδίαν καινὴν καὶ πνεῦμα καινὸν δώσω ἐν ὑμῖν καὶ ἀφελῶ τὴν καρδίαν τὴν λιθίνην ἐκ τῆς σαρκὸς ὑμῶν καὶ δώσω ὑμῖν καρδίαν σαρκίνην. 27) καὶ τὸ πνεῦμά μου δώσω ἐν ὑμῖν καὶ ποιήσω ἵνα ἐν τοῖς δικαιώμασί μου πορεύησθε καὶ τὰ κρίματά μου φυλάξησθε καὶ ποιήσητε. 28) καὶ κατοικήσετε ἐπὶ τῆς γῆς, ἧς ἔδωκα τοῖς πατράσιν ὑμῶν, καὶ ἔσεσθέ μοι εἰς λαόν, καὶ ἐγὼ ἔσομαι ὑμῖν εἰς θεόν. 29) καὶ σώσω ὑμᾶς ἐκ πασῶν τῶν ἀκαθαρσιῶν ὑμῶν καὶ καλέσω τὸν σῖτον 30) καὶ πληθυνῶ αὐτὸν καὶ οὐ δώσω ἐφ' ὑμᾶς λιμόν· καὶ πληθυνῶ τὸν καρπὸν τοῦ ξύλου καὶ τὰ γενήματα τοῦ ἀγροῦ, ὅπως μὴ λάβητε ὀνειδισμὸν λιμοῦ ἐν τοῖς ἔθνεσι. 31) καὶ μνησθήσεσθε τὰς ὁδοὺς ὑμῶν τὰς πονηρὰς καὶ τὰ ἐπιτηδεύματα ὑμῶν τὰ μὴ ἀγαθὰ καὶ προσοχθιεῖτε κατὰ πρόσωπον αὐτῶν ἐν ταῖς

ἀνομίαις ὑμῶν καὶ ἐν τοῖς βδελύγμασιν αὐτῶν. 32) οὐ δι' ὑμᾶς ἐγὼ ποιῶ, λέγει κύριος, γνωστὸν ἔσται ὑμῖν· αἰσχύνθητε καὶ ἐντράπητε ἐκ τῶν ὁδῶν ὑμῶν, οἶκος Ισραηλ.

24) And I will take you out from the nations and will gather you out of all the lands and will bring you into your own land: 25) and I will sprinkle clean water upon you, and you shall be purged from all your uncleannesses, and from all your idols, and I will cleanse you. 26) And I will give you a new heart, and will put a new spirit in you; and I will take away the heart of stone out of your flesh and will give you a heart of flesh. 27) And I will put my Spirit in you and will cause you to walk in mine ordinances and to keep my judgments and do them. 28) And ye shall dwell upon the land which I gave to your fathers; and ye shall be to me a people, and I will be to you a God. 29) And I will save you from all your uncleannesses and I will call for the corn and multiply it, and will not bring famine upon you. 30) And I will multiply the fruit of the trees. and the produce of the field, that ye may not bear the reproach of famine among the nations. 31) And ye shall remember your evil ways, and your practices that were not good, and ye shall be hateful in your own sight for your transgressions and for your abomination. 32) Not for your sakes do I this, saith the Lord God, as it is known to you: be ye ashamed and confounded for your ways, 0 house of Israel.

Stone tablets

According to Ezekiel 11:19 and 36:26, the counterpart of the heart of flesh is the heart of stone. However, in II Cor. 3:3 the first member of Paul's "οὐκ/ἀλλ'" construction is not "heart of stone," but "tablet of stone." This lack of exact correspondence with the Ezekiel texts proposed as the source of the expression "καρδίαις σαρκίναις," as well as the fact that the end of the comparison in II Cor. 3:3 reads "ἐν πλαξὶν καρδίαις σαρκίναις" in distinction from Ezekiel 11:19 and 36:26, points out the need for a further inquiry into the source of Paul's expression.

The phrase "ἐν πλαξὶν λιθίναις" of II Cor. 3:3 carries clear echoes of the stone tablets of the testimony given to Moses in the wilderness when the covenant was made at Sinai. Jeremiah 38:32 (LXX) has already spoken of this covenant made with the fathers when they were brought out of Egypt. The particular formula, "πλάκες λίθιναι" is, in fact, typical of Exodus and Deuteronomy in the Septuagint,[33] referring exclusively to those stone tablets given to Moses twice, before and after the incident of the golden calf in Exodus 32. Those tablets were the written witness to (πλάκες τοῦ μαρτυρίου, Ex. 31:18, etc.), or proof of, the words of the covenant spoken to Moses alone. Once again, then, the text of the Septuagint is the source of Paul's vocabulary in II Corinthians 3.

---

[33] Occurring only at Exod. 31:18; 32:15; 34:1,4 and their parallels in Deut. 4:13; 9:10,11; 10:1,3.

Paul may have had any or all of the occurrences of "πλάκες λίθιναι" from the story of the covenant-making at Sinai in mind as he wrote II Corinthians 3:1-6. Solely on the basis of that single phrase, no choice can be made among them. However, in II Cor. 3:7-18 Paul begins to focus on a scene which immediately follows the giving of the second set of stone tablets in Exodus 34. Therefore, Paul probably intended primarily the stone tablets of Exodus 34:1-4, 27-28 in II Cor. 3:3, on the basis of their closer contextual proximity to the Exodus text with which he was shortly to be explicitly engaged.[34]

Exodus 34:1-4,27-28

1) Καὶ εἶπεν Κύριος πρὸς Μωυσῆν Λάξευσον σεαυτῷ δύο πλάκας λιθίνας καθὼς καὶ αἱ πρῶται καὶ ἀνάβηθι πρὸς μὲ εἰς τὸ ὄρος, καὶ γράψω ἐπὶ τῶν πλακῶν τὰ ῥήματα ἃ ἦν ἐν ταῖς πλαξὶν ταῖς πρώταις αἷς συνέτριψας. 2) καὶ γίνου ἕτοιμος εἰς τὸ πρωί, καὶ ἀναβήσῃ ἐπὶ τὸ ὄρος τὸ Σινά, καὶ στήσῃ μοι ἐκεῖ ἐπ' ἄκρου τοῦ ὄρους. 3) καὶ μηδεὶς ἀναβήτω μετὰ σοῦ μηδὲ ὀφθήτω ἐν παντὶ τῷ ὄρει· καὶ τὰ πρόβατα καὶ αἱ βόες μὴ νεμέσθωσαν πλησίον τοῦ ὄρους ἐκείνου. 4) καὶ ἐλάξευσεν δύο πλάκας λιθίνας καθάπερ καὶ αἱ πρωται· καὶ ὀρθρίσας Μωυσῆς ἀνέβη εἰς τὸ ὄρος τὸ Σινά, καθότι συνέταξεν αὐτῷ Κύριος· καὶ ἔλαβεν Μωυσῆς τὰς δύο πλάκας τὰς λιθίνας.

---

[34] As against most commentators who select Exod. 31:18 as Paul's reference, because it is the first occurrence of the term in the biblical narrative. PLUMMER, *II Corinthians*, p. 82 cites both; HUGHES, FALLON, COLLANGE, BULTMANN and PRÜMM choose Exod. 31:18. ALLO cites Exod. 24:12 quite in error, since the expression does not occur there at all, although the idea does. The gift of the first stone tablets does, however, contain a single, but very important, contrast with the gift of the second set which may be important in II Cor. 3. While the broken first set of tablets was written by God himself, according to Exod. 31:18, the second set was written by Moses (Exod. 34:27-28). Paul's expression, "πνεύματι θεοῦ ζῶντος" may be intended as an evocation and reinterpretation of the phrase "τῷ δακτύλῳ" of Exod. 31:18. *Like* the first set of tablets, Paul's "letter" is written by God, *unlike* the second set of tablets which were written by Moses. There is even a late tradition within Judaism that Moses wrote the second set of tablets with ink. See GINZBERG, *Legends of the Jews*, Vol. III, p. 143; VI, notes 309 and 310, pp. 60-61. If such an interpretation of Moses' writing had been current in Paul's time (as GINZBERG seems to presume, although I see no evidence early enough to prove it), the first contrast of II Cor. 3:3b — οὐ μ ελανι ἀλλὰ πνεύματι θεοῦ ζῶντος — would imply a comparison between the way Moses wrote his "letters," i.e., the law, and the way Paul was given his "letter", i.e., the Corinthians. Paul received his "letter" by the power of God, just as Moses received the *first* tablets of the law. The second contrast — οὐκ ἐν πλαξὶν λιθίναις ἀλλ ἐν πλαξὶν καρδίας σαρκίναις — then would imply a comparison between even those first tablets of stone and the "letter" of the new covenant. This is an interesting theory, but the late date of the sources for this particular Moses tradition make it impossible to confirm.

27) καὶ εἶπεν Κύριος πρὸς Μωυσῆν Γράψον σεαυτῷ τὰ ῥήματα ταῦτα·
ἐπὶ γὰρ τῶν λόγων τούτων τέθειμαι σοὶ διαθήκην καὶ τῷ Ἰσραήλ. 28)
Καὶ ἦν ἐκεῖ Μωυσῆς ἐναντίον Κυρίου τεσσεράκοντα ἡνέρας καὶ
τεσσεράκοντα νύκτας· ἄρτον οὐκ ἔφαγεν καὶ ὕδωρ οὐκ ἔπιεν· καὶ
ἔγραψεν τὰ ῥήματα ταῦτα ἐπὶ τῶν πλακῶν τῆς διαθήκης, τοὺς δέκα
λόγους.

1) And the Lord said to Moses, Hew for thyself two tables of stone, as
also the first were and come up to me to the mountain; and I will write
upon the tables the words which were on the first tables, which thou
brokest. 2) And be ready by the morning and thou shalt go up to the
Mount Sinai, and shalt stand there for me on the top of the mountain. 3)
And let no one go up with thee, nor be seen in all the mountain; and let
not the sheep and oxen feed near that mountain. 4) And Moses hewed two
tables of stone, as also the first were; and Moses having arisen early, went
up to the Mount Sinai, as the Lord appointed him; and Moses took the
two tables of stone.

27) And the Lord said to Moses, Write these words for thyself, for on these
words I have established a covenant with thee and with Israel. 28) And
Moses was there before the Lord forty days, and forty nights; he did not
eat bread and he did not drink water; and he wrote these words upon the
tablets of the covenant, the ten sayings.

Engraved on the heart

A final unusual notion occurs in v. 2 of II Corinthians 3, that of
writing on hearts, expressed with an equally unusual vocabulary,
"ἐγγεγραμμένη ἐν ταῖς καρδίαις ἡμῶν." The idea of keeping the Law or
the word of God in one's heart occurs occasionally in the Old Testament
in the sense of "to remember" or "to be faithful to." [35] The idea of
writing on hearts occurs very rarely, only at Proverbs 7:3 [36] and Jeremiah
38:33 (LXX), the key text already displayed as the source of the phrase
"καινὴ διαθήκη." The appearance of the *theme* of writing on the heart in
II Corinthians 3:2, therefore, may be explained by its assimilation from
the promise of Jeremiah.

The verb in the relevant Septuagint text, Jeremiah 38:33 is not,
however, reflected by the Pauline "ἐγγεγραμμένη." The reading in
Jeremiah 38:33 is from the simple γράφω. Although ἐπιγράφω does
appear as a variant in Jer. 38:33,[37] ἐγγράφω does not appear in the
manuscript traditions which we possess. There is, of course, always the

---

[35] Deut. 30:14 and Prov. 3:3, for example.

[36] Although some older commentators cite Prov. 7:3 as part of the background of II
Cor. 3:2-3 (ALLO, WINDISCH, PLUMMER), I have not found that it is influential in Paul's
composition as the other texts cited here will be shown to be.

[37] A, Arab.

possibility that Paul is reflecting a Greek text of Jeremiah 38 which we no longer possess, or that he is translating from the Hebrew text of Jeremiah himself and has preferred the compound. We have already seen that Paul has exhibited considerable correspondence with known Septuagint texts, however, and the hypothesis of a lost Greek version does not help in our interpretation of II Corinthians 3. Leaving these hypotheses aside, therefore, another explanation for Paul's verb "ἐγγράφω" can be suggested. The verb "ἐγγράφω," may reflect the influence of another Septuagint text, Exodus 36:21, a text once again in fairly close contextual proximity to Exod. 34:29-35 which is treated explicitly in II Cor. 3:7-18.

Exodus 36:21 (LXX)

> 21) καὶ οἱ λίθοι ἦσαν ἐκ τῶν ὀνομάτων τῶν υἱῶν Ἰσραὴλ δώδεκα, ἐκ τῶν ὀνομάτων αὐτῶν, ἐνγεγραμμένα εἰς σφραγῖδας, ἕκαστος ἐκ τοῦ ἑαυτοῦ ὀνόματος, εἰς τὰς δώδεκα φυλάς.[38]

> 21) And the stones were twelve according to the names of children of Israel, graven according to their names like seals, each according to his own name for the twelve tribes.

This verse occurs within an extended description of the ceremonial clothing of Aaron, the priest of the Mosaic covenant. In particular, according to this text, the names of the twelve tribes of Israel were engraved upon the stones in the breastplate which Aaron wore when he ministered before the Lord, so that he might bring their names into the presence of God. It was suggested long ago that this text is the source of the compound verb present in II Corinthians 3:2 and 3[39] with which Paul has altered his reference to Jeremiah 38:33. Although this suggestion

---

[38] The Codex Vaticanus text used for the other selections from Exodus does not use the reading "ἐγγεγραμμένα εἰς σφραγῖδας." It reads "ἐνγεγραμμένα εἰς σφραγῖδας." The fact that we are dealing here with what is only a variant spelling of the compound does not significantly weaken the case for Paul's dependence upon Exod. 36:21. See *A Greek Grammar of the New Testament and Other Early Christian Literature*, F. BLASS and A. DEBRUNNER, Tr. and rev. by Robert W. FUNK (Chicago: The University of Chicago Press, 1961), pp. 11-12. Moreover, the presence of the word "σφραγίς" in Exod. 36:21 (LXX) strengthens the lexical argument for Paul's use of it. In II Cor. 3:2 Paul says that the Corinthians are his letter, engraved on his heart. This chapter will argue that this metaphorical "letter" is parallel to the breastplate, or seal, worn by Aaron, engraved with the names of the tribes of Israel. In the only text truly parallel to II Cor. 3:2, noted above, I Cor. 9:2, Paul describes the Corinthians as the seal (σφραγίς) of his apostleship. The presence of σφραγίς in I Cor. 9:2 and of ἐγγράφω in II Cor. 3:2 and 3 argues strongly for the presence of the image of the engraved seal of Aaron's ministry behind Paul's image in both cases.

[39] This was suggested by H. OLSHAUSEN in his 1840 commentary, which has not been available to me. An English translation of his work done in Edinburgh in 1855 is mentioned by PLUMMER in *II Corinthians* and used extensively by HUGHES in *Second*

has received no critical acceptance, I must agree that Paul has indeed used Exod. 36:21 in the course of his argument in II Cor. 3:1-6. The compound does not occur frequently in the Septuagint.[40] Although it is not immediately apparent why Exodus 36:21 (LXX) should be selected from among its few appearances, the argument which follows will make clear how Paul has used this description of Aaron's breastplate to create one of his famous mixed metaphors.

Summary

This completes the initial group of texts from the Septuagint which Paul's unusual vocabulary in II Corinthians 3:1-6 indicates as the background for his argument there. In fact, one need only glance at the apparatus of any good critical edition of II Corinthians to see these very texts, with the exceptions of Ex. 34:1-4,27-28 and 36:21 (LXX), noted for reference with this passage.[41] The phrases "καινὴ διαθήκη," "καρδία σαρκίνη," and "πλάκες λίθιναι" are so clearly biblical and so easily traced to their exact sources that they can hardly be missed by someone familiar with the Greek text of the Old Testament. It is extremely likely that Paul's allusions to Jeremiah 38:31-34 (LXX); Ezek. 11:19 and 36:26, and Exod. 34:1-4,27-28, at least, would have been easily recognized by his audience if they had been converted to Christianity through the kerygmatic preaching of the fulfillment of scripture texts, such as C. H. Dodd long ago envisioned,[42] or if they came to Christianity as Hellenistic Jews accustomed to hearing or reading the scriptures in Greek.

Epistle. HUGHES cites OLSHAUSEN's theory regarding Paul's reference to Aaron's breastplate on pp. 91-92 of his own commentary, but dismisses it. PLUMMER also rejects this theory, but without due credit, on p. 80. OLSHAUSEN is certainly wrong in saying that Paul alludes to Aaron's breastplate *rather than* to the stone tablets of the old covenant, but I see no reason to deny an *auxiliary* reference to Exod. 36:21 (LXX).

[40] Only at Exod. 36:21 (39:14); III Ki. 22:46 (LXX); II Ch. 34:31; Jer. 17:13; 28 (51):60; Dan. 12:1 and I Ma. 13:40.

[41] The Revised Standard Version, surprisingly, does not note the texts from Ezekiel.

[42] C. H. DODD, *The Apostolic Preaching*, pp. 10-17, for Paul, and *According to the Scriptures*, pp. 11-12, 23, 59-60, passim. It is true, however, that Dodd's broad outline of the OT background of large sections of the NT text needs to be filled in careful detail and that this has not been satisfactorily done. The present study attempts to analyze II Cor. 3-4 from just that viewpoint. FITZMYER, "Glory Reflected on the Face of Christ," pp. 630-631 remarks that "it is surprising that Paul, in writing to such a Greek community, would indulge in the midrashic sort of argumentation that he employs here (2 Cor. 3-4). One wonders whether the Corinthian Christians would have appreciated the subtlety of his argument, since it is so closely based on an Old Testament passage and utilizes figures and motifs that turn up in Palestinian Jewish writings." Having accepted DODD's theory of the nature of the earliest Christian preaching and acknowledging the high degree of interpretation that existed between Palestinian and Diaspora Judaism, I am not as surprised by Paul's method. Dr. Bruce MALINA has suggested to me, in

Many modern commentators recognize allusions to these scriptural texts as well.[43] To some extent, however, Christian interpreters of the New Testament have "lost their ear" for Old Testament references or have begun to regard such allusions as mere window-dressing for the more basic and independent New Testament text.[44] For many commentators on II Cor. 3:1-6, Paul merely mentions a variety of scriptural passages as he pursues his own line of argument, as a form of decoration or secondary support, much as a modern preacher might do today. On the contrary, these verbal traces of the biblical texts assembled above are not random or secondary in II Cor. 3:1-6. *There is no line of argument without the full force of this scriptural background*, as the scholarly confusion over Paul's meaning amply attests. Jeremiah 38 (LXX) and Ezekiel 11 and 36 have affected Paul's composition, not only on the level of vocabulary, but on the levels of structure and content as well. It is necessary, therefore, to discover, not only *that* Paul alludes to these various texts, but *why*, and how he uses them. The next step in my analysis, then, will be to show how these texts are related to one another. The following section of this chapter will show that there is a pattern and purpose to their association which parallels both contemporary and later Jewish exegetical procedure, that is, the hook-word association of scriptural texts around a central theme.[45]

The Structure and Operation of the Text-Complex

The previous pages have brought to light some of the unarticulated background of II Corinthians 3:1-6 through an investigation of its voca-

---

conversation, that it would have made no difference to Paul whether or not his audience did understand his argument. In his social milieu it was far more important to *impress* than to *convince*. While I cannot agree with Dr. MALINA without reservation, I must admit that Paul may have been trying to impress the Corinthians with his skill as an interpreter of scripture.

[43] The tradition of German scholarship has been particularly sensitive to the OT references in II Cor. 3:1-6, but has done very little with its awareness of this background. BULTMANN, for example, notes Exod. 31:18; Jer. 38 (31):33; Ezek. 11:19 and 36:26 (LXX) but does not ask why just these texts should be reflected in II Cor. 3:3-6 (*Der zweite Brief*, p. 76; so also PLUMMER, *II Corinthians*, p. 82 and many others).

[44] W. C. VAN UNNIK expresses a more correct view: "We who have 19 centuries of Christianity behind us and are used to read [sic] things more or less from a christological point of view, hardly realize that these patent facts [the realities of the new covenant] were not theory for the Christians, but the lifeblood of happiness and strength. The texts from the OT were collected not for a pass-time, but for their joy that the Lord had realized his promises, to defend their faith, against attacks that it was not make-believe." "Ἡ καινὴ διαθήκη," *Studia Patristica* IV, ed. F. L. CROSS, TU 79 (Berlin: Akademie-Verlag, 1961) p. 223.

[45] RICHARD, "Polemics," p. 347.

bulary. The evidence of this vocabulary indicates a set of Septuagint texts which stand behind the text we possess and endow the terms used therein with specific meaning and a particular frame of reference. To fully understand the background uncovered, however, it is necessary to ask whether and, if so, how these texts are related to one another. Does this background of Paul's discourse form a coherent system which might help to explain the disparate elements of its Pauline reflection?

It is, of course, *possible* that snatches of these assorted Old Testament passages simply popped into Paul's mind as he wrote. This is the position frequently taken, even in scholarly treatments of the passage — Paul is "reminded" of Jeremiah 38 (LXX),[46] one these "evokes" another;[47] Paul's ideas "develop one out of another in an essentially unsystematic and spontaneous manner..."[48] This is not, however, to do justice to Paul either as a writer or as a student of the scriptures of the Jews. It provides no clue to the reason why just these selections were relevant, and so it offers no real help in explaining the passage.

As we have seen in the Introduction to this study, Paul certainly was a student of the scriptures, in fact, a skilled interpreter of them by training. His letters provide ample evidence of intricate exegesis of texts of the Old Testament, a fact which is becoming better recognized in the literature of current Pauline scholarship.[49] Therefore, the methods of exegesis available in first-century Judaism should be of considerable use in analyzing the organization of the text-group to which he refers, as well as his use of it. Besides being an exegete in his own time, Paul was, at least in his pre-Christian days, also a worshipping Jew. Therefore, the uses of scripture in the synagogue, insofar as they can be discovered, should also be informative.

As we have also seen in my Introduction, the exegetical method of *gezera shava*, or the hook-word association of texts, was very possibly the simplest, earliest and most frequently used exegetical and literary technique of Paul's time. As you recall, according to this method, two texts may be associated with each other through the common occurrence of the same word in each text. For example, Jeremiah 38:31 ff. (LXX) could be associated with Ezekiel 11:16 ff. through the hook word,

---

[46] HUGHES, *Second Epstle*, p. 89.

[47] BARRETT, *Second Epistle*, pp. 107-108.

[48] C. J. A. HICKLING, "The Sequence of Thought," p. 384.

[49] Both FITZMYER, "Glory Reflected in the Face of Christ," p. 632 and HOOKER, "Beyond the Things that are Written?", p. 297 agree that II Cor. 3:7-18 is the passage in the Pauline corpus that is most aptly named exegetical, or "midrashic." However, there are numerous other Pauline passages that are obviously exegetical. FITZMYER suggests Gal. 3-4 and I Cor. 10. I would add Rom. 1-3, 4, 9-11 and the body of II Corinthians. Scratch any "theological" passage and you will probably find exegesis underneath.

καρδία. Jeremiah 38:33 says "I will put my laws into their mind and I will write them on their *hearts,*" while Ezekiel 11:19 reads "I will give them a different *heart.*" Heart, "καρδία," is the common term. A review of the texts in the group assembled above reveals that each of them can be associated with one or more of the others through a significant hook word.

Verbal links

Thematically, the primary text of the group is Jeremiah 38:31-34 (LXX). Paul has cited its key phrase, "καινὴ διαθήκη," at the close of his argument in 3:6, thereby emphasizing its importance for him. My example of the application of the method of *gezera shava* has already indicated that Jeremiah 38:33 can be connected to Ezekiel 11:19 through the hook word, καρδία. In fact, all of the prophetic texts in the group can be associated with one another through καρδία. This verbal connection of Jeremiah 38:33/39:39 (LXX) with Ezekiel 11:19/36:26 also establishes the primary thematic link within the system, that between the covenant of Jeremiah and the spirit of Ezekiel. Jeremiah 38 and 39 (LXX) are connected through covenant (διαθήκη), while spirit (πνεῦμα) is the most significant link between Ezekiel 11 and 36.

The texts displayed from Exodus do not share these verbal links through καρδία or πνεῦμα. Exodus 34:27-28, however, does contain the hook word διαθήκη. The presence of this link is another reason why Exod. 34 should be considered Paul's primary referent for πλάκες λίθιναι. However, a link with all of the Exodus texts — 34:1-4,27-28; 36:21 (LXX) — can be drawn to both of the Ezekiel texts with the key word "stone" (λίθος), and its adjective "stony" (λίθινος). It can equally well be drawn to Jeremiah 38:33 (LXX) with the key word "write" (γράφω and its compound, ἐγγράφω). Figure 1 illustrates visually the proposed relationships among the texts.

Each text of the complex shares a hook-word link with each other text in the group with the exception of Jeremiah 39 (LXX) which has no link with Exod. 36. The links between the prophetic texts in the group are complementary in Paul's treatment of them. On the other hand, the relationships of the Jeremiah/Exodus texts and of the Ezekiel/Exodus texts within the complex are a set of contrasts through the links, γράφω and λίθος. The Jeremiah/Exodus texts are contrasted on the basis of two different types of writing, while Ezekiel's spirit and flesh are contrasted with the stones of Exodus.

The assertion that this group of texts has been exegetically related through a hook-word process does not, of course, deny that they are

Figure 1

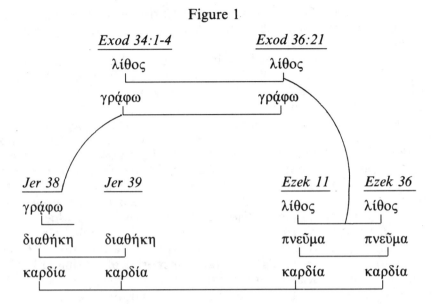

thematically related as well.[50] In fact, it emphasizes their obvious thematic correspondence, centering around the covenant concept in various ways. The texts from Exodus are derived from the story of the covenant-making at Sinai. The promises of Jeremiah rest upon the religious heritage conveyed in those same stories. Ezekiel draws his own theological conclusions regarding a future renewed covenant relationship between Israel and its God on the basis of that same Exodus tradition. The repetition of the covenant formula, "καὶ ἔσονταί μοι εἰς λαόν, καὶ ἐγω ἔσομαι αὐτοῖς εἰς θεόν" in Jeremiah 38:33 and 39:38 (LXX), Ezekiel 11:20, 36:28, which had appeared for the first time in Exodus 6:7 at the beginning of the events of the exodus confirms this covenant theme in all the passages in the complex. In using such a text-group, Paul certainly was aware of, and primarily interested in, its most fundamental theme, God's covenant with Israel. However, though the thematic correspondence is certainly present and, for the modern reader, is possibly more persuasive of the unity of the group than are the verbal links, those verbal links were for the first-century interpreter the indispensable indicators of a complementary meaning present in all

---

[50] Nor does it deny that these background texts themselves may have been dependent on one another in composition or redaction. An analysis of such dependence is not, however, the purpose of this study.

the texts included. For the Jew of early Christian, and certainly post-Christian, times the theological unity of scripture was primarily conveyed through its verbal expression.[51]

From the foregoing analysis it can be concluded, then, that the individual texts unearthed on the basis of the Pauline vocabulary in II Corinthians 3:1-6 actually form a cohesive group in themselves on the basis of hook-word linkage. All of the key linking words — διαθήκη, καρδία, λίθος and γράφω — are present in Paul's text, but they have also become integral parts of his own composition. One of the common mistakes of even the finest interpretations of this passage — those which do recognize Paul's contact with some sort of a scriptural background and even draw attention to possible hook-word connections — is the attempt to view Paul's own text as a direct exegesis of, or a hook-word association of, this group of Old Testament texts.[52] Paul does indeed reflect such a hook-word association of the texts assembled above, but the exegetical process itself cannot be traced in II Corinthians 3:1-6. The attempt to trace it there ends in the familiar morass of missing links. The hook-word links exist between the texts which form the *background* of his text. It is the resulting structure of the background of II Cor. 3:1-6 which has been analyzed here.[53] The structure of Paul's own text hangs on a

---

[51] Even a cursory reading of Jewish exegetical material is enough to convince on this point. For example, although stemming from a somewhat later period, the very first argument contained in the *Genesis Rabbah* is based solely on a verbal relationship between texts hinging on the word "beginning" in Gen. 1:1, "In the *beginning* God created the heavens and the earth," variously vocalized. See *Midrash Rabbah*, I, translated by H. FREEDMAN and M. SIMON (London: The Soncino Press, 1938) pp. 1-3 and TOWNER, *Rabbinic Enumeration*, pp. 154ff. for an analysis of further rabbinic examples of this type.

[52] For example, RICHARD, "Polemics," pp. 348-349.

[53] It is not possible to enter into the question which follows naturally upon this analysis: what is the *Sitz im Leben* of this background? This is the same problem that the Schulz/Georgi hypothesis of an opponents' midrash standing behind II Cor. 3:7-18 was intended to solve, but on a wider scale. I reject that hypothesis on three grounds: first, its limitation to verses 7-18, second, its too precise definition of the content of such a midrash and its "Pauline" interpolations and third, its insistence on the *anti-Pauline* origins of the exegesis. Yet I must admit that the argument of II Cor. 3:1-6 does not appear to me to be *ad hoc*, nor does its complicated exegetical background. FITZMYER and LIETZMANN feel that Paul composed the midrash of II Cor. 3:7-18 himself for another occasion (see my Introduction, note 41). MOULE has suggested that Paul has incorporated a synagogue sermon into II Corinthians, *Birth of the New Testament* (New York: Harper & Row, 1962) p. 54, n. 1. Both of these opinions are entirely hypothetical, as was that of SCHULZ and GEORGI. Nevertheless, it will become clear that the argument and exegetical background of II Cor. 3-4 are too intricate and extensive to be occasional. Some evidence will be offered in the course of this study for the independent existence of the cluster of OT texts Paul reflected. Very little evidence has come to light, however, because none has been sought. The search is the material for another study. My hypothesis would be that of DODD in *According to the Scriptures*. On p. 23 he states his thesis: "The impression ... that we derive from examination of such applications of Old Testament Scripture to the events

single link with the text-group discovered, γράφω, and consists of an
argument which relies heavily on ideas drawn from the group.[54] This use
that Paul has made of the text-group which has been discovered will be
discussed after the nature of the background text-group has been more
fully explored.

A pool of covenant characteristics: Paul's Prophetic background

An exegetical model

The exegetical procedure, *gezera shava*, as it is illustrated in the later
works of the rabbis, is usually performed on legal, or halakic, texts, but
does occur as well in haggadic, or narrative, midrashim. The verbal
linkage between two or more texts is performed in either case for the sake
of mutual interpretation. What one text lacks in detail, or in clarity, is
supplied from the other, or others, with which it shares specific verbal
affinity.[55] Although the rabbinic texts which most clearly illustrate this
procedure are admittedly later than II Corinthians 3, they do provide an
excellent model with which to understand the background which we can
now see standing behind II Corinthians and the operations which we will
shortly observe have been performed upon it. It seems reasonable then, in
spite of their late compilation, to suppose for the sake of this analysis
that these later Jewish exegetical texts may be a continuation of exegetical
practice in use in Paul's time.[56] If one will grant this assumption for the

---

of the *kerygma* by the New Testament theologians is that they are working upon certain
accepted assumptions, and that *they have behind them a good deal of fundamental work
upon the subject which must have gone on in very early days* (emphasis my own). This
impression must be tested by closer inspection of the *data*." The data still needs closer
inspection than Dodd himself, Lindars in *New Testament Apologetic*, or Ellis in his
various works have gaven it. See also van Unnik, "Ἡ καινὴ διαθήκη," p. 223. What I
have discovered standing behind II Cor. 3:1-4:6 is simply very early Christian exegesis,
probably not limited to Paul, but, on the other hand, not the exclusive property of his
opponents. It is likely, however, that those who opposed Paul handled such kerygmatic
exegesis very differently. To this extent, Schulz and Georgi are correct.

[54] Richard, "Polemics," p. 349 recognizes the central importance of *letter* for Paul's
argument, as most thematic analyses do, but he does not use the concept in the same way
as I do in this chapter.

[55] Strack, *Introduction*, p. 94; Mielziner, Introduction, p. 143; Longenecker,
Biblical Exegesis, p. 34; Bloch, "Midrash," pp. 32-34.

[56] The rabbinic "enumerations" discussed by Towner, because they do not deal with
legal matters, are good examples of this model. In a paper presented at the February,
1982 Regional Meeting of the SBL, Dr. William R. Stegner used such a passage to
understand the pattern of Paul's thought in Romans 9 in a paper entitled "Romans
9:6-29—A Midrash." I am grateful to Dr. Stegner for allowing me to use this unpublished
material. He argued using *Midrash Rabbah* Leviticus II, 1. This text interprets the
Pentateuchal text using Jer. 31:20, "Is Ephraim a precious son unto me? Is he a child that
is dandled? For as often as I speak of him, I do repeatedly mention him still." Stegner

sake of argument, the results are very rewarding for the understanding of II Corinthians 3. The following reconstruction emerges.

Once a chain of scriptural texts has been established through such a hook-word procedure as I have illustrated with the Jeremiah/Ezekiel texts above, a further exegetical operation may be performed on them. The texts, now related through specific verbal links, may be further related in any of their themes. They become mutually explanatory as a whole. The key themes in one can be applied to its partner, and vice versa. Each text may be used to expand the interpreter's understanding of any of the others.

A schematic expression of this procedure is presented in Figure 2. Each numbered block represents a single text and each letter of the alphabet represents a term/concept present in that text.

According to this diagram, a relationship of identity exists between Text #2 and Text #3. Text #1 is related both to Text #2 and to Text #3 because all three contain terms "B, D, and G." Once this relationship has been established through B, D and/or G, however, the term "H," contained in #2 and #3, but not in #1, may be predicated of #1 on the basis of the established relationship. Texts #2 and #3 are then being used to interpret Text #1. Similarly, the term "C," which is contained in Text #1, but not in Texts #2 and #3, may be associated with them in exactly the same way. When this procedure is performed in all of its possible variations on a particular set of texts, a pool of terms and the concepts which they express is formed, drawn from all of the texts in the set. The individual texts have become a mutually interpreting group and their individual aspects form a pool around their leading concept, the notion of greatest, or originating, interest to the interpreter.

---

quotes the rabbis' exposition as follows: "Ten things are designated as precious, and these are they: The Torah, prophecy, understanding, knowledge, folly, riches, the righteous, the death of the pious, lovingkindness, and Israel. As to the Torah, whence [do we learn that it is called precious]?—*She is more precious than rubies* (Prov. III, 15). Prophecy, whence?—*And the word of the Lord was precious in those days* (I Sam. III, 1). Understanding, whence?—*That which is precious of the spirit of man, is understanding* (Prov. XVII, 27). Knowledge, whence?—*The lips of knowledge are a precious jewel* (ib. XX, 15). Folly, whence?—*A little folly is more precious than wisdom and than honor* (Eccl. X, 1). Riches, whence?—*Precious is the substance of a diligent man* (Prov. XII, 27). The righteous, whence?—*How precious are Thy friends unto me, O God!* (Ps. CXXXIX, 17). The death of the pious, whence?—*Precious in the sight of the Lord, is the death of his saints* (ib. CXVII, 15). Lovingkindness, whence?—*How precious is Thy lovindkindness, O God!* (ib. XXXVI, 8). Israel, whence?—'*Is Ephraim a precious son unto me?*' (Jer. XXXI, 20), which means, I set a great price upon Israel." *The Midrash Rabbah* II, Exodus and Leviticus; translated by J. Israelstam (London: The Soncino Press, 1977) p. 19, STEGNER, "Romans 9," p. 4. The link between all of the scripture texts quoted is the word "precious" and the interpretation of the Leviticus text is based on the information provided by the catena thus obtained.

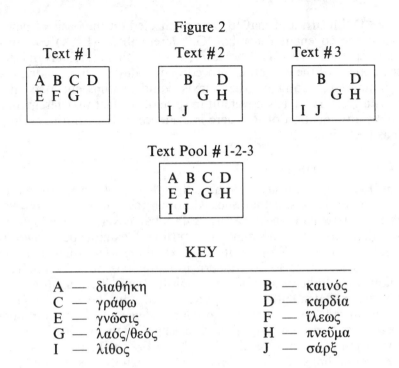

Figure 2

Text # 1

| A | B | C | D |
| E | F | G | |

Text # 2

	B		D
		G	H
I	J		

Text # 3

	B		D
		G	H
I	J		

Text Pool # 1-2-3

A	B	C	D
E	F	G	H
I	J		

KEY

A — διαθήκη	B — καινός
C — γράφω	D — καρδία
E — γνῶσις	F — ἵλεως
G — λαός/θεός	H — πνεῦμα
I — λίθος	J — σάρξ

The foregoing is admittedly an abstraction from the exegetical procedure of the later rabbis as it is expressed in the midrashim. I am confident, however, that the New Testament itself is the most fruitful ground for the eventual discovery of numerous other instances of such a procedure in the first century. Moreover, the value of the model is that it works very well in explaining Paul's otherwise illogical jumps in II Cor. 3:1-6. Once its usefulness for II Cor. 3 has been illustrated, its corroboration in later rabbinic sources is more welcome than suspicious.

The bare bones of the diagram can be fleshed out from the text-complex developed from II Cor. 3:1-6. At this time I am concerned only with the positive correlation to be found between the Prophetic texts in the group. Furthermore, I am concerned only with those verses in which the key terms used to identify the text occur — Jeremiah 38:31-34 (LXX), Ezekiel 11:19-20, 36:26-28. Finally, the terms and ideas selected here for emphasis do not necessarily exhaust the thematic content of each text. They have been selected on the basis of their importance to Paul's composition.

Text # 1 is Jeremiah 38:31-34 (LXX); Text # 2 is Ezekiel 11:19-20; Text # 3 is Ezekiel 36:26-28. All have previously been connected on the basis of "D," heart, and may also be connected on the basis of newness, "B," and the covenant formula, "G." Jeremiah 38 (LXX) contains no reference to the spirit, "H," however, while both Ezekiel 11 and 36 do. On the pattern of the exegetical procedure just described, an individual or a community reflecting on these texts could legitimately associate the spirit with Jeremiah's new covenant in spite of the fact that Jeremiah does not make any mention of it. There is evidence in II Corinthians 3:6 that this has been done.

The spiritual covenant

In II Cor. 3:6 Paul says that he is the minister of a new covenant, not a written one, but a spiritual one. Although the phrase "new covenant" stems from Jeremiah, the deceptively familiar covenant theology which knows that the new covenant is "spiritual" cannot be drawn from Jeremiah 38:31-34 (LXX) or its context alone. The question that II Corinthians 3:6 poses to its modern interpreter is how Jeremiah's new covenant came to be understood as a spiritual one. We must not take the extraordinary statement "οὐ γράμματος ἀλλὰ πνεύματος" for granted, simply because it has become so familiar. I suggest that the combination of the notions "καινὴ διαθήκη" and "πνεῦμα" is the result of the mutual interpretation of Jeremiah 38:31 (LXX) and Ezekiel 11:19/36:26-27 based on their verbal links. The pool developed through the association of these texts contains both "new covenant" and "new spirit" and so the notions have been combined.[57]

Written on hearts of flesh

Similarly, term "C" in the abstraction, the notion of writing (γράφω), could legitimately be associated with the Ezekiel texts from Jeremiah 38 (LXX) on the basis of their established connections, even though Ezekiel does not talk about writing. There is evidence in II Cor. 3:3 that this application has been made, even though the process itself is not articulated in the Pauline text. In II Cor. 3:3, Paul speaks of a letter written on tablets which are hearts of flesh. It has been well established that the phrase "hearts of flesh" stems from Ezekiel. In Ezekiel, however, nothing is to be written on them; they are to receive the spirit. It is in

---

[57] The contrast between "letter" and "spirit," then, is certainly a contrast between covenant benefits or characteristics rather than between hermeneutical principles. Therefore, the tradition of interpretation which begins with Tertullian and runs through John Chrysostom and Augustine is more correct than the tradition, stemming from Origen, that Paul refers to two levels of meaning in the Old Testament text. The relevance of Origen's theory to Paul's argument, however, will become clear in Chapter Two of this study.

Jeremiah 38:33 (LXX) that something is to be written on a heart. Paul's expression is not a mixed metaphor. It is an interpretation of Ezekiel 11:19/36:26 by Jeremiah 38:33 (LXX). The pool of concepts which their text-group creates includes both "written-on hearts" and "hearts of flesh" and the two notions have been combined.

Covenant theology

The key and the alphabet notation in Figure 2 and Figure 3 below describe the components of the concept-pool formed by the combination of the Prophetic texts, Jeremiah 38:31-34 (LXX); Ezekiel 11:19-20; 36:26-28. As I have said before, the notion of covenant is dominant in this group. The pool, then, is a set of covenant characteristics which eventually come to form a unified Christian notion of covenant carefully drawn exegetically from the Old Testament, rather than taken up whole from any single Old Testament text. The Christian covenant has the following characteristics, if drawn from this pool: it is new (B); it is written on hearts (C, D) which are not stone but flesh (I, J). It imparts individual knowledge of God (E); it involves the forgiveness of sins and is a divine mercy (F). It reconstitutes the people of God (G). It imparts the spirit and is itself a spiritual reality (H).

It would be extremely interesting to trace the presence and the influence of this particular pool of concepts within the Pauline letters. W. C. van Unnik has begun to do just that in his brief article with regard to Jeremiah 31:31-34, with extremely provocative results.[58] It is furthermore important to remember that the theological themes listed are *covenant* characteristics and *covenant* benefits, because of their origin in the exegesis of Prophetic covenant texts dominated by Jeremiah 31 (38 LXX), and not random, unrelated theological concepts. For example, the possession of the spirit, an idea widely considered to be particularly Pauline, has been firmly anchored here from scripture as a paramount characteristic of the new covenant through the articulation of the exegetical origin of the idea. It has not simply occurred to Paul, and Paul only. It is not just a facet of his unique personal experience in Christ, although it may well be that. The possession of the spirit can be recognized, as a result of this exegetical analysis, as a predictable effect of the inauguration of the new covenant of Jeremiah.[59]

---

[58] VAN UNNIK, "La conception de la nouvelle alliance."

[59] That other Christians of the New Testament period expected and experienced the outpouring of the spirit on the basis of OT prophecy is of course obvious from Acts 2:16ff. and its use of Joel 2:28ff. But with Ezekiel 11 and 36 we are closer to Paul's particular appropriation of the idea in II Cor. 3:3-6. A relationship between Joel 2:24-27 and Ezekiel 36:8-15 is most probable and certainly worthy of further thought. What is encountered here is the ever-present tendency of the OT to re-think and re-present in a

The ultimate result of the foregoing exegetical investigation of the scriptural background of II Corinthians 3:1-6, then, has results on the literary level, but also on the historical and the theological levels as well. This study is concerned mainly with exegetical results, conclusions on the literary level about II Corinthians 3:1-4:6 specifically. I will return to that level shortly, but I wish to point out briefly that this exegetical task has results which reach into all areas of theology. The foregoing analysis has brought to light something about the process through which "theology" arose in the New Testament period. With the exegetical formation of the pool of covenant concepts around Jeremiah 31 (38 LXX) and its companion texts, a Christian understanding of covenant came into being. So the modern interpreter has gained historical insight into the process through which biblical theology is born. The "covenant pool" *is* Paul's covenant theology. It is not produced by Paul's text in II Cor. 3:1-6; it lies behind it. Biblical theology is exegetically produced in its origins in the New Testament period, and then conveyed to us in and through the texts we possess, at least in the particular case brought to light here from II Corinthians 3. Through further exegetical work done along the pattern exhibited in this study, I am confident that this model for the formation of "theology" in the New Testament period will be validated for a larger field of documents and theological themes.

Evidence for the Conceptual Pooling of Covenant Texts Outside of II Cor. 3:1-6

Jeremiah 39:38-40 (LXX) and II Cor. 3:11; 5:11

If a fourth text were added to the abstract in Figure 2, Jeremiah 39:38-40 (LXX), two more covenant characteristics could be added to the conceptual pool which they produce. Jeremiah 39 (LXX) was cited in the establishment of Paul's background text-complex, but its influence

---

literary mode the tradition handed down from the past. This tendency continues, as I am trying to show, in the formation of the New Testament itself. Furthermore, Thomas E. PROVENCE has very recently pointed out the clear connection between Paul's question in II Cor. 2:16: καὶ πρὸς ταῦτα τίς ἱκανός; and its answer in II Cor. 3:5: ἡ ἱκανότης ἡμῶν ἐκ τοῦ θεοῦ ("Who is Sufficient for These Things?," pp. 55-57). The question of II Cor. 2:16 may well reflect Joel 2:11—καὶ τίς ἔσται ἱκανὸς αὐτῇ. See WINDISCH, *Der zweite Korintherbrief,* p. 100. Joel 2:12 enjoins Israel to turn (ἐπιθτρέφω) to God with their whole heart (καρδία). This verse alone contains two key verbal links with the scriptural background to be discussed in this study and considerable thematic similarity to II Cor. 3:16. Moreover, Joel 2 contains the military and sacrificial imagery that is so unexpectedly present in II Cor. 2:14-16 as well. The relationship of Joel 2, II Cor. 2-3 and the rest of its scriptural background, which is the focus of this study, definitely calls for further investigation, but cannot be undertaken in the context of the present inquiry.

cannot be seen in II Cor. 3:1-6. Nevertheless, it can be connected with Jeremiah 38:31-34 (LXX) on the basis of the key words διαθήκη and καρδία, as has been indicated in Figure 1. When it is added, Jeremiah 39:38-40 (LXX) contributes the ideas of the eternity of the covenant and of fear of the Lord as a characteristic of God's renewed people to the conceptual pool. The text is visually expressed as Text #4 in Figure 3.

Figure 3

| Text #1 | Text #2 | Text #3 | Text #4 |

Text Pool #1-2-3-4

KEY

A — διαθήκη	B — καινός
C — γράφω	D — καρδία
E — γνῶσις	F — ἵλεως
G — λαός/θεός	H — πνεῦμα
I — λίθος	J — σάρξ
K — φόβος τοῦ θεοῦ	L — αἰώνιος

There is evidence that this text was part of the background which influenced Paul's composition at II Cor. 3:11. In II Cor. 3:7-11, Paul is in the midst of a series of contrasts between the new covenant and his ministry of it and the earlier covenant and Moses' ministry. These contrasts will be fully discussed in Chapter Two of this study. For now, however, I can point out that he states in verse 11 that the new covenant and its ministry will remain or last (τὸ μένον μένει...). Nothing *explicit* in Jeremiah 38 (LXX) or Ezekiel 11 and 36 tells him that this is the case, but Jeremiah 39:40 (LXX) does explicitly assert that the promised covenant will be everlasting. The conviction on Paul's part expressed in II Cor. 3:11 that his new covenant will last is easily explained on the basis of the pooling of the ideas contained in Jeremiah 39:38-40 (LXX) with those of the other texts in the group and his appropriation of this theme from the pool. Jeremiah 39:40 (LXX) elaborates the contrast drawn in Jeremiah 38:32 (LXX) between the new covenant and the covenant in which the fathers did not remain (ὅτι αὐτοὶ οὐκ ἐνέμειναν ἐν τῇ διαθήκῃ μου). What was once a choice made wrongly by the recipients of God's covenant has become a divine gift in the new covenant. God has now promised the eternity of his new covenant. This covenant characteristic is traceable to Jeremiah 39:40 (LXX).

The eternity of the covenant is guaranteed in Jeremiah 39:38-40 (LXX), not only by the divine promise of faithfulness, but by the divinely bestowed "fear of the Lord," which will be characteristic of his people. The idea of fear of the Lord occurs also in II Corinthians 5:11, within the proximate context of II Cor. 3. Although fear of the Lord is traditionally the prescribed attitude for men in the face of eventual judgment as described in 5:10,[60] the couplet rests uneasily within the surrounding discussion. It is possible that it is germane there as dictated by the structure of Paul's scriptural background. If this is the case, the complex of Prophetic texts discussed above may have influenced a section of II Corinthians far more extensive than II Cor. 3:1-11 alone. Man's righteous stance before the ultimate judgment would therefore be another gift of the new covenant.[61] His acquittal or indictment would depend upon his faithfulness to the new covenant, just as Israel's judgment had always depended on its adherence to the covenant of Moses. Under the new covenant, however, his faithfulness itself has been promised to him.

The New Testament itself contains other instances of such exegetical operations as are under investigation in this study, although it is impossible to discuss them here. As I have mentioned in the context of locating the source of the expression, "καινὴ διαθήκη" in Jeremiah 38:31-34 (LXX), the Epistle to the Hebrews contains the only explicit and lengthy citations of that text in the New Testament, at Heb. 8:8-12 and 10:16-17. Chapters 8-10 of Hebrews contain an extended discussion of the new covenant from a soteriological and liturgical point of view. The phrase "καινὴ διαθήκη" occurs alone at Heb. 9:15 and 12:24. The argument of Hebrews concerning the new covenant is important for the purposes of this study because it suggests knowledge and use of the complex of prophetic texts which has just been shown to lie behind II Corinthians 3 and define the notion of the new covenant revealed in it. At Hebrews 10:22 there is verbal evidence, not present in II Corinthians, which shows an awareness of Ezekiel 36:25 in association with the idea of

---

[60] PLUMMER, *II Corinthians, p. 168.*
[61] VAN UNNIK, "La conception de la nouvelle alliance," p. 121.

a new covenant, as well as an appreciation of the exegetical operations performable with it. The particular application made of Ezekiel 36 is not traceable directly through II Corinthians, and so must indicate the independent status of the exegetically based new covenant tradition. I will explore this very early confirmation of the exegetical method proposed in this study as the background for II Corinthians 3 in a forthcoming article entitled "Hebrews 10:22 and the New Covenant: An Exegetical Analysis."

Further evidence for Paul's use of his scriptural background

A conclusion from context

Thus far, we have seen that a group of Septuagint texts is reflected in the vocabulary of II Corinthians 3:1-6 and that several unusual phrases present there, rather than being mixed metaphors, are in fact evidence of the dynamic exegetical structure of that text-group. One of those unusual phrases previously discussed was "... καινῆς διαθήκης, οὐ γράμματος ἀλλὰ πνεύματος..." of II Cor. 3:6. Several of the elements of this highly significant phrase have already been discussed. The "καινῆς διαθήκης" refers to the promised new covenant of Jeremiah 38:31-34 (LXX). This new covenant is considered to be "πνεύματος" because of the exegetical combination of Jeremiah 38 (LXX) with Ezekiel 11 and 36. The contrast between "γράμματος" and "πνεύματος" will be discussed in the following section. For the moment, however, I would like to concentrate on the final segment of the verse, "τὸ γὰρ γράμμα ἀποκτέννει, τὸ δὲ πνεῦμα ζῳοποιεῖ". The ensuing discussion will show that this statement is also traceable to the complex of Prophetic texts assembled earlier. In this case, the second member of the parallelism is a direct recalling of a passage from the context of Ezekiel 36:26, that is, Ezekiel 37:6,10 and 14.[62]

As I have said in my Introduction, for the Jew of the New Testament period the scripture was a unity as the message of God for Israel. Although the scriptures were already old at this time, that message was not perceived as directed only to the men of the past for whom it was originally composed. On the contrary, the whole of scripture continued to be perceived as directed to the Israel of each present day. Passages were therefore not understood on the basis of the original intention of the authors, so much as they were understood according to the needs of the contemporary interpreting community. Similarly, passages were related

---

[62] As David DAUBE pointed out in his seminal article "Rabbinic Methods of Interpretation and Hellenistic Rhetoric," HUCA 22 (1949), pp. 239-264, it was common legal practice in the Hellenistic age — whether in Rome, Jerusalem or Alexandria — to clarify an ambiguous passage with what precedes or follows it (pp. 257-258).

to one another, as the preceding section has amply illustrated, on the basis of verbal similarity.[63] In this way each single text could have a sort of magnetic field of verbally similar passages, drawn from the surrounding material or from other biblical books, through which it could be explained. These verbally related passages can correctly be called the proper interpretative context of the single text.

In II Corinthians 3:6 Paul has drawn a conclusion from such a context surrounding Ezekiel 36:24-32, already cited as a background text, and applied it to expand his understanding of Ezekiel 36:26-27. The verses following the background text cited close Chapter 36 of Ezekiel with no discernible thematic or verbal link with the preceding verses or with the Pauline text. But Chapter 37 of Ezekiel opens with the famous "dry bones" vision, linked with the material quoted from Chapter 36 through the word "spirit" (πνεῦμα). Ezekiel 37:1-14 is a scenario depicting the realization of the promise of Ezekiel 36:26b-27a (... and I will give you a new spirit ... καὶ πνεῦμα καινὸν δώσω ἐν ὑμῖν ... and I will put my spirit in you ... καὶ τὸ πνεῦμά μου δώσω ἐν ὑμῖν). Ezekiel 37:1-14 reads as follows:

1) Καὶ ἐγένετο ἐπ᾽ ἐμὲ χεὶρ κυρίου, καὶ ἐξήγαγέ με ἐν πνεύματι κύριος καὶ ἔθηκέ με ἐν μέσῳ τοῦ πεδίου, καὶ τοῦτο ἦν μεστὸν ὀστῶν ἀνθρωπίνων · 2) καὶ περιήγαγέ με ἐπ᾽ αὐτὰ κυκλόθεν κύκλῳ, καὶ ἰδοὺ πολλὰ σφόδρα ἐπὶ προσώπου τοῦ πεδίου, ξηρὰ σφόδρα. 3) καὶ εἶπε πρὸς με Υἱὲ ἀνθρώπου, εἰ ζήσεται τὰ ὀστᾶ ταῦτα; καὶ εἶπα Κύριε, σὺ ἐπίστῃ ταῦτα. 4) καὶ εἶπε πρός με Προφήτευσον ἐπὶ τὰ ὀστᾶ ταῦτα καὶ ἐρεῖς αὐτοῖς Τὰ ὀστᾶ τὰ ξηρά, ἀκούσατε λόγον κυρίου 5) Τάδε λέγει κύριος τοῖς ὀστέοις τούτοις Ἰδοὺ ἐγὼ φέρω εἰς ὑμᾶς πνεῦμα ζωῆς 6) καὶ δώσω ἐφ᾽ ὑμᾶς νεῦρα καὶ ἀνάξω ἐφ᾽ ὑμᾶς σάρκας καὶ ἐκτενῶ ἐφ᾽ ὑμᾶς δέρμα καὶ δώσω πνεῦμά μου εἰς ὑμᾶς, καὶ ζήσεσθε · καὶ γνώσεσθε ὅτι ἐγώ εἰμι κύριος. 7) καὶ ἐπροφήτευσα καθὼς ἐνετείλατό μοι. καὶ ἐγένετο ἐν τῷ ἐμὲ προφητεῦσαι καὶ ἰδοὺ σεισμός, καὶ προσήγαγε τὰ ὀστᾶ ἑκάτερον πρὸς τὴν ἁρμονίαν αὐτοῦ. 8) καὶ εἶδον καὶ ἰδοὺ ἐπ᾽ αὐτὰ νεῦρα καὶ σάρκες ἐφύοντο, καὶ ἀνέβαινεν ἐπ᾽ αὐτὰ δέρμα ἐπάνω, καὶ πνεῦμά οὐκ ἦν ἐν αὐτοῖς. 9) καὶ εἶπε πρός με Προφήτευσον ἐπὶ τὸ πωεῦμα, προφήτευσον, υἱὲ ἀνθρώπου, καὶ εἶπον τῷ πνεύματι Τάδε λέγει κύριος Ἐκ τῶν τεσσάρων πνευμάτων ἐλθὲ καὶ ἐμφύσησον εἰς τοὺς νεκροὺς τούτους, καὶ ζησάτωσαν. 10) καὶ ἐπροφήτευσα καθότι ἐνετείλατό μοι · καὶ εἰσῆλθεν εἰς αὐτοὺς τὸ πνεῦμα, καὶ ἔζησαν καὶ ἔστησαν ἐπὶ τῶν ποδῶν αὐτῶν, συναγωγὴ πολλὴ σφόδρα. 11) καὶ ἐλάλησε κύριος πρός με λέγων Υἱὲ ἀνθρώπου, τὰ ὀστᾶ ταῦτα πᾶς οἶκος Ισραηλ ἐστί, καὶ αὐτοὶ λέγουσι Ξηρὰ γέγονε τὰ ὀστᾶ ἡμῶν, ἀπόλωλεν ἡ ἐλπὶς ἡμῶν, διαπεφωνήκαμεν. 12) διὰ τοῦτο προφήτευσον καὶ εἶπον Τάδε λέγει κύριος Ἰδοὺ ἐγὼ ἀνοίγω ὑμῶν τὰ μνήματα καὶ ἀνάξω ὑμᾶς ἐκ τῶν μνημάτων ὑμῶν καὶ εἰσάξω ὑμᾶς εἰς τὴν γῆν τοῦ Ισραηλ, 13) καὶ γνώσεσθε ὅτι ἐγώ εἰμι κύριος ἐν τῷ

---

[63] Renée Bloch, "Midrash," pp. 32-33; Addison Wright, *Midrash*, pp. 59-75.

ἀνοῖξαί με τοὺς τάφους ὑμῶν τοῦ ἀναγαγεῖν με ἐκ τῶν τάφων τὸν λαόν μου. 14) καὶ δώσω πνεῦμά μου εἰς ὑμᾶς, καὶ ζήσεσθε, καὶ θήσομαι ὑμᾶς ἐπὶ τὴν γῆν ὑμῶν, καὶ γνώσεσθε ὅτι ἐγὼ κύριος λελάληκα καὶ ποιήσω, λέγει κύριος.

1) And the hand of the Lord came upon me, and the Lord brought me forth by the Spirit, and set me in the midst of the plain, and it was full of human bones. 2) And he led me round about them every way, and behold, there were very many on the face of the plain, very dry. 3) And he said to me, Son of man, will these bones live? and I said, O Lord thou knowest this. 4) And he said to me, Prophesy upon these bones, and thou shalt say to them, Ye dry bones, hear the word of the Lord. 5) Thus saith the Lord to these bones, Behold I will bring upon you the breath of life, 6) and I will lay sinews upon you, and will bring up flesh upon you, and will spread skin upon you and will put my Spirit into you, and ye shall live, and ye shall know that I am the Lord. 7) So I prophesied as the Lord commanded me, and it came to pass while I was prophesying, that behold, there was a shaking and the bones approached each one to his joint. 8) And I looked, and behold, sinews and flesh grew upon them, and skin came upon them above, but there was no breath in them. 9) And he said to me, Prophesy to the wind, prophesy, son of man, and say to the wind, Thus saith the Lord, Come from the four winds and breathe upon these dead men and let them live. 10) So I prophesied as he commanded me, and the breath entered into them and they lived, and stood upon their feet a very great congregation. 11) And the Lord spoke to me saying, Son of man, these bones are the whole house of Israel, and they say our bones are become dry, our hope has perished, we are quite spent. 12) Therefore prophesy and say: Thus saith the Lord: Behold, I will open your tombs and will bring you up out of your tombs and will bring you into the land of Israel. 13) And ye shall know that I am the Lord, when I have opened your graves, that I may bring up my people from their graves. 14) And I will put my Spirit within you, and ye shall live, and I will place you upon your own land, and ye shall know that I am the Lord; I have spoken, and will do it, saith the Lord.

In this text in verses 6, 10 and 14, the promise of Ezekiel 36:26,27 is repeated in an only slightly modified form: v. 6 καὶ δώσω πνεῦμά μου εἰς ὑμᾶς; v. 10 καὶ εἰσῆλθεν εἰς αὐτοὺς τὸ πνεῦμα; v. 14 καὶ δώσω πνεῦμά μου εἰς ὑμᾶς. Each time the promise is followed by the same qualification: καὶ ζήσεσθε v. 6; καὶ ἔζησαν v. 10; καὶ ζήσεσθε v. 14. The result of the gift of the spirit is life — "And you (they) will live." Therefore, the spirit gives life. This is a direct conclusion from Ezekiel 37:6,10, 14, but it is also exactly what Paul says in II Cor. 3:6c — τὸ δὲ πνεῦμα ζῳοποιεῖ. The earlier vocabulary analysis has shown that Paul is in contact with Ezekiel 36:26,27 in this section of his text. Its context has just as surely provided Paul with his concluding remark.[64] The concept of life and its association with the spirit is thereby added to the pool of covenant characteristics previously developed.

Of course, the spirit is instrumental in giving life in other places in the Old Testament, most obviously in the whole of the creation narrative of Genesis on the basis of Gen. 1:2. That this is so is undeniable, but it is illustrative of the dependency of Ezekiel's prophecy upon the creation tradition, rather than of Paul's dependence on Genesis for his imagery. Paul's verbal link with Ezekiel 36:26,27, the verbal links between Ezekiel 36:26,27 and Ezekiel 37:1-14, and the similarity of expression between Paul's "τὸ δὲ πνεῦμα ζῳοποιεῖ" and Ezekiel's "δώσω πνεῦμά μου εἰς ὑμᾶς, καὶ ζήσεσθε" all indicate clearly that Paul has based his statement directly on Ezekiel 37. There is a great difference between thematic similarity alone and the type of contextual proximity and verbal reflection present between Paul and Ezekiel here.

It is important to notice as well that the life that the spirit gives in Ezekiel 37:1-14 is precisely the recreation of "dead" Israel into a new people of God. This theme was already implicit in the other Jeremiah and Ezekiel texts, but it is much more dramatically and emphatically stated in Ezekiel 37. I would argue that it is just this sort of a "recreation" of a new Israel that Paul sees as the task of the spirit which is given in the new covenant. That new covenant, ministered by him and communicating the divine life-giving spirit, has created a new Israel, the Corinthian Christians.[65]

Summary

The investigation of the unarticulated scriptural background of II Corinthians 3:6 and its *implicit* use is now almost completed. The clues provided by the unusual vocabulary and expression of the section have led to the hypothesis that a cluster of Old Testament texts stands behind

---

[64] Several authors have suggested that the prophecy of Ezekiel 37 might stand behind II Cor. 3:6, especially M. A. CHEVALLIER who calls it "une glose fulgurante sur Ez. 37" in his work on the spirit, *Esprit de Dieu, paroles d'hommes*, Bibliothèque théologique (Neuchâtel: Editions Delachaux et Niestle, 1966) p. 90. CHEVALLIER emphasizes that Paul's reference to Ezek. 37 serves to underline his role in the creation of a new people of God by the spirit in his own day. In this CHEVALLIER is quite correct, but he offers no exegetical rationale for this reference to Ezekiel's "dry bones" vision, on his own part, or for Paul. Similarly, the following authors mention a possible reference to one or other verse of Ezek. 37 without following the suggestion up with any substantiating argument: Boaz COHEN, "Note on Letter and Spirit," p. 200; H. J. SCHOEPS, *Paul* (London: Lutterworth Press, 1961) p. 212; Jean VANDERHAEGEN, "2 Corinthiens, 3,1-3," *Bible et Terre Sainte* 68 (1964) p. 23; M. H. SCHARLEMANN, "Of Surpassing Splendor," *Concordia Journal* 4 (1978) p. 112; RICHARD, "Polemics," p. 350.

[65] So also CHEVALLIER, *Esprit de Dieu*, p. 90.

Paul's composition. A hook-word structure for this exegetical background has been proposed based on valid exegetical procedure in Judaism and has been confirmed by the presence of the key words themselves in II Corinthians 3:1-6. The exegetical implications of such a hook-word text group have been explored, such as the pooling of concepts to produce a unified notion under the leading concept of covenant and an elaboration of that notion drawn from a context created through extension of the hook-word process.

The results of an application of these exegetical models to Paul's text have been rewarding. Paul's unusual vocabulary is explained by the scriptural texts adduced. His metaphors are un-mixed by an understanding of the pooling interpretative process, as in the case of the writing on hearts of flesh in v. 3, for example. The context of Ezekiel 36:26-27 has provided the background for Paul's unexpected statement that the spirit gives life in II Cor. 3:6. The remaining task, then, is to explain the argument as it stands in II Corinthians 3:1-6 in the light of this enabling background. The next section of this chapter will explore Paul's *explicit* use of the Prophetic and Pentateuchal texts so far assembled.

The Argument of II Corinthians 3:1-6
in Light of its Scriptural Background

A Preliminary Outline

In order to reach a proper understanding of the argument of II Corinthians 3:1-6, the interpreter must still take several more steps after discovering and investigating the background of Paul's discourse. First, he must find and describe the specific link between the arguments in II Cor. 3:1-6 and this background. He must discover the particular way in which Paul has brought the background scriptures into play. This link is not, properly speaking, the unique vocabulary discussed in the preceding section. This vocabulary is rather a reflection of the background and thereby an evidence of it. It is not the pivot on which Paul's use of the scriptural background hangs and turns. In the case of II Corinthians 3:1-6, the key word, $\gamma \rho \acute{\alpha} \varphi \omega$, is the thread on which Paul's argument from scripture is strung.

Second, the ways in which that background has been brought into play against the particular problem that II Corinthians 3:1-6 sets out to solve must be better understood. In the course of his argument, Paul sets out a series of contrasts between the actual writing of the Mosaic covenant and the unwritten, spiritually written, or interiorly written realities of the new covenant which he ministers. In these contrasts, written letters of recommendation fall implicitly on the side of the superceded Mosaic writing, clearly inappropriate for a minister of the new covenant. For him, the interior recommendation of a heart enlivened by the divine spirit suffices, along with the obvious existence of a new people of God created by that same spirit.

So, after Paul's particular link with his scriptural source is discovered and his uses of it described, his answer to the critics who question his credentials and behavior can finally be adequately appreciated in the light of the external scriptural authority that he has chosen to employ. The modern reader, like his better informed first-century counterpart, will be enabled to feel the full force of Paul's argument because the conceptual world of the original writer and readers has been recovered for him. With the key to that conceptual world provided by the scriptures which echo through II Corinthians 3:1-6, we can see that Paul's confidence rests solidly on his divine commission as a minister of the new covenant. His defense is the conformance of his behavior to the demands of that covenant. We shall see in the final section of this chapter that Moses remains the model for such a defense.

The Hook Word, γράφω, as Link between II Corinthians 3:1-6 and its Scriptural Background

A re-reading of II Corinthians 3:1-6 reveals that the terms and concepts appearing most frequently are those having to do with writing and written things.[66] I have indicated previously that γράφω and its compounds are an important link between the key covenant text, Jeremiah 38 (LXX) and the texts from Exodus that Paul's vocabulary reflects. Continuity between the Exodus traditions and the Prophetic traditions which Paul employs is established and maintained by the key verbal and conceptual link, διαθήκη, shared by Exodus 34:27-28 and Jeremiah 38:31-34; 39:40; (LXX). But, Paul has engaged his scriptural background in support of his argument precisely at the point at which the new covenant of Jeremiah can be compared and contrasted with the Exodus covenant — the way that they are written. His consistent reference to written things — in his own situation (μὴ χρῄζομεν ... συστατικῶν ἐπιστολῶν, v. 1) and in his background ([θεός] ὃς καὶ ἱκάνωσεν ἡμᾶς διακόνους καινῆς διαθήκης, οὐ γράμματος ἀλλὰ πνεύματος ... v. 6) at the beginning and the end of the section especially — indicates the significance of the theme. It is also used in verses 2 and 3 as the basis for their comparisons. Therefore, the word "γράφω" is the

---

[66] ἐπιστολή in v. 1, 2 and 3; ἐγγράφω in v. 2 and 3; γράμμα in v. 6. Even μέλας and πλάξ in v. 3 and v. 2 are associated with writing.

single most important verbal and thematic hook through which Paul works with his background. It is on the basis of the contrast between the new unwritten covenant and the written Exodus covenant that he rests his rejection of written letters of recommendation in contrast to his adversaries' possession of them. A decision for the superiority of the new covenant in its unwritten, interior and spiritual form is a decision for Paul and a dismissal of his need for any written recommendations.

In order to fully appreciate this argument, the next step is the analysis of his exploitation of the contrasts afforded by this particular link with his background. It is a giant step because his use of it is constant and multiple. It is uniformly one of contrast, contrast between the heart-writing of Jeremiah and the stone-writing of Exodus. Throughout the ensuing analysis it is important to remember, moreover, that Paul has brought the whole of the discovered scriptural background into play by linking into it through "writing" once and for all, in a process parallel to the pooling effect discussed above. He does not take a snatch of it here and a tidbit there, so that Ezekiel 11:19; 36:26 would only be relevant in v. 3 and Jeremiah 38:33 (LXX) only in v. 6. Rather, he is in dialogue with the whole of the established background at all times, evoking it through his reflection of its key terms. He works freely within it, having once entered into it at the point at which the Exodus covenant can be compared unfavorably with the new covenant of Jeremiah. It is the presupposition which informs and dominates his text as a whole. The tone of his treatment is entirely positive to the Prophetic side of this contrast and, with only two exceptions — its original and inviolable status as διαθήκη and the divine commission of Moses as minister — negative to the Exodus side.

The Contrasts of II Corinthians 3:1-6

Written in hearts, not on stones

In discussing the hook-word structure of the background in the earlier part of this chapter I have said that Exodus 34:1-4,27-28 and Exodus 36:21 (LXX) are linked with Jeremiah 38 (LXX) through γράφω and with Ezekiel 11 and 36 through λίθος. These are positive links on the exegetical level, but negative links conceptually. The intention of Jeremiah 38:31-34 (LXX) is clearly to contrast its promised new covenant with the covenant of the fathers. The crucial point of this contrast is that the new covenant will be differently written (Jer. 38:33 LXX) and will therefore have different results. The new covenant will be written in the hearts of God's people. The covenant of the fathers was written on stone tablets. This contrast is expressly repeated by Paul in II Corinthians 3:2-3 with a clear preference for the mode of writing used in the new over that used in the old.[67] Paul's letter is written in his heart. Paul's covenant is written in his heart.

The intention of Ezekiel is also a contrast — new hearts of flesh against the hardened hearts of Israel. Hearts which have turned to stone do not live, that is, have not received the spirit. Upon inclusion in the covenant text-complex, this contrast is referred to the stone tablets of Exodus. In combination with Jeremiah 38 (LXX), Ezekiel's hearts of flesh become hearts which can be written on to receive the new covenant, identified through this very combination within the text-group as the spirit. Paul repeats this contrast also in II Corinthians 3:3 and 6. He is a minister of Jeremiah's new covenant. He is in possession of a heart of flesh, just as promised by Ezekiel. The spirit has been written in that heart.

Known by all, not by one alone

In II Corinthians 3:2, the phrase "γινωσκομένη καὶ ἀναγινωσκομένη ὑπὸ πάντων ἀνθρώπων" implies another comparison between Jeremiah and Exodus. A decision is made in favor of Jeremiah, and the prophecy of Jeremiah 38:34 (LXX) is applied to Paul's situation directly. In Exodus after Moses received the words of the covenant, he communicated them to the people (Exod. 24:3; 34:32). The following section of II Corinthians 3, vv. 7-18, is an exegesis based on the report of just such a proclamation.[68] This mediation of Moses becomes the pattern of the relationship of Israelites to the covenant. It is not the case that all Israelites received it directly. Moses gave it to them. It is subsequently read to them through the ages on selected cultic occasions of the utmost importance, right down to Paul's own day, when the Torah was read in sections each week in the synagogue service.[69] This situation had arisen not only due to the inability of the general populace to read the Hebrew of the Torah, but ultimately on the example of Moses himself, who had become the mediator between God and Israel at the time of the Sinai covenant at the express request of Israel itself, according to Exodus 20:19

---

[67] RICHARD, "Polemics," p. 350 suggests that Paul's "antithetical style" is derived from Jeremiah 38:31-33 (LXX). Where Jeremiah has οὐ ... ὅτι, however, Paul has οὐ ... αλλὰ.

[68] The verb "ἀναγινώσκω" in the Septuagint almost always refers to the cultic reading of the covenant, and if not that, at least to the public announcement of royal letters or to prophetic pronouncements, never to private reading. In the NT it refers almost exclusively to the formal or liturgical reading of scripture (Exod. 24:7; Deut. 17:19; 31:11; Jo. 8:34,35; Neh. 8:3,8,18; 9:3; 13:1; Mt. 19:4; 21:16; Mk. 12:10 par; 26 par; 13:14 par; Lk. 6:3 par; 10:26; Acts 13:15,27; 15:21,31; Eph. 3:14; Col. 4:16; I Th. 5:27; I Tim. 4:13).

[69] John BOWKER, The Targums and Rabbinic Literature, pp. 12, 13. In addition to this general pattern of public recitation, however, there were a few private bibles in NT times.

and subsequent Jewish legend.[70] In Exodus 20 the people stand well clear while Moses bears the divine presence and speech, because they are terrified of the divine manifestations that they do witness.

It is precisely this state of affairs that Jeremiah 38:34 (LXX) promises to alter and which Paul exploits here. Unlike the covenant given at Sinai, written on stone and known and read by Moses alone unless and until he revealed it to Israel, the new covenant is one that is written on hearts and so directly available to all men. Like the covenant he ministers, Paul's letter of recommendation is directly available to all men. They need only look into his heart. Paul repeats this idea in II Cor. 4:2; 5:11 and 6:11. It is the link of "written thing" and of "writing" in general that allows this transfer from covenant to letter and from letter to covenant, but it is the promise of Jeremiah in contrast to the Exodus model that justifies the conclusions drawn. Paul is more faithful to the biblical texts than he is responsive to the demand for mundane commendatory letters.[71] This is because he is in the process of redefining letter of recommendation as covenant commission. In that process, the scriptural background is what is most significant.

Written with the spirit, not with ink

II Corinthians 3:3 closes with another contrast between the Prophetic promises and the events of the Exodus. The origin of the phrase "ἐν πλαξὶν καρδίαις σαρκίναις" in the combination of Ezekiel 11/36 with Exodus 34 has already been discussed, as has its conceptual combination with Jeremiah's heart-writing. The explicit contrast with the

---

[70] GINZBERG, *Legends*, III, pp. 106-109, 124-128, 131-134; Renée BLOCH, "Quelques aspects de la figure de Moïse dans la tradition rabbinique," *Cahiers Sioniens* 8 (1954) pp. 211-285.

[71] This is not to deny that Paul uses the figure of the letter of recommendation consistently. BAIRD has convincingly argued that he does. After having established the reading ἡμῶν as the correct one in II Cor. 3:2, BAIRD goes on to describe Paul's application of the technical designation "ἐπιστατικὴ συστατική" which he uses in II Cor. 3:1. He concludes that "1) Paul views himself as the courier, not the amanuensis of the letter. ... the epistle of recommendation is normally by the one recommended. ... 2) ... Paul is not to be understood as either the writer or the ultimate recipient of the letter. ... 3) ... By describing the epistle as written on his heart, Paul is not referring to the receiving of the letter but the carrying of it. ... 4) When Paul says that 'you are a letter *from Christ*' (v. 3), he is attempting to clarify his interpretation of the author of the epistle of recommendation. ... Christ ... is the author of the letter of recommendation." All of this is entirely accurate usage of the metaphor of the Greek epistle of introduction. ("Letters of Recommendation," pp. 169-170). However, although his use of the metaphor of the letter of recommendation is consistent, his denial of his need for one is based entirely on the authority of the scriptural background he employs, and not upon a logical justification of his indifference to what were probably expected credentials on the basis of that metaphor.

tablets of stone from Exodus 34:1,4 embodied in the couplet with which verse 3 closes (οὐκ ἐν πλαξὶν λιθίναις/ἀλλ' ἐν πλαξὶν καρδίαις σαρκίναις) is also now clear. One further Pauline interpretative statement is also present in the verse, however, in the first couplet, "οὐ μέλανι/ἀλλὰ πνεύματι θεοῦ ζῆντος."

The "οὐ μέλανι" of II Cor. 3:3 is the last verbal remnant of Paul's mundane situation and the complaint against him with its clear reference to the materials of ordinary letter-writing. But its partner "ἀλλὰ πνεύματι θεοῦ ζῆντος" creates another of Paul's so-called mixed metaphors. The comparison is between one writing material and another, just as it is in the couplet which follows — there the papers or stone, here the ink. Opposed to the stone tablet is the heart; opposed to the ink is the spirit of God. This strange comparison is easily explained with reference to Ezekiel. It is the literal application of the prophecy of the gift of the spirit from Ezekiel 36:27 to the promise of Jeremiah, and from there to Paul's situation.[72]

Ezekiel 36:27 reads "καὶ τὸ πνεῦμά μου δώσω ἐν ὑμῖν." II Cor. 3:2 has already indicated that writing is going on in hearts. In ordinary letters, the ink as agent of the writing becomes the writing itself when applied to parchment or paper. If a similar agent is found for the writing of the new covenant, it too can be understood as "being" or constituting the writing on analogy with μέλας. The agent or the material of this writing is sought and found in Ezekiel's text because it mentions something in addition to writing that is put into hearts. This is another instance of the pooling or transference effect that the linkage of the Jeremiah and Ezekiel texts has and of the options for interpretation that it opens up. The spirit is identified with the writing of the new covenant and contrasted with the writing of the first covenant on the basis of the interpretation of the promise of Jeremiah 38 (LXX) by the promise of Ezekiel 36, as much in this first couplet in II Cor. 3:3 as in the second one already discussed. The writing of the first covenant was the law; the writing of the new covenant is the spirit of God. The well-known Pauline contrast between the law, or letter, and the spirit can be seen here in its exegetical origins.[73] The spirit itself in all its manifestations is then the verification of the reality of the new covenant, Paul's recommendation.

---

[72] RICHARD, "Polemics," pp. 348, 351 also sees the agency of the spirit as derived from Ezekiel 11/36. However, he seems to bypass the step in which I see Ezek. 11/36 combined with Jer. 38 (LXX) and move directly from Ezekiel to Paul's situation. This is the case for the phrase "καρδία σαρκίνη" but not for "ἐγγεγραμμένη ... ἐν πλαξὶν καρδίαις σαρκίναυ" which requires not only Jer. 38 (LXX) but also Exod. 34.

[73] What Paul is saying *theologically* has been clear since Tertullian (Adv. Marc. 5,11); see B. SCHNEIDER's article reviewing the history of the interpretation of II Cor. 3:6, "The Letter and the Spirit," pp. 165-187. The point of this study, however, is to

A spiritual covenant, not a written one

The foregoing analysis has revealed that verses 2 and 3 should be taken together to be properly understood because of their consistent and interdependent use of the scriptural background of the section. Verse 6ab should be taken with them as well for a similar reason. Once again, this verse is related to the scriptural background in many and various ways in combination. The clearest statement of Paul's intentions in the whole passage comes only in v. 6b in which the καινὴ διαθήκη of Jeremiah is explicitly stated to be the object of Paul's ministry. My analysis has shown that the new covenant has been of paramount importance all along, but it is mentioned explicitly only at the end.[74]

The last half of the couplet "οὐ γράμματος/ἀλλὰ πνεύματος" has been discussed in conjunction with the "pool" concept earlier. It does involve the application of Ezekiel 36:26-27 (11:19-20) to Jeremiah 38:33 (LXX) as I have suggested. It is also dependent, however, on the interrelation done in vv. 2-3 as just described. Once the "writing in the heart" of Jeremiah has been identified with the gift of the spirit of Ezekiel, the idea of physical writing is gradually left behind in an exclusive emphasis on the spirit in the new covenant. The ideas of epistolary writing, and of letter as alphabetic symbol, are relegated to the Sinai covenant alone. The written covenant made at Sinai assumes in verse 6 all the negative aspects of Paul's comparison of the two covenants.[75] The choice of this aspect of the Sinai covenant as its

---

understand what he is saying exegetically. Most exegetical studies of II Cor. 3 in the past have used their own critical methodology to determine what Paul said theologically, and, in the main, they have been correct. Paul does believe that the old covenant, characterized by the written law, failed to give life and therefore resulted in death. He does believe that the new covenant is characterized by the gift of the spirit which brings with it eternal life. But, *this* exegetical study intends to use modern critical methodology in order to understand *Paul's* exegetical methodology. I do not expect, therefore, to make a new statement about the meaning of II Corinthians 3-4 on a theological level, so much as I want to discuss *how* and *why* Paul said what he did.

[74] RICHARD, "Polemics," p. 350.

[75] SCHNEIDER, "'Letter and the Spirit,'" pp. 188-191 contains a brief philological survey of the use of the term "γράμμα" in literature antecedent and contemporary to Paul with significant bibliography noted. He concludes that γράμμα was used frequently as a designation for any written law, or written law taken as a whole. Boaz COHEN, in an article "Letter and Spirit in Jewish and Roman Law" argues that the expression "ῥητὸν καὶ διάνοια" was a commonplace in ancient Greek rhetoric and is imitated by Paul in his γράμμα/πνεῦμα contrast. The classical distinction referred to the written form of a law and the ordinary interpretation of such a written document according to its intention. See also COHEN's article, "Note on Letter and Spirit" and DAUBE "Rabbinic Methods," pp. 248, 258-259. Therefore, as I read these authors, it is not the couplet, "not letter, but spirit," used by Paul that is exceptional, but the application of the pair to the Exodus tablets and the new spirit of Ezekiel specifically, as well as the negativity that comes to be attached to the first member of the pair.

epitome serves Paul's purpose well, since it both maintains the consistency of his theme, and also bears directly on his own problem with written letters. In verse 6, then, the new covenant is defined as a spiritual one, while the Sinai covenant is defined as a written one.

Gradually, in the course of verses 2-3 and 6 the change of level has taken place which has produced so much confusion in the interpretation of this text. The earlier elucidation of its exegetical background has now enabled us to follow it more easily. The idea of writing remains the connecting link, but Paul's uncomfortable situation regarding the use of letters of recommendation has been left behind in favor of his exalted status as minister of Jeremiah's promised covenant. Two parallel events, the ministry of the Mosaic covenant at Sinai and the ministry of the new covenant at Corinth, are alive in Paul's text from 3:3 on, quite explicitly so in II Cor. 3:7-18. When the transfer is made back into Paul's uncomfortable social milieu in II Cor. 4:1, his situation has been thoroughly redefined as a covenant-making situation, one dominated by the characteristics of the Jeremiah-Ezekiel covenant, rather than by the covenant characteristics which were in force at Sinai.

The letter kills, but the spirit gives life

The close of verse 6, a transition between this section of the chapter and the next, which anticipates the antitheses of II Cor. 3:7-11, has already been discussed with respect to its conclusion from context, "τὸ δὲ πνεῦμα ζῳοποιεῖ." It also presents a further contrast between Ezekiel and Exodus, however. Paul's statement in II Corinthians 3:6c that "what is written kills" comes as a surprise to his reader, however familiar we may have become today with Paul's negative evaluation of the law of Moses. Nothing in the preceding verses has prepared for this radically negative assessment of the "written thing" with which Paul is now concerned, the Sinai covenant mediated by Moses.

As I have previously shown, "τὸ δὲ πνεῦμα ζῳοποιεῖ" of II Cor. 3:6c is directly dependent on Ezekiel 37:1-14 and its narrative presentation of the promise of Ezekiel 36:26-27. A contrast between Ezekiel 36:26 and Exodus 34:1-4 has already been drawn, wherein the stone of Exodus was replaced by the flesh which is able to receive the spirit of Ezekiel. In an interpretative process parallel to the pooling effect of hook-word linkages between two texts, but running in the opposite direction, Paul's "τὸ γὰρ γράμμα ἀποκτέννει" has simply excluded from the devalued Exodus covenant, epitomized by its physically written aspect, a quality characteristic of the Jeremiah/Ezekiel covenant, that is, life. That is to say, the phenomenon of mutual interpretation, which I have illustrated in its positive function in the development of the covenant conceptual pool, can here be seen working negatively. Because the basic relationship in which Paul apprehends the Exodus material vis-à-vis the Jeremiah/Ezekiel material is one of contrast, the Exodus texts and the whole covenant narrative of which they are a part are radically excluded from the covenant conceptual pool developed from the prophets. Nothing which is true of Ezekiel's promise, then, will be true of Exodus' covenant. Nothing which is proper to the new covenant may be present in the old covenant. If Ezekiel 36:26-27, 37:1-14 show that life, in dependence on the gift of the spirit, is a characteristic of the new covenant (τὸ δὲ πνεῦμα ζῳοποιεῖ II Cor. 3:6c), then life cannot be a property of the written covenant. The negative is expressed first by Paul as it is in the preceding couplet (οὐ γράμματος/ἀλλὰ πνεύματος) on which the concluding one depends. If the new spirit gives life, then the old letter has taken life. Paul's statement "τὸ γὰρ γράμμα ἀποκτέννει" is nothing but the logical outcome of the interpretation of the Exodus covenant by the Jeremiah/Ezekiel covenant complex.[76]

This sort of negative assessment of the covenant of Moses on the basis of the covenant of Jeremiah/Ezekiel is carried on extensively in the section of II Corinthians which immediately follows, vv. 7-18. In the following chapter, which will deal with that section, the same negative interpretative procedure will be seen at work, especially in verses 7, 8, 9, 10 and 11 of II Corinthians 3. The Prophetic promises themselves give warrant for this negative interpretation of the Mosaic covenant when they describe the situation of Israel as their promises are made. Jeremiah 38:32 (LXX) states that the fathers did not remain in their covenant and were disregarded by the Lord. This is death for Israel. In Jeremiah 39:37 (LXX) we find Israel scattered into every land by God's fury. Again this is a national death, also described in Ezekiel 11:16. The abominations reported in Ezekiel 36:25,31 were a spiritual death from which the divine spirit resurrects Israel in Ezekiel 37. A stone heart does not beat. Paul expresses these prophetic condemnations very radically when he says in effect that the Exodus covenant kills.[77] But, he believes he has seen the

---

[76] RICHARD, "Polemics," p. 351, assumes the same conclusion. It is Paul's knowledge that the life promised by Ezekiel has been received through the new covenant which causes him to so devalue the ancient one. Such a condemnation of the Mosaic covenant would be impossible outside of the realization of the prophetic promises.

[77] Amusingly, Chrisostom says that Paul "adds something really apt to startle them when he says that the one kills, while the other gives life." II ad. Cor. Ep. Comment, Hom. 6, 2, and SCHNEIDER, "'The Letter and the Spirit,'" pp. 172-173. Paul may have gone to excess in claiming that the letter kills, but he has certainly gotten his readers' attention for the last 1900 years. In explaining this radically negative statement, most authors have recourse to Pauline passages about the law from Galatians and Romans, especially, since the 'letter/spirit" contrast occurs only twice more in the NT, at Rom. 2:29 and 7:6. See SCHNEIDER. "The Letter and the Spirit;" K. PRÜMM, "Rom. 1-11 und 2 Kor. 3," Biblica 31 (1950) 164-203 and Diakonia Pneumatos, pp. 116-122; HUGHES, Second

arrival of the new life of the spirit in the new covenant. Only because he perceives these prophecies fulfilled can he depart so radically from the reverence in which the Mosaic covenant was universally held in Judaism.

An internal ministry, not an external ministration

The presentation of the contrasts of II Corinthians 3:1-6 is now almost complete. One contrast is done on the level of ministry, however, rather than on the level of covenant, as all of the others have been. The noun "διάκονος" appears in verse 6 for the first time,[78] but the accusations against Paul, reflected in verse 1, were already accusations made against his ministry in Christ. The fact that Paul's substitution of the verb "ἐγγράφω" in II Cor. 3:2 and 3 indicates an intended reference to Exodus 36:21 (LXX) has already been mentioned.[79] It also presages this ministry theme and brings another aspect of the Exodus story into play, the role of Aaron as liturgical minister of the Sinai covenant in contrast to Paul as liturgical minister of the new covenant. Cultic imagery has already been present in II Corinthians just prior to chapter 3, at II Cor. 2:14-16, so its use here is not totally unexpected. Exodus 36 (LXX) is a description of the ceremonial robes and ornaments of Aaron to be made in accordance with instructions received by Moses. In particular, Exodus 36:14-25 (LXX) is a description of the breastplate Aaron was to wear on his chest when in the tabernacle of the Lord. Fixed upon this breastplate were twelve stones with the names of the tribes engraved on them. By wearing this device Aaron brought the people itself ceremonially into the presence of God as he performed his duties for them.

The correspondence between the imagery of this section of ritual law and the imagery of the law engraved on stone with its reinterpretation by Jeremiah and Paul is striking. Aaron is depicted in Exodus 36:21 (LXX) as wearing a stone object on top of his heart, an external written thing that he bore before the Lord. This picture is evoked by Paul with ἐγγράφω, but in the light of Jeremiah's promise. The occurrence of ἐγγράφω in v. 2 implies that rather than wearing an external stone engraving, which in its day resembled the stone tablets of the law on which it was based, Paul bears an internal heart-engraving, which in his

---

Epistle, p. 96; PLUMMER. *II Corinthians*, p. 88. It is not true, however, as PLUMMER says, that "this verse would have been very obscure if we had not possessed Romans..." The material from Romans may indeed be relevant and helpful, but it is Paul's Old Testament background that really explains II Cor. 3:6.

[78] The verb "διακονέω" has appeared in verse 3, somewhat out of place in a discussion of the delivery of letters, but very much in place in a discussion of ministering to God's people.

[79] Contra PLUMMER, *II Corinthians*, p. 80 and HUGHES, *Second Epistle*, p. 92.

day matches his new covenant. Paul carries the Corinthians themselves before the Lord in his heart as his "letter," not just the letters of their names on a stone tablet. A second deliberate use of ἐγγράφω in verse 3 reinforces this reinterpretation.

The recognition of this application of Exodus 36:21 (LXX) un-mixes the metaphor of a letter engraved on a heart just a bit more by making an intended contrast more easily visible. In II Cor. 3:1-4:6 Paul presents himself as improving on the ministry of the first covenant in many ways. The application of Exodus 36:21 (LXX) gives a cultic cast to Paul's improvements. Interpretative alteration of text is another available exegetical method of Paul's time, especially among more radically eschatological groups such as the Essenes of Qumran. It allows the exegete to insert his interpretation into the text he is interpreting itself.[80] In II Cor. 3:2-3, Jeremiah 38:33 (LXX) though not completely cited, has been interpreted by Exodus 36:14-25 (LXX). The comparison with Aaron is not a main point of Paul's argument. It does add a distinct nuance to the emerging new covenant/Sinai covenant contrast, however, and does so through the unexpected use of a single word.

An appreciation of this reference to the ministerial role of Aaron helps us to become aware of a second shift in focus within II Cor. 3:1-6. The shift in focus from letter to covenant in verses 2-3 is accompanied by a second shift, especially toward the end of the section in verses 4-6, between covenant and the ministry dependent upon it. This second shifting focus is another cause of ambiguities in the text. It is a function of Paul's answering an accusation regarding ministry on the basis of the covenant which is ministered. The argument of II Cor. 3:7-18 operates on the level of covenant and the level of ministry simultaneously in much the same way and a similar confusion results. The realization that Paul's method answered a difficulty in ministry on the basis of covenant alleviates this difficulty. In II Cor. 3:1-6, focus has been largely on

---

[80] E. Earle ELLIS is a major proponent of this interpretation of first-century exegetical practice. See *Paul's Use of the Old Testament,* pp. 139-149, "How the New Testament Uses the Old," pp. 147-149 and "Midrash Pesher in Pauline Hermeneutics," pp. 173-181 in *Prophecy and Hermeneutic in Early Christianity* (Grand Rapids, Michigan: Wm. B. Eerdmans Publishing Co., 1978). ELLIS has been criticized for this theory by A. T. HANSON, who charges that he maintains "an undue measure of arbitrary alteration on Paul's part." According to HANSON, Paul "uses the same license of interpretation that contemporary rabbinic exegesis allowed itself, no more and no less," *Studies in Paul's Technique and Theology* (London: SPCK, 1974) pp. 147-148. Whether or not ELLIS' application of this technique to Paul's OT citations is excessive, one must also wonder how HANSON has determined what license was allowed in contemporary rabbinic exegesis. At any rate, the technique of interpretation through textual selection and alteration was certainly in existence in Paul's time and available to him. See also BOWKER, *The Targums and Rabbinic Literature,* pp. 5-16 and BROWNLEE, *The Midrash Pesher of Habakkuk,* pp. 33-34.

covenant as the characteristics of the new covenant have been described in contrast to the characteristics of the Sinai covenant. In II Cor. 3:7-18, the focus is on ministry, as the challenge to Paul's conformance to a Mosaic pattern of ministry is met head on. Nevertheless, the principle of the solution remains the same there — the superiority of the new covenant ministered by Paul. The contrasts discussed above have had as their purpose the establishment of this superiority of Paul's covenant, and, in the last one using Exod. 36 (LXX), of Paul's ministry before God. This evocation of the role of Aaron signals the presence of the theme of ministry throughout the argument, and the enduring validity of Old Testament figures as models of behavior in the day of the new covenant.

Paul's final contact with a scriptural background in II Cor. 3:1-6 breaks the foregoing pattern of contrasts by appropriating an element from the Sinai covenant in a positive way. It is not a covenant characteristic which is positively adopted but the role of Moses as minister, regardless of the eventual status of his covenant vis-v-vis the realized new covenant. This unique case signals the final solution to Paul's problem when combined with the superiority of his new covenant, already established through scripture. Both his proper conformance to the pattern which Moses provided for the ministry of God's covenants with his people and the evidence of the superior characteristics of the new covenant in his behavior argue for Paul's authentic apostleship.

Paul and Moses as Covenant Ministers

The dense theological summary of the nature of the new covenant in contrast to the Sinai covenant of II Cor. 3:6bc has been introduced in II Cor. 3:6a by the statement that God has also made Paul competent to minister a new covenant, II Cor. 3:6a ([θεός, v. 5] ὃς καὶ ἱκάνωσεν ἡμᾶς διακόνους [καινῆς διαθήκης]). It is on this simple assertion that the giant edifice of his defense rests. II Cor. 3:5 has referred to competence as well, in a fairly back-handed manner: οὐχ ὅτι ἀφ' ἑαυτῶν ἱκανοί ἐσμεν λογίσασθαί τι ὡς ἐξ ἑαυτῶν, ἀλλ' ἡ ἱκανότης ἡμῶν ἐκ τοῦ θεοῦ.

ἱκανός, ἱκανότης are clearly the key words in this verse, and they are usually taken to refer to the competence conferred either by the possession of adequate references and/or the indisputable power of the θεῖος ἀνήρ. The verse is then itself referred to the *Sitz im Leben* reflected in 3:1 regarding letters of recommendation. Paul is thought to be reflecting on his own situation directly, a situation in which he has been reproached for recommending himself instead of possessing proper recommendations from others or the proper legitimating works. The text is usually left at that.[81] The

---

[81] Dieter GEORGI, *Die Gegner*, pp. 220-225, 241-246; COLLANGE, *Enigmes*, p. 60; FALLON, *2 Corinthians*, p. 29.

point is that Paul's confidence (ἡ πεποίθησις), expressed in v. 4, is unfounded in reality from the point of view of his opponents.

While this may be true of Paul's situation, it does not exhaust the meaning which lies underneath the surface of verse 5. In the case of ἐγγράφω, and of ἀναγινώσκω as well, Paul's vocabulary has led to an awareness that he has gone to aspects of the Exodus story beyond the gift of the stone tablets alone. The word "ἐγγράφω" is not so strikingly unusual that one would be led to Exodus 36:21 (LXX) to explain its use in II Cor. 3:2 and 3 if other clear references to Exodus 34 were lacking. This is the case with ἱκανός and its cognates in verses 5 and 6 as well.

ἱκανός is not solely a business term or one that could necessarily be expected to occur in a letter of recommendation, although that it might occur in such a context is quite possible. It was a term used frequently in common speech and in the Greek Old Testament, simply meaning "enough," — enough people, enough food, enough time, and, especially in Leviticus, enough wealth.[82] In its uses with regard to specific persons, parallel to Paul's use of it in II Cor. 3:5 and 6, it means, as he does, "competent to, or sufficient for, an assigned task."[83] The vocabulary analysis done early in this chapter, however, has inclined us to expect the source of Paul's significant vocabulary in the scriptures. Only one parallel use of the word occurs in the Septuagint, and that is at Exodus 4:10. This is a most unusual use of the term within biblical literature because it refers to the competence of a person, Moses. It is this use of ἱκανός which determines Paul's appropriation of it in II Corinthians 3.

Exodus 3 begins the story of the burning bush, the vision which first acquaints Moses with the Lord's name (Exod. 3:14) and which commissions him to bring the children of Israel out of Egypt eventually to receive the covenant in the wilderness (Exod. 3:10-12). Moses lacks the confidence to take on this task, however, and in Exodus 4 he argues with the Lord about it and denies his own ability. Exodus 4:10 reads:

Εἶπεν δὲ Μωυσῆς πρὸς Κυριον Δεομαι, Κύριε, οὐχ ἱκανός εἰμι πρὸ τῆς ἐχθὲς οὐδὲ πρὸ τῆς τρίτης ἡμέρας οὐδὲ ἀφ' οὗ ἤρξω λαλεῖν τῷ θεράποντί σου· ἰσχνόφωνος καὶ βραδύγλωσσος ἐγώ εἰμι.

And Moses said to the Lord, I pray, Lord, I have not been sufficient in former times, neither from the time that thou hast begun to speak to thy servant; I am weak in speech, and slow tongued.

---

[82] Leviticus 5:7; 12:8; 25:26, 28.

[83] According to RENGSTORF in his article "ἱκανός" in the *Theological Dictionary of the New Testament* III, p. 293, it is simply a typical Hellenistic word in the New Testament and has no particular emphasis.

God's answer to Moses' humility is the assurance in vv. 11-12 that God himself will tell Moses what to say.

11) εἶπεν δὲ Κύριος πρὸς Μωυσῆν Τίς ἔδωκεν στόμα ἀνθρώπῳ, καὶ τίς ἐποίησεν δύσκωφον καὶ κωφόν, βλέποντα καὶ τυφλόν; οὐκ ἐγὼ ὁ θεός; 12) καὶ νῦν πορεύου, καὶ ἐγὼ ἀνοίξω τὸ στόμα σου καὶ συμβιβάσω σε ὃ μέλλεις λαλῆσαι.

11) And the Lord said to Moses, Who has given a mouth to man, and who has made the very hard of hearing and the deaf, the seeing and the blind? have not I, God? 12) And now go and I will open thy mouth and will instruct thee in what thou shalt say.

The competence that Moses feels that he lacks in himself will be supplied to him by God.

Although the use of ἱκανός in the Septuagint is too widespread to have led in itself to Exodus 4:10-12 as the background of Paul's thought in II Cor. 3:4-6a, the situations reported in the two texts are so similar that a relationship must be assumed. In Exodus 3-4 Moses is commissioned to minister to Israel, ultimately to minister what Paul will call in II Cor. 3:14 the "old covenant," the covenant made with the fathers when they came out of Egypt of Jeremiah 38:32 (LXX). Although he rightly denies that he is competent even to accomplish the exodus, God assures Moses that he himself will provide the competence to do so. II Corinthians 3:5-6 mimics Moses' attitude in this scene from Exodus perfectly. Exodus 4:10-12 is appropriated and paraphrased in the Pauline version: "Not that we are competent in ourselves so as to reckon anything as coming from our selves" — like Moses in Exod. 4:10; "rather our competence is from God" — like Moses in Exod. 4:11-12.[84]

The "καὶ" of II Cor. 3:6 reinforces the obvious similarity and the signal verbal correspondence through ἱκανός. God has "*also* made us competent to be ministers of a new covenant," just as he first made Moses competent to be the minister of the old covenant in the scene in Exodus 4 which Paul has had in mind. There is nothing in the Pauline text to which the καὶ refers. Without this reference to a previous making-competent by God, the καὶ of II Cor. 3:6a is superfluous.[85]

---

[84] This correspondence has also been hesitantly suggested by JONES in "The Apostle Paul," pp. 40-41 and earlier by A. M. FARRER, "The Ministry in the New Testament," in *The Apostolic Ministry*, 2nd ed. (London: Hodder & Stoughton, 1957) p. 173.

[85] According to LIETZMANN as well as ALLO and COLLANGE, who both translate it *réellement*, the καὶ simply emphasizes the following verb. BARRETT, *Second Epistle*, p. 111 acknowledges this interpretation, but admits that the καὶ should be translated "also," making the sentence "grossly repetitive." This is to miss the point—there was someone else who was "made competent" by God to be the minister of a covenant, Moses.

Verses 5-6 of II Cor. 3, then, mirror a text from Exodus to which the word "ἱκανός" has led, once the relationship of II Cor. 3:1-6 to Exodus 34 and 36 (LXX) specifically and to the Exodus tradition as a whole was recognized, even though it is not an unusual expression in itself.

Moses as the minister of the old covenant in contrast to Paul as minister of the new covenant is a theme explicitly carried out at length in the following section, II Cor. 3:7-18, and implicit also in II Cor. 4:1-6. Just as Moses was commissioned by God and recognized in humility that his competence to fulfill that commission came, not from himself, but from God, so Paul declares, that he has boundless confidence because his competence to fulfill his commission as the minister of the new covenant stems from God also.

Paul's Answer to his Critics: Implications of II Cor. 3:1-6

Paul's definitive answer to those who accuse him of lacking adequate recommendations and spiritual authority for carrying on his preaching of the gospel is given with this positive comparison drawn between Moses and himself. On the mundane level, Moses had no letter of recommendation, in spite of the fact that the covenant which he ministered was a written one. He feared that he would not be either believed or followed (Exod. 4:1). God's power alone enabled him to carry the Israelites out of Egypt despite opposition. Paul, like Moses, is the minister of a covenant, a new and unwritten one. Surely then, although he encountered opposition, he has no need of written letters from men to recommend and enable him. Moses had none. No human authority stood behind him. In answering this way, Paul has set himself as an equal beside Moses, the greatest and most authoritative figure in the religious history of Judaism. On this basis he has denied his need for any human legitimation of his work.

He has done even more than that. He has, through this positive comparison of himself and Moses, appropriated to himself a divine commission and empowerment parallel with Moses' own. Moses was made competent to minister his covenant by God. Paul has been made competent by God as well.

Finally, the argument of verses 2, 3 and 6bc regarding the superior nature and benefits of the new covenant, when coupled with the positive correlation of Paul and Moses in verses 4, 5 and 6a, allows Paul to see himself as superior to Moses as the minister of a better covenant than Moses' own. This superior status and its ramifications are elaborated in the following section, II Cor. 3:7-18, using the veiling of Moses as evidence of his acknowledged inferiority. The basis of Paul's superiority remains the same. The nature and quality of his ministry rest upon the nature of the new covenant ministered by him.

Moses did possess several proofs of his competence as a covenant minister, however, to which Paul possesses counterparts. Moses received the stone tablets of the law as a witness to his reception of the covenant on Mount Sinai on behalf of the people, and he possessed the people itself, created by the Exodus which he led and the covenant which he received. The possession of the spirit of the new covenant and the existence of the Corinthian Christian community are the parallel proofs which Paul has adduced in II Cor. 3:2-6 to guarantee that his ministry was a valid one. Both are witnesses to the divine commission he had fruitfully carried out. The exegetical argument of the foregoing chapter has enabled us to see how Paul understands the spirit written into his heart as the new covenant counterpart of the law engraved on stone tablets which Moses carried to the Israelites. That same spirit has enlivened the Corinthian Christians just as the spirit of God was expected to recreate out of the Old Israel, dead in sin, a new people of God.

Without a familiarity with the scriptural background of Paul's argument and without an awareness of what he could, and did, do with that background, that argument cannot be followed and these implications cannot be logically drawn. In the following chapter of this study, I will investigate II Corinthians 3:7-18 from the same point of view. There Paul is dealing explicitly with a continuation of the Exodus text against which his contrasts have been primarily drawn, Exodus 34:29-35. The implicit scriptural background discovered for II Cor. 3:1-6 also controls his explicit use of this continued text. Once again the pattern of his argument is one of contrast between the covenant ministered by Moses and the new covenant he himself ministers. The comparison between Paul and Moses is continued. Another proof of the validity of Moses' ministry was the glorious appearance of his face as he descended the mountain after seeing the glory of God. Paul asserts that he possesses a similar glory in II Cor. 3:18, but in verses 7-18 Paul's superiority over Moses even in glory is also emphasized. As evidence of this superiority over his model, Paul exploits a single unusual facet of Moses' behavior as it is reported in the Exodus text: the veiling of Moses' glorious face following the proclamation of the old covenant.

CHAPTER TWO

II CORINTHIANS 3:7-18

Introduction

The Text [1] and its Boundaries

And if the ministry of death, which was engraved in letters on stones, began in glory so that the sons of Israel were not able to look steadily [2] into the face of Moses, because of the glory of his face, a glory which is being brought to an end, [3] how much more should not the ministry of the

---

[1] This translation, like that of II Cor. 3:1-6 with which Chapter One began, is my own rendering of the Greek text into English. It is intended neither to be slavishly literal nor interpretative, but to fully convey the thought expressed by the author in Greek into English.

[2] In verses 7 and 13 I have tried variously to convey the sense of "ἀτενίζω." The basic meaning of the verb is "to look intently" (LIDDELL-SCOTT, *Lexicon*, p. 269). The idea of "staring" or "straining the eyes" to see attaches to the verb. Paul's intention in using ἀτενίζω may have been to convey the idea that Moses' veil protected the eyes of Israel from the strain and damage that might have resulted from gazing at too dazzling a light for too long. A.T.HANSON has suggested that the proper translation of the verb is "to recognize" ("The Midrash in II Corinthians 3," p. 18). The only reference he provides for this is a citation of COLLANGE, *Enigmes*, pp. 75-76, but I do not find that COLLANGE supports him, although he does put considerable emphasis on the verb. With COLLANGE I have also noted that PHILO uses the same verb in his discussion of Exod. 34:29-35 in *Vita Mosis*. COLLANGE may be more correct, therefore, when he traces the rather odd verb to a traditional interpretation of the scene which emphasized the appearance of Moses' face rather than the reaction it evoked. HANSON's translation exceeds the linguistic evidence in the service of his own interpretation of the passage.

[3] It is important to notice that the verb "καταργέω" is used in the present tense in verses 7, 11, 13 and 14. Whatever "ending" or "passing away" Paul is referring to, therefore, is taking place at the time of his writing and not at the time of this incident in the life of Moses. Contra PLUMMER, *II Corinthians*, pp. 90, 92, 97. As Collange says, authors are divided over which sense to give to the present participle, imperfect or future. He concludes, however, that it is a simple present participle. The participle, "τὴν καταργουμένην," is attribution, not supplementary or adverbial, and therefore related to the noun phrase "δόξα τοῦ προσώπου αὐτοῦ" and as such future to the main verb; see *A Greek Grammar of the New Testament and Other Early Christian Literature*, F. BLASS and A. DEBRUNNER, Tr. and rev. by Robert W. FUNK (Chicago: The University Press, 1961) p. 212. Therefore, COLLANGE correctly argues that the fading of Moses' glory is a present reality for Paul, but a future reality from the point of view of the Exodus text itself (*Enigmes*, p. 76). One can only conclude that Paul does not assert that Moses' glory faded during the wilderness period. He is not in contradiction to, but in agreement with, his religious tradition and the text of Exodus on this point.

spirit be in glory? For if there was glory in the ministry of condemnation, how much more does the ministry of righteousness abound in glory.[4] For, indeed, that which was glorified has not been glorified, that is,[5] in view of the glory which surpasses it. For if what is being brought to an end came with glory,[6] how much more does that which remains remain in glory. Having, therefore, so great a hope, we are very bold,[7] and not like Moses who put a veil over his face so that the sons of Israel might not continue to gaze upon the end of what is being brought to an end. Rather, their minds were hardened, for until the present day the same veil remains on the reading of the old covenant, lest it be revealed that[8] in Christ it is being

---

[4] The textual variant "ἡ διακονία" versus "τῇ διακονίᾳ" makes no real difference to the meaning. The external evidence seems stronger on the side of τῇ διακονίᾳ and it produces as well a nicer antithetical parallelism of construction (ministry, dative—glory, nominative/glory, dative—ministry, nominative) for the verse.

[5] The somewhat awkward expression, "ἐν τούτῳ τῷ μέρει" is, I think, adequately represented in English as "that is." It means literally "in this respect," or "to this extent," but its use is somewhat redundant with the "εἵνεκεν" that follows, so the translation simplifies Paul's Greek.

[6] Verse 11a appears to me to be a shortened repetition of v. 7a, so I have supplied the verb "γίνομαι" from there. The verb "μενει," has similarly been supplied in verse 11b on the basis of τὸ μένον.

[7] παρρησία is a term most at home in the political realm. Often associated with the term "ἐλευθερία," which occurs here in II Cor. 3:17, it refers first of all to the right to "say everything" freely and openly that came with the status of a freeborn citizen of a Greek city-state. See the recent, very readable article, "*Parrhesia* and the New Testament," by Stanley B. MARROW, S.J. in *CBQ* 44 (1982) pp.431-446 and the bibliography available there. MARROW cites several texts from JOSEPHUS which are reminiscent of Paul's use of the term in II Corinthians. JOSEPHUS speaks of the "perfect confidence before God and man arising from a good conscience" (p.439) and his expression recalls Paul's attitude as it is expressed in II Cor. 3:4, 12; 4:2; 5:11-12; 7:2-4.

[8] There is a lack of scholarly agreement concerning the proper translation of the end of verse 14: μὴ ἀνακαλυπτόμενον, ὅτι ἐν Χριστῷ καταργεῖται. Frankly, I can find no commentator who agrees with me in translating "μή" as "lest," so I offer this translation as provisional and argue here for its cogency. Other major problems occur in the translation of the phrase, however, and these should be dealt with first. PLUMMER, *II Corinthians*, p.100, PRÜMM, *Diakonia Pneumatos*, pp.140-145 and COLLANGE, *Enigmes*, pp.98-99 all contain good summaries of the problems with the verse. These revolve around the form "ἀνακαλυπτόμενον." Is it a simple participial modifier of κάλυμμα or is it a nominative or accusative absolute which refers to παλαιᾶς διαθήκης? With COLLANGE and PRÜMM and against PLUMMER, I have translated the participle as absolute referring to παλαιᾶς διαθήκης. This translation receives some specific support in BLASS-DEBRUNNER, #424, p.219 and also M. ZERWICK and M. GROSVENOR, *A Grammatical Analysis of the Greek New Testament* II (Rome: Biblical Institute Press, 1979) p.540. This decision produces the translation, "because it has not been revealed that it [the old covenant] is being brought to an end in Christ," if "μή" is taken as a simple negative. I realize that "μή" is the negative expected with participles and that Paul customarily follows this usage, see James MOULTON, *A Grammar of New Testament Greek*, III (Edinburgh: T. & T. Clark, 1963) pp.284-285. Nevertheless, both C.F.D. MOULE in *An Idiom Book of New Testament Greek* (Cambridge: The University Press, 1953) p.155 and LIDDELL-SCOTT, *Lexicon*, p.1124 have "lest" as the primary meaning of "μή" without further particles. If

brought to an end. Rather, until this day whenever Moses is read a veil lies
on their heart, but whenever it turns toward the Lord,[9] the veil is lifted.
Now the Lord is the spirit, and where the spirit of the Lord is, there is
freedom. And we all, [10] with unveiled face reflecting [11] the glory of the

---

this is added to the foregoing translation, the text reads: "lest it be revealed that in Christ
it [the old covenant] is being brought to an end." BARRETT, *Second Epistle*, p. 121, as well
as BLASS-DEBRUNNER, *Grammar*, p. 219 note that either of the above translations are valid
only if they are qualified by "to them," since Paul cannot be arguing that it is not revealed
at all that the older dispensation is ended in Christ, or else he himself could not know it.
This is true! But I think that the addition of "lest" lessens this difficulty. First of all, Paul
is certainly referring to "the sons of Israel" in verses 14 and 15 with "αὐτῶν," so the
qualification "to them" is not unwarranted. In addition, however, this chapter will argue
for the influence of Isaiah 6:9-10 on these verses. Without anticipating my later argument,
it can be pointed out that Isaiah 6:9-10 was used by early Christianity to express the
mystery of Israel's rejection of Jesus. In Mk. 4:11-12, for example, Isaiah 6:9-10 is applied
with the sense that Israel *is prevented from* understanding because the secret, or mystery,
has not been given to them by God. The situation of Israel is like that of Pharaoh in
Exodus, whose heart was hardened lest he relent, so that the glory of God would appear
beyond all measure in his rescue of Israel from Egypt. Paul's expression in II Cor. 3:14
may correspond to and lean upon such ideas. The veil remains on Israel's reading of the
old covenant *so that* they will not see its end in Christ. In fact, they do not see this, any
more than the crowd understood Jesus' Parables in Mk. 4; cf. Rom. 11:7-32 as a parallel
within the Pauline corpus.

[9] The subject of verse 16 is intentionally ambiguous. Although Paul is working
directly with the text of Exodus 34:34, his omission of the expected subject, "Moses,"
extends the reference of the verse to *anyone* who turns toward the Lord, and, probably,
the proximate reference is to the "heart"of Israel in verse 15; cf. COLLANGE, *Enigmes*,
p. 103; RICHARD, "Polemics," pp. 356-357. It is possible, furthermore, that the sentence
should end "he removes the veil," referring to the κύριον which immediately precedes
the last phrase, as BARRETT, *Second Epistle*, p. 122 and RICHARD, "Polemics," p. 357
translate it.

[10] The "we all" with which this verse begins has caused some confusion and critical
debate. Does Paul speak in his own name, using a sort of "regal we," or does he speak for
a select group of apostles, for a particular variety of Christian over against others, or for
the Christian community as a whole? Paul's earlier use of "we" in II Cor. 3:1, 2, 3, 4, 5, 6
and 12 poses a similar problem. In a recent article, M. CARREZ has tried to analyze the use
of the pronouns "I/we/you," in II Corinthians: "Le 'Nous' en 2 Corinthiens," *NTS* 26
(1980) pp. 474-486. Although he attempts a task much too large for the format such an
article provides, CARREZ does point out the importance of the distribution of these
pronouns for Paul's self-identification in II Corinthians. He concludes that Paul speaks in
the name of the whole Christian community in II Cor. 3:18—all Christians reflect the
Lord's glory (p. 476). I agree that this is probably the case in II Cor. 3:18, but his meaning
in the earlier verses of Chapter 3 is less certain. Since this issue is part of the larger debate
concerning Paul's opponents and the various parties active in Corinth at the time, it is
beyond the scope of this study. Therefore, I will simply make my own usage clear and
leave the problem of sorting it all out to other scholars more interested in that aspect of
the text. Whomever Paul means when he says "we," he certainly includes himself. So, in
this study, I will customarily just refer to Paul in discussing those passages in which he
says "we." I do acknowledge the existence of a particular group or groups with which he
is identifying himself in at least some of these cases, but I regard their identification as an
open question.

Lord, are being transformed into that same image, from glory to glory,[12] in a similar way by the Lord who is the spirit.[13]

This second section of II Corinthians 3 can be distinguished from the surrounding material by its constant and pivotal reference to Exodus 34:29-35. Chapter One of this study has shown that II Cor. 3:1-6 is dependent upon and in exegetical dialogue with a cluster of scriptural texts dominated by Jeremiah's promise of a new covenant. In the case of the preceding section, it was necessary to reconstruct this scriptural background through the vocabulary of the Pauline text alone. In the

---

[11] The verb "κατοπτρίζω" has an ambiguous meaning—either to view in a mirror or to reflect as a mirror. No absolute choice can be made between them on linguistic grounds. I have chosen the latter for this translation, because it is of primary importance in Paul's dialogue with Exodus 34, in agreement with J. DUPONT in "Le Chrétien, miroir de la gloire divine." The other possible meaning is relevant also, but not primary in Paul's *argument* in II Cor. 3. Its relevance is as a *presupposition* of Paul's argument.

[12] There are two alternatives in the interpretation of the phrase "ἀπὸ δόξης εἰς δόξαν." Either it refers to the "continual and gradual progress" of the Christian toward eternal, inner, spiritual glorification (PLUMMER, *II Corinthians*, p. 107) or the "ἀπὸ δόξης" could be taken to refer to the divine glory as source and the "εἰς δόξαν" to that gift as received. PLUMMER (p. 107) regards the second alternative as less likely, as do most other commentators. See especially COLLANGE, *Enigmes*, pp. 122-123; PRÜMM, *Diakonia Pneumatos*, pp. 193-195; SCHARLEMANN, "Of Surpassing Splendor," p. 117. As is the case with many aspects of this section of II Cor., a certain ambiguity is intentional, and both interpretations grasp essential elements of Paul's point.

[13] The end of verse 18, "καθάπερ ἀπὸ κυρίου πνεύματος," is traditionally viewed as an exceptionally difficult phrase. In a critical note, "2 Cor. 3:18b, καθάπερ ἀπὸ κυρίου πνεύματος," in *Neues Testament und Geschichte*, Festschrift Oscar Cullmann, ed. H. BALTENSWEILER and B. REICKE (Tübingen: J. C. B. Mohr, 1972) pp. 231-237, C. F. D. MOULE has described it as the "cryptic phrase" which ends one of the "most elaborately studied of all New Testament cruces," p. 231. There are two perfectly acceptable translations, however: 1) from the Lord who is the spirit and 2) from the Lord of the spirit. There is nothing so unusual about this construction. Some time ago, Rendel HARRIS noted in "Enoch and 2 Corinthians," *Expository Times* 33 (1921-1922) pp. 423-424, that the phrase "Lord of the Spirits" is one that should be familiar to us from the books of Enoch, wherein it is the favorite designation for God. He referenced in particular I En. 38 and Marcion's reading of II Cor. 3:18 which was "καθάπερ ἀπὸ κυρίου πνευμάτων." The Enoch material has to do with the transformation of the elect and righteous by the light of the "Lord of Spirits." This theme certainly has significant rapport with II Cor. 3:18. I too had often been struck by the constant repetition of the somewhat odd title in I Enoch and its resemblance to Paul's phraseology in II Cor. 3:18. I would not go so far as Harris suggests, however, and adopt the Marcionite text of II Cor. 3:18. The real difficulty with the text stems not from "κυρίου πνεύματος" but from "ἀπὸ" and "καθάπερ:" What is from the Lord? Just as what? It is important to be clear about these difficulties. In general it seems that v. 17, plus the scripture texts discussed in the chapter are the best clues to Paul's meaning, and only a review of the passage as a whole will (may) extricate us from its problem. I have produced a simple translation of the Greek words, but not a full rendering of their meaning. A full understanding of this difficult phrase is dependent on the interpretation of the whole section which it concludes. Justification for my translation, therefore, is best saved for the conclusion of the ensuing analysis.

second section formed by verses 7-18, however, the primary scriptural narrative which Paul is engaged in interpreting is clear on the surface of his text. Here, therefore, it will not be necessary to do such extensive digging to recover Paul's most important Old Testament context. The relationship of Exodus 34:29-35 to II Corinthians 3:7-18 can be established on the basis of obvious verbal and thematic echoes in Paul's composition. Then, we need only describe the dialogue between Paul and his scriptural source.

The Method and Goals of this Inquiry

That relationship of interpreter and text is best described in terms of the exegetical methodologies Paul has employed in order to make this particular Exodus tradition relevant to his own situation and meaningful to his first-century Corinthian readers.[14] An analysis of II Cor. 3:7-18 from the viewpoint of the exegetical techniques which it uses with regard to Exodus 34 reveals that verses 7-18 can be divided on this basis into two discrete subsections, verses 7-11 and verses 13b-18, with verses 12 and 13a forming a bridge between them.[15] The later rabbinic method of

---

[14] See BLOCH, "Midrash," pp. 32-33 and WRIGHT, *Midrash*, pp. 49-75 on this as the major goal of scriptural interpretation in this period. In a recent work, *Midrash in Context* (Philadelphia: Fortress Press, 1983), Jacob NEUSNER presumes a similar starting-point, although his focus is on the later literature of the Mishnah, Talmud and Midrash. He says, for example, on p. 7 that "It was in the medium of writing that, in the view of all Israel until about 200 C.E., God had been understood to reveal the divine word and will. The Torah was a written book. People who claimed to receive further messages from God usually wrote them down. They had three choices in securing acceptance of their account. All three involved linking the new to the old. In claiming to hand on revelation, they could, first, sign their books with the names of biblical heroes. Second, they would imitate the style of biblical Hebrew. Third, they could present an exegesis of existing written verses, validating their ideas by supplying proof-texts for them. ... Insofar as a piece of Jewish writing did not find a place in relationship to scripture, its author laid no claim to present a holy book." According to NEUSNER, the Mishnah, produced in the late second century C.E., did none of these things and made no claims *for itself* as a holy book. As far as I can see, however, on the basis of NEUSNER's summary, Paul *did* make the claim to be writing a "holy book" for Israel insofar as he tried to connect the new revelation of Christ that he had received to the written Torah, as he does in II Cor. 3:1-18 via exegesis. His effort, from NEUSNER's perspective would have been both to win acceptance for his own ideas by placing them in the context of the older Torah and also to bring the Torah itself into active dialogue with the Judaism of his day (*Midrash in Context*, pp. xix-xx).

[15] The text is not always divided up in this way, although the exegetical techniques are frequently recognized. WINDISCH separated verses 7-11 on the basis of the three arguments *a minori ad maius* (*Der zweite Korintherbrief*, p. 112) as do many scholars following him. See very recently on the structure of the whole section 2:14-4:6, LAMBRECHT, "Structure and Line of Thought," pp. 354-362 especially. J. D. G. DUNN isolates verse 17 as a *pesher* in "2 Corinthians III. 17 — 'The Lord is the Spirit'," but no other scholars to my knowledge see *pesher* exegesis as the determining structure of verses

kal va-homer or the classical *a minore ad majorem* argument, is the major exegetical, as well as structural, feature of the first subdivision. A *kal va-homer* pattern structures verses 7-11. The second exegetical technique which emerges in an analysis of II Cor. 3:13-18 is *pesher* exegesis. A specific *pesher* interpretation, "ὁ δὲ κύριος τὸ πνεῦμά ἐστιν," appears in verse 17a. But, as a conceptual pattern, a *pesher*-type interpretative approach structures verses 14-18 as a whole.

This investigation into the meaning of II Cor. 3:7-18 using the approach described above has four specific goals. The first is to recognize and fully describe Paul's dialogue with Exodus 34:29-35. This has frequently been tried before, with various degrees of success.[16] I hope to make my contribution to this continuing endeavor to understand II Cor. 3:7-18 as a "midrash"[17] on Exodus 34 through a more thorough analysis

---

12-18 as a whole, even though they are customarily grouped together. W. C. van Unnik deals with just verses 12-18 in his influential article, "'With Unveiled Face,' An Exegesis of 2 Corinthians iii 12-18," following, but ultimately rejecting, the received scholarly opinion that they form a "loosely connected digression" (p. 154). Although Van Unnik comes close (p. 158), he does not explicitly view verse 12 as a bridge between Paul's earlier argument and his further exegesis of Exod. 34. Prümm calls verse 12 "Die Einführung des neuen Abschnitts... eine Hoffnungsformel" (*Diakonia Pneumatos*, p. 132). Collange sees it as rigorously pursuing the argument of verses 7-11! (*Enigmes*, p. 85). I call it a bridge because it concludes the preceding section *and* introduces a *specific, contemporary application* of the scriptural background of both the preceding and following sections.

[16] The origin of this approach is usually traced to Windisch, who was followed by Schulz and Georgi, Dunn, Hooker, Fitzmyer and Richard, all of whom have made explicit attempts to analyze verses 7-18 as a midrash on Exodus 34:29-35.

[17] The more I have worked on this text, the more I have come to feel that the term, "midrash" should probably not be applied to it or any NT text. *Pace* Fitzmyer, "Glory Reflected on the Face of Christ," p. 632 and Hooker, "Beyond the Things that are Written?," p. 297. This is in part because I agree with Addison Wright and others (*Midrash*, pp. 21-22) that the term has become a catch-all and is used with considerable imprecision in biblical studies today. Furthermore, it is properly used to refer specifically to the rabbinic *midrashim* which are commentaries, continuous interpretations of single books of the Hebrew scriptures. As such, it is not a term which can be properly applied to NT works which do not share this genre. Such usage is both anachronistic and imprecise. My objection is not, however, that "midrash" as thus applied does an injustice to the genre in the Jewish materials, but that it doesn't do full justice to the genre of the NT materials. I will use it occasionally here, therefore, to reflect an awareness of the exegetical nature of the passage present in current scholarship, but I prefer to describe II Cor. 3 otherwise, perhaps as an "exegetical composition." In my view Paul is indeed concerned to interpret scripture, and so were the rabbis. Paul shares much of their point of view on scripture, as well as some of their methodology. But he does not share their genre because he is writing a letter. The question for Paul is, therefore, "How do you handle scripture when you are writing a letter, trying to convince someone else of your point of view?" The question for the gospels is, "How do you handle scripture when you are writing a theologically motivated biographical narrative, trying to describe its protagonist in terms of your tradition?" These are very complicated questions, and it is easy to see that from the point of view of *genre* there are no truly midrashic documents in the NT as it stands.

and elaboration of the exegetical forms used in that midrash than is usually done. In the course of this more thorough analysis of the exegesis contained in verses 7-18, the second and third goals of this chapter will be achieved as well.

A careful look at the terms of the *kal va-homer* arguments contained in the first subsection of the text reveals that they involve the opposition of positive, "new covenant" characteristics, drawn from the covenant "pool" described in Chapter One of this study, and negative, "old covenant" characteristics inferred from it. Therefore, this chapter will highlight and discuss the relationship between II Cor. 3:7-18 and 3:1-6 to a much greater degree than is usually done.[18] II Cor. 3:1-6 and the scriptural background discovered for it are absolutely determinative for Paul's interpretation of Exodus 34 and, therefore, for the meaning of II Cor. 3:7-18 as well. The frequent isolation of II Cor. 3:7-18 from its preceding context by regarding it as an essentially unrelated interpolation by Paul of an *opposing* group's exegesis of Exodus 34:29-35 has, therefore, frequently prevented an adequate understanding of the text by excluding material needed to explain it.

In the process of working through the implications of the *pesher* methodology of verses 14-18, a scriptural background for these verses, in addition to Exodus 34, comes to light. This additional background is largely from the Book of Isaiah, especially Isaiah 6:9-10 and 29:10-14. In a way similar to the discovery of the scriptural background of verses 1-6 in Chapter One of this study, Paul's slightly strange vocabulary leads to these new scriptural sources via parallel New Testament passages which confirm their use and combination. The texts from Isaiah to be used here to explain Paul's contemporization of Exodus 34:29-35 have close verbal contacts with the text-complex discussed in Chapter One as background for Paul's introduction to his treatment of the Exodus text. The explanation of this further prophetic background, therefore, besides unlocking the meaning of II Cor. 3:14-17, also provides additional validation of the exegetical model used to explain II Cor. 3:1-6. This chapter will show, then, that II Cor. 3:1-18 presents a single, carefully constructed argument based on intricately interwoven scriptural authorities.

With NEUSNER in his recent work cited, however, in avoiding the use of the term "midrash," I am forced to use some "somewhat awkward circumlocutions" (*Midrash in Context*, p. xvi). NEUSNER's Preface, pages xvi-xvii, provides a good summary of the proper meaning and reference of the term in Judaism.

[18] Except in the short work of Earl RICHARD already extensively noted. The obvious reason for the isolation of these verses — the SCHULZ/GEORGI hypothesis of their source in an opposing document — has already been mentioned in the Introduction to the present study.

The fourth goal of the present chapter is, in a way, the most important, because it has to do with that single argument itself, rather than with its sources or its structures. The previous chapter has shown that a comparison between himself and Moses as covenant ministers is an important aspect of Paul's argument in II Cor. 3:1-6. Therefore, if II Cor. 3:1-18 does indeed present a unified argument, it is important to discover how this most basic issue is continued and addressed in verses 7-18. Is Paul like Moses?

II Cor. 3:13 and 18 each give an explicit answer to this most important question. Paul is both like Moses and unlike Moses. Paul is not like Moses because he may be bold and does not need to veil himself in either shame or humility. Paul is like Moses because he too has a share in the glory which is given to the minister of God's covenant with Israel.[19]

It is not only II Cor. 3:13 and 18 which address this comparison with Moses. Verses 13 and 18 simply provide summary statements. The whole of II Cor. 3:7-18 explains just when and how the new covenant minister resembles his Old Testament prototype, as well as when, how and *why* he does not. The realization of the promised new covenant is the basis for both the similarities and the differences. Because Paul is the minister of a superior new *covenant,* he shares in Moses' glorification. Because Paul is the minister of a *superior* new covenant, he need not veil that glorification. It will never end. To explore all of the ways in which Paul's similarity to and difference from Moses are developed in II Cor. 3:7-18 is not only to interpret the passage itself but to touch on Paul's intention in writing it in his own defense.

---

[19] The fact that the new covenant is a covenant between God and *Israel* should not be overlooked. A new, or renewed, covenant relationship between God and Israel is what Jeremiah promised, and there is no indication in II Cor. 3 that Paul understood that promise incorrectly. Therefore, both Paul's viewpoint and the reaction he probably elicited are put into focus. In II Cor. 3:2-18, Paul was attempting to relate two different expressions of Israel's covenantal relationship with God, redefining the old in terms of the new, while at the same time relying heavily on the old. Because that covenantal relationship was the bedrock of the very life of Israel, however, Paul's reinterpretation, if not accepted, necessarily would have been regarded as a subversion of and a threat to the national religious and cultural existence. See the recent works by E. P. SANDERS, *Paul, the Law and the Jewish People* (Philadelphia: Fortress Press, 1983) and W. D. DAVIES, *Jewish and Pauline Studies* (Philadelphia: Fortress Press, 1984) pp. 91-152 especially. These works reflect the consciousness in current Pauline studies of the continuing existence of Israel as the people of God for Paul and of his role as an interpreter *within its community* of the shared traditions of Judaism from a Christological perspective.

II Corinthians 3:7-18 and Exodus 34:29-35

The Text

Paul's reference to Exodus 34 is made explicit immediately in verse 7. The beginning of Moses' ministry in glory and the reluctance of the sons of Israel to approach him is a direct and unmistakable reference to the narrative account of Moses' second descent down the mountain with the stone tablets of the covenant and of the events which followed which is preserved in Exodus 34:29-35. For the convenience of the reader I will display the Septuagint version of this text here as I have done in Chapter One with other relevant texts.

I have already displayed Exod. 34:27-28 in Chapter One as part of the referent of "stone tablets" in II Cor. 3:3. I will include it once again here in order to point out the continuity of both Paul's scriptural sources and of his own argument. A close tie with verse 6 is indicated by the "εἰ δὲ" which begins verse 7. The "δὲ" indicates a continuation of what has preceded, and so the "εἰ" must also posit a condition dependent, at least to some degree, on what has been previously stated. What *has* just been stated in 3:6 is that Paul has been made a minister of a new covenant which gives life, and not of one that kills. The correspondence of "ἀποκτέννει" in verse 6 and "θανάτου" in verse 7 is obvious. The "γράμμα" which brings death has already been identified in Chapter One of this study as the covenant made through Moses at Sinai. II Cor. 3:7, then, clearly contains explicit connections both to the preceding material in II Corinthians and to a specific narrative of the Exodus tradition

Exodus 34:29-35 [20]

29) Ὡς δὲ κατέβαινεν Μωυσῆς ἐκ ὄρους, καὶ αἱ δύο πλάκες ἐπὶ τῶν χειρῶν Μωυσῆ· καταβαίνοντος δὲ αὐτοῦ ἐκ τοῦ ὄρους, Μωυσῆς οὐκ ᾔδει ὅτι δεδόξασται ἡ ὄψις τοῦ χρώματος τοῦ προσώπου αὐτοῦ ἐν τῷ λαλεῖν αὐτὸν αὐτῷ. 30) καὶ ἴδεν Ἀαρὼν καὶ πάντες οἱ πρεσβύτεροι Ἰσραὴλ τὸν Μωυσῆν, καὶ ἦν δεδοξασμένη ἡ ὄψις τοῦ χράματος τοῦ προσώπου αὐτοῦ· καὶ ἐφοβήθησαν ἐγγίσαι αὐτοῦ. 31) καὶ ἐκάλεσεν αὐτοὺς Μωυσῆς, καὶ ἐπεστράφησαν πρὸς αὐτὸν Ἀαρὼν καὶ πάντες οἱ ἄρχοντες τῆς συναγωγῆς· καὶ ἐλάλησεν αὐτοῖς Μωυσῆς. 32) καὶ μετὰ ταῦτα προσῆλθον πρὸς αὐτὸν πάντες οἱ υἱοὶ Ἰσραήλ· καὶ ἐνετείλατο αὐτοῖς πάντα ὅσα ἐνετείλατο κύριος πρὸς αὐτὸν ἐν τῷ ὄρει Σεινά. 33) καὶ ἐπειδὴ κατέπαυσεν λαλῶν πρὸς αὐτούς, ἐπέθηκεν ἐπὶ τὸ πρόσωπον αὐτοῦ

---

[20] Like the texts cited from the Book of Exodus in Chapter One of this study, this passage is taken from the critical text of Exodus in *The Old Testament in Greek* from the Cambridge University Press and the English translation is that of the Bagster edition of 1851.

κάλυμμα. 34) ἡνίκα δ' ἂν εἰσεπορεύετο Μωσῆς ἔναντι κυρίου λαλεῖν αὐτῷ, περιῃρεῖτο τὸ κάλυμμα ἕως τοῦ ἐκπορεύεσθαι· καὶ ἐξελθὼν ἐξάλει πᾶσιν τοῖς υἱοῖς Ἰσραὴλ ὅσα ἐνετείλατο αὐτῷ κύριος. 35) καὶ ἴδον οἱ υἱοὶἸσραὴλ τὸ πρόσωπον Μωσῆ ὅτι δεδόξασται· καὶ περιέθηκεν Μωυσῆς κάλυμμα ἐπὶ τὸ πρόσωπον ἑαυτοῦ, ἕως ἂν εἰσέλθῃ συλαλεῖν αὐτῷ.

29) and when Moses went down from the mountain, there were the two tables in the hands of Moses — as then he went down from the mountain. Moses knew not that the appearance of the skin of his face was glorified when God spoke to him. 30) And Aaron and all the elders of Israel saw Moses and the appearance of the skin of his face was made glorious, and they feared to approach him. 31) And Moses called them and Aaron and all the rulers of the synagogue turned towards him, and Moses spoke to them. 32) And afterwards all the children of Israel came to him and he commanded them all things whatsoever the Lord had commanded him in the mount of Sinai. 33) And when he ceased speaking to them, he put a veil on his face. 34) And whenever Moses went in before the Lord to speak to him, he took off the veil till he went out and he went forth and spoke to all the children of Israel whatsoever the Lord commanded him. 35) And the children of Israel saw the face of Moses, that it was glorified, and Moses put the veil over his face, till he went in to speak with him.

In distinction to the Prophetic promises which were used by Paul to define his ministry in II Cor. 3:1-6, the text he interprets in II Cor. 3:7-18 is a narrative. Exodus 34:29-35 is a *story* about what happened to Moses as he came down from Mount Sinai, about the reaction that the people had to his theophanic appearance, and about further actions that Moses regularly performed in Israel following his reception of the covenant. This story has all the elements that every story has, at least potentially. It has actors (Moses, the sons of Israel). It has props (the stone tablets, the veil). It has action (Moses descends the mountain; he calls the people to him and communicates the commandments to them; he veils his face). It has motivation (Moses is ignorant of the glorious appearance of his face; the people are afraid to come near him because of that appearance).

Il Corinthians 3:7-18 evidences numerous verbal contacts with this Exodus narrative. Because it is narrative, however, it is important to remember that those verbal echoes call to mind the whole *story* and not just isolated snatches of it. The props, actors, action and motivation of this particular Pentateuchal narrative enter into Paul's own composition as they are verbally recalled by him. He accepts and enters into the story as he retells and interprets it. As story, Exodus 34:29-35 lacks one important narrative element. Moses' motivation for the veiling of his face is left unexplained, or at least implicit.[21] It is ultimately this problem in the story that Paul exploits in II Cor. 3:13 when he explicitly assigns a motivation to Moses not present in the original story, even implicitly. Here we will begin by discussing Paul's appropriation and understanding of the simpler narrative elements as they are indicated verbally in his text.

Points of Contact Between Exodus 34:29-35 and II Corinthians 3:7-18

The Props

The most important aspect of the story from Paul's point of view, glory (δόξα), is introduced into verse 7a from Exod. 34:29 where it occurs in its verbal form, "δοξάζω," which appears again in Exodus 34 in verses 30 and 35. The nominal form, "δόξα," appears in II Corinthians in verses 7b, 8, 9, 10, 11 and 18. The verb, "δοξάζω," is also present in II Cor. 3:10 in a clear echo of the specific wording of Exod. 34:29 and 35. Paul's passive participle "δεδοξασμένον" reflects the passive "δεδόξασται" of Exod. 34:29 and 35. The important reality of glory, then, enters into Paul's argument from the text of the Old Testament story. Whenever it appears, therefore, a dialogue of some sort is taking place between Paul and his Old Testament narrative context.

The veil, the counterpart of the glory of Moses, is similarly introduced into Paul's composition directly from Exodus. The noun, "κάλυμμα," appears in II Cor. 3:13, 14, 15 and 16, while the related verb form "ἀνακαλύπτω" appears in II Cor. 3:14 and 18. The veil of Moses is a primary feature of the Exodus narrative. The noun, "κάλυμμα" is present in Exod. 34:33, 34 and 35. The veil dominates much of the last half of Paul's text, verses 13-16, just as glory dominates the first half of the section, verses 7-11. This literary structure follows that of Exodus 34 itself, in which Moses' glory is predominant in verses 29-30, while his veil is of greater importance in verses 33-35. As is the case with Paul's use of δόξα in his composition, whenever κάλυμμα appears in II Corinthians 3, some sort of dialogue with its narrative source is in evidence.

The Actors

Besides appropriating its two major props, II Corinthians 3:7-18 also incorporates the actors from the dramatic narrative of Exodus 34. The "sons of Israel" appear somewhat unexpectedly in II Cor. 3:7 directly from Exodus 34:32ff. The phrase "οἱ υἱοὶ Ἰσραήλ" itself, since it is not

---

[21] One might infer, on the basis of certain details given in Exodus such as the fear Israel displayed when Moses descended (Exod. 34:30), that Moses put on the veil in order to spare the sons of Israel the frightening spectacle of his glorious appearance. This is not a necessary inference, however, and Paul may not have made it.

at all typical for Paul, is a very clear verbal indication of dependence on an Old Testament narrative, even for a reader who does not expect it.[22]

On the basis of the previous chapter of this study, however, the appearance of Moses himself in II Cor. 3:7 should come as no surprise. In II Cor. 3:5-6 the commissioning of Moses stood implicitly behind Paul's view of his own commission and authority. Through his inevitable association with the stone tablets of the Sinai covenant, the figure of Moses lurked behind II Cor. 3:2-3 as well. But in II Cor. 3:7 Moses first emerges explicitly as a character, not only in his own drama as it is reported in Exod. 34:29ff., but also in the present-day situation between Paul and his Corinthians. II Corinthians 3:7-18 becomes somehow dynamically involved with the events which transpired between Moses and the sons of Israel in the wilderness, and those events become relevant to Paul's contemporary readers, through their incorporation into his argument here.

The Action

Numerous aspects of the scenario of Exodus 34 are incorporated into Paul's discussion. II Cor. 3:7 presumes a covenant-making setting with the phrase "ἐν γράμμασιν ἐντετυπωμένη λίθοις." As before, the general reference is to the two tablets of stone on which the words of the Sinai covenant were twice written. However, the following references to the unusual scene which ensues as Moses descends from the mountain the second time pinpoint Exod. 34:28-29 as the particular referent.

The reality of the shining glory of Moses' face is the backbone of Paul's treatment of the incident. It is explicitly accepted in II Cor. 3:7, 9, 10, and 11.[23] Its equally important negative counterpart, Moses' veiling of his face, is reported in II Cor. 3:13 (ἐτίθει *κάλυμμα ἐπὶ τὸ πρόσωπον αὐτοῦ*) in a clear echo of Exod. 34:33 (ἐπέθηκεν *ἐπὶ τὸ πρόσωπον αὐτοῦ κάλυμμα*)[24] and alluded to in II Cor. 3:18 (ἀνακεκαλυμμένῳ προσώπῳ). Paul readily accepts both Moses' glorified condition and the difficult phenomenon of his veil.[25] He takes the story told in Exodus 34:29-35 absolutely seriously.

---

[22] II Cor. 3:7 and 13 are the only uses of the phrase "οἱ υἱοὶ Ἰσραήλ," in the Pauline corpus, although it is a frequent designation for the people of God in the Septuagint.

[23] The glory of Moses' face is even enhanced, in the way that a developing legend often is, in verse 7. In Exodus it is never stated that the sons of Israel were not able to look on Moses' face, only that they were quite naturally afraid to do so.

[24] Italicizing is added here and also below to highlight similarities. Although at other times I have made much of verbal substitutions in the form of quoted texts and will do so again very shortly, the variant in the verb here seems to me to be innocent. Either Paul is reflecting a variant Greek text of which we have no knowledge or he simply prefers the more common verb.

[25] This incident of Moses' veiling is otherwise rarely or never mentioned in either

In II Cor. 3:16-18 another dramatic feature of the narrative of Exodus 34 is appropriated into its Pauline interpretation. According to Exodus 34:34f., Moses' veil was removed when he spoke with the Lord in the Tent of Meeting. The *"ἡνίκα δὲ ἐὰν ἐπιστρέψῃ πρὸς κύριον, περιαιρεῖται τὸ κάλυμμα"* of II Cor. 3:16 repeats *"ἡνίκα δ᾽ ἂν εἰσεπορεύετο Μωσῆς ἔναντι κυρίου λαλεῖν αὐτῷ, περιῃρεῖτο τὸ κάλυμμα"* of Exodus 34:34 with sufficient verbal similarity to indicate dependence in a conclusive manner. Paul's interpretation of this facet of the story is contained in the variations within the quotation itself and continues in verses 17 and 18. The order of the Exodus narrative is again followed in II Corinthians: first Moses' descent and glorification (II Cor. 3:7-11), then his regular converse with the Lord and continued glorification (II Cor. 3:13-18).

Two final narrative features drawn from Exodus are also reflected in the Pauline text in verses 7 and 13 and in verses 14 and 15. Exodus 34:30 reports a reluctance on the part of the people to approach Moses because of the glory of his face. In II Cor. 3:7 and again at II Cor. 3:13, Paul picks up this feature of the incident, accepting it from his source but adapting it to his own purpose. I have already noted the enhancement of Moses' glory which II Cor. 3:7 contains. Moses' glorification was so overpowering that the sons of Israel *could not* gaze upon it. In II Cor. 3:13 an apparently different reason is given for the inability of the sons of Israel to see that glory. It was veiled from their eyes. This sequence in II Corinthians 3:7-13 again follows the order of the Exodus story, but supplies detail. Although Exodus 34:30 does say that the people were afraid, it does not say that they could not bear the glory of Moses. Paul does. Exodus 34:35 does not say that Moses donned his veil because of Israel's continued fear. One might infer that from Exod. 34:30. In II Cor. 3:13 Paul begins to focus on a different explanation — Moses' veil concealed it. The pattern of glory/fear and then glory/veiling is there in II Corinthians, but in altered form.[26]

Secondly, the climax of the scene as it is presented in Exodus is the communication from Moses to Israel of the words of the covenant (Exod. 34:28), all that God had spoken to him on the mountain (Exod.

---

pre-or post-Pauline Jewish sources, according to STRACK-BILLERBECK, *Kommentar* III, p. 516, and I can find no evidence to the contrary. On the other hand, Moses' glorification is fairly frequently discussed. See STRACK-BILLERBECK, *Kommentar* III, pp. 513-516 and GINZBERG, *Legends* III, pp. 143-144 for summaries of these references.

[26] In verses 14-15 Paul offers yet another explanation—Israel could not, and still cannot, see Moses' glory because their hearts are covered and their minds are hardened. II Cor. 3:7-15, then, appears to be a series of increasingly sophisticated explanations for the meaning of Moses' veiling, beginning with one probably more or less common in Paul's day (v. 7; cf. PHILO, *Vit. Mos.* II, 70) to one that is unique to Paul (v. 15).

34:32). Indeed, although the present form of the story in Exodus preserves the puzzling phenomena of glorification and veiling as valuable remnants of an earlier form of the narrative, it does little to explain or expand them. In fact, it probably has intentionally subdued them.[27] In its present context, the focus of the story is entirely on Moses as the mediator of God's covenant and its legislation.[28]

The most important of Moses' activities, according to Exodus 34:32-33, are the initial communication of God's words to Israel, as reported in Exod. 34:32, and his continuing mediation of divine commands from the Tent of Meeting, as presumed in Exod. 34:33. This particular aspect of Moses' ministry is echoed in the Pauline text in verses 14 and 15. As I have noted in Chapter One, the verb "ἀναγινώσκω," generally refers to the public and cultic reading of the scriptures. It refers to the reading of the "old covenant," [the books of] "Moses" explicitly in II Cor. 3:14 and 15. In Exodus 34, and indeed in the whole of Exodus and Deuteronomy particularly, Moses himself speaks. In Paul's day, of course, Moses no longer spoke as a living person. However, the books of the Pentateuch were called the "books of Moses" and considered to be a message for Israel in every age mediated originally through Moses himself.[29] Therefore, to "read Moses" was to read the Law, the first five books of the scriptures, and still to receive the words of God through Moses. The figure, Moses, had in a sense become the book, Moses. Paul saw the mediatorial role of Moses, as it is reported in Exodus 34:32-33 and elsewhere, as continued in the contemporary world in the *reading* of the narratives and laws written by him.

Summary

In this section I have not explained Paul's interpretation of Exodus 34 in II Corinthians 3. I have, however, assembled all of the narrative elements which he has taken from Exodus 34:27-35, as well as the verbal evidence for his absorption of them.[30] Paul has so

---

[27] J. MORGENSTERN, "Moses With the Shinning Face," *HUCA* 2 (1925) pp. 1-27; VON RAD, *Old Testament Theology* I, p. 234 and CHILDS, *Exodus*, pp. 356-359, 533-534, 607-620 agree that Chapters 33-34 contain some of the oldest material in Exodus. It has been considerably reworked and various strands have been combined to produce a narrative that plays down the aspects of the story that probably originally (at least according to MORGENSTERN) portrayed the divinization of Moses.

[28] CHILDS, *Exodus*, p. 617.

[29] Other New Testament usage of the word "Moses" to refer to the written Torah, in addition to its use as a personal name supports Paul's usage. Lk. 16:29,31; 24:27; Jn. 5:45,46; Acts 15:21; 21:21 and Rom. 10:19 all provide examples of an identical use of the term. Mt. 19:7 par; 22:24 par; and Mk. 1:44; 7:10 presume that Moses' commands, once given orally and then personally written down, are contained in the written Torah which can be referred to using his name alone.

[30] I have approached Paul's use of Exodus 34 from a viewpoint somewhat different

extensively appropriated facets of the Exodus story that his own text cannot be explained without constant reference to its Old Testament counterpart.[31] It is this interpenetration of II Cor. 3:7-18 and Exodus 34:29-35 that so distinguishes II Cor. 3:7-18 from its context, not the origin of those verses in an *opposing* exegetical document.[32] Paul himself knows the narrative of Moses' glorious descent from the mountain in every detail. He follows its structure closely. He accepts the story unreservedly. He wants to understand it. He wants to explain it to his Corinthian readers. He wants to use it to support his argument to them. To do all of these things he must find the true meaning of Exodus 34:29-35, solve its difficulties, and make it relevant to his contemporary audience. In short, he must interpret it. Most of the remainder of this chapter of my own study is concerned with presenting just how he does so. First, however, I would like to discuss very briefly several considerations which make the appearance of this interpretation of Exodus 34:29-35 in its present context much less surprising than it is usually considered to be.

Why Exodus 34:29-35?

Before going on to discover the intricacies of Paul's interpretative use of Exodus 34:29-35, one background question may be asked

---

from the one usually taken. Those commentators noted above who have done specific studies of II Cor. 3:7-18 as "midrash" have taken as their starting points those verses of Exodus 34, vv. 33-34 especially, which Paul has cited, viewing their partial quotation in II Cor. 3:13 and 16 as the best evidence for and the high point of Paul's exegesis. The commentaries share this perspective. It is certainly true that the citations are good evidence for Paul's use of Exod. 34, but that can hardly be missed in any case. I have tried to emphasize in contrast Paul's total involvement with the events that are recounted in Exodus 34:29-35, his appropriation of the story as a whole and its importance for him, by approaching his use of it from this "narrative" perspective. Moses and his mysterious actions are significant for Paul. He cares about the sons of Israel and their unwillingness or inability to partake of the vision of glory. Paul is not proof-texting from Exodus. He is trying to understand it. While other interpretations of II Cor. 3 might agree with this in principle, their approach tends to draw attention away from the event retold again and again in each reading of Exod. 34:29-35 and focus it instead on a more modern, but less Pauline, "bits and pieces" approach to a text that is not *story*, but only literature *data* to be analyzed.

[31] J. GOETTSBERGER already argued this forcefully in "Die hülle des Mose nach Ex. 34 und II Cor. 3," *BZ* 16 (1924) pp. 1-17 in response to J. B. NISIUS, "Zur Erklärung von 2 Kor 3,16ff.," *ZKT* 40 (1916) pp. 617-675 whose focus was limited to Exod. 34:29ff. insofar as it illumined the meaning of Paul's "ὁ δὲ κύριος τὸ πνεῦμά ἐστιν" only.

[32] Contra the work of SCHULZ, GEORGI, ULONSKA and others following them (FALLON, for example) who have adopted the hypothesis of an inserted opponents' midrash as an unquestioned presupposition. I absolutely reject the presupposition of ULONSKA's study: "Die Frage nach der Bedeutung des Alten Testaments in 2. Kor. 3 ist unlöslich verbunden mit der nach den paulinischen Gegnern. ..." ["Die Doxa des Mose," *EvTh* 26 (1966) p. 380.

concerning the presence of this final section of Exodus 34 in Paul's argument. Why is it there at all? We have seen that critical opinion has frequently held that it is an intrusion into Paul's own argument, included only for the sake of refutation. Such a challenge to the relevance of Exod. 34:29-35 must be met. Why discuss the glory and veiling of Moses in conjunction with the new covenant? Does Paul's subtle argument in II Cor. 3:1-6 lead naturally to Exodus 34:29-35? Answers to these questions are available on several levels: thematic, exegetical and historical.

Thematic considerations

Chapter One of this study has shown that in the first six verses of his argument in II Corinthians 3 Paul is dependent on and in dialogue with a set of texts from the prophets Jeremiah and Ezekiel centered around the promise of a new covenant. All of these prophetic texts direct attention naturally to a consideration of the first covenant, both as the basis for their promises for the future and as a contrast to them. These Prophetic promises are themselves intrinsically related to the Book of Exodus to which Paul explicitly turns in II Cor. 3:7. In their visions of the future we can see a much earlier interpretation and contemporization of the stories told in ancient times and recorded in the books of the Pentateuch.

Jeremiah 38:31-32 (LXX) refers specifically to a new covenant, not like the covenant made with the fathers at the time they were led out of Egypt. Obviously, Jeremiah's idea of covenant was based upon the stories of the covenant preserved in Exodus which offered him form and content for his own hope for the future. Jeremiah's promise is a reappropriation, not only of the religious beliefs embodied in the story of the Exodus and the making of the covenant at Sinai, but also of the text in which those beliefs were conveyed to him. Without the Book of Exodus, which tells the story of the events which created Israel as a nation and gave birth to the Mosaic covenant, the promise of Jeremiah is without foundation and cannot be made. The prophecy of Jeremiah is, in this instance, a continuation of the Book of Exodus into another age. My purpose here is not to propose a literary critical analysis of the relationship between Jeremiah and Exodus, but only to point out the fundamental similarity between the process whereby Jeremiah has reinterpreted Exodus traditions and the presuppositions under which Paul has approached them both. Paul knew of and appreciated Jeremiah's general reference to the Exodus narratives and so could have been led naturally to the text of Exodus through the prophet.[33]

---

[33] Part of the mistake which led to the hypothesis of an opposing document as the source for Paul's exegesis of Exod. 34 was the failure to delve deeply enough into Paul's use of Jer. 38 (LXX) and Ezek. 11 and 36 to appreciate the extent of his involvement with the ideas contained in them.

Furthermore, Exodus 34, Jeremiah 38 (LXX) and II Corinthians 3 all share a single characteristic which binds them together and makes recourse to this particular pair of Old Testament texts even more appropriate for Paul. In each case the subject under discussion is a new covenant, a replacement covenant for one previously given and broken. While Moses received the first stone tablets of the covenant on the mountain, Exodus informs us that the people were involved in the apostasy of the golden calf (Exod. 32:1-35). The first covenant was therefore rejected by its recipients and, in a sense, void from the first moment it was given. Moses' shattering of the tablets in Exodus 32:19 expresses this shattering of Israel's relationship with God.[34] The rupture required forgiveness and atonement (Exod. 32:30-35) and the covenant had to be given a second time (Exod. 34:1-28). This story of the second giving of the covenant is, therefore, a natural parallel for the new covenant of which both Paul and Jeremiah speak. The literary peculiarity of a second giving of the Mosaic covenant is just the sort of exegetical problem which frequently gave rise to considerable later interpretation.[35]

Jeremiah was prophesying at a time of extreme national stress, when the religious beliefs of his people and even that people itself were threatened with dissolution. He condemned the sinfulness and error of the people, which he experienced as idolatry and to which he ascribed

---

[34] Later Jewish legend sometimes held that Moses broke the tablets because he knew that the covenant had been forfeited by the idolatry of the calf. It is also argued that Moses saved Israel by breaking the tablets and so postponing the ratification of the covenant. Since their sin was then one committed in ignorance rather than as a deliberate transgression of the law, they were spared the punishment of total annihilation that they would otherwise have deserved. See L. SMOLAR and M. ABERBACH, "The Golden Calf Episode in Postbiblical Literature," *HUCA* 39 (1968) pp. 98, 114 and Terrance CALLAN "Pauline Midrash: The Exegetical Background of Gal. 3:19b," *JBL* 99 (1980) pp. 562-563.

[35] I cannot enter here into the history of the Book of Exodus itself. Modern criticism tells us that a report of a double giving of the covenant indicates a doublet within the textual history of the book, arising very probably from separate and different covenant traditions which were absorbed and accommodated to the narrative flow more or less smoothly. Contemporary exegesis then produces theories to account for the doublet and analysis of the theological and compositional tendencies of its redactions. See above, Note 27. But that is not to the point here. My study is aimed at the exegetical activity such as an anomaly would have produced in the centuries before Christ and especially in the first century of the Christian era. For readers in that age, the doublet is not a literary peculiarity, but an historical fact, an event in God's story the significance of which must be discovered. In this study, therefore, I will always take the Book of Exodus as it stands, as they did in the first century. The Introduction to Brevard CHILDS' *Introduction to the Old Testament as Scripture* (Philadelphia: Fortress Press, 1979) pp. 27-106, and the section on Exodus, pp. 159-179, offer some profound reflections on the theoretical differences between these two points of view and open an avenue through which the modern critic might begin to reappropriate the earlier understanding of scripture in a critical age.

their imminent destruction.[36] He speaks explicitly about the rupture of a covenant bond in that section of his text with which Paul is in dialogue: the fathers did not remain in the covenant. So, although Jeremiah was experiencing a contemporary apostasy, he turned to an apostasy of the past in 38:32 (LXX) — [οἱ πατέρες] αὐτοὶ οὐκ ἐνέμειναν ἐν τῇ διαθήκῃ μου — as a parallel to his own situation. He refers to the "murmurings" and disobedience of the wilderness period of which the apostasy of the golden calf was the epitome[37] in order to understand the contemporary scene. In justification for his hope for a better covenant, Jeremiah goes back to an ancient flawing of the old covenant and its repair, rather than concentrating only on the apostasy of his own age. The pattern of the old covenant drawn from Exodus thus gives form to the promise of the new. An inadequacy of the first covenant also supplied the details of Jeremiah's hope.

The new covenant will not be like the one given to the fathers (Jer. 38:32 LXX) precisely because that covenant failed in its recipients, not only in the wilderness, but in Jeremiah's own day. It will be better, because it will not fail. Certainly Jeremiah also personally *experienced* the conviction that the Lord would preserve his people in their distress and reestablish his love and his covenant with them in a new and better way. Nevertheless, it is to the story of the old covenant that he looks for the details that he chooses to describe the advantages of the new covenant. He pinpoints the inadequacy of the first one that led to the failure of the fathers, and in so doing envisions the proper solution to the problems of his present experience.

Jeremiah 38:33-34 (LXX) describes this proposed solution. The new covenant will of course be accompanied by a new promulgation of the law, since it was, and is, by breaking the law that the covenant has been broken on the side of Israel. The new promulgation of the law, however, will be different in a specific way from the first law-giving. This time the law will be given inside of each man, *written on hearts,* not on a pair of stone tablets (Jer. 38.33 LXX). As a result of this interiority of the law of the new covenant, it will be known by everyone. Men will learn it directly from God who gives it (Jer. 38:34 LXX). Thus placed in the heart, it will be "remembered"[38] and so obeyed. If the law of the covenant is thus known, remembered and kept, the covenant will stand forever. When this covenant appears, sins under the former covenant will be forgiven (Jer. 38:34 LXX) and Israel will begin its covenant relationship with God anew (Jer. 38:33 LXX).

---

[36] CHILDS, *Introduction,* p. 350; J. LINDBLOM, *Prophecy in Ancient Israel* (Philadelphia: Fortress Press, 1962) pp. 311-312, 320; EISSFELDT, *The Old Testament,* p. 348; VON RAD, *Old Testament Theology* II, pp. 191-219.

[37] GINZBERG, *Legends* III, p. 120.

[38] Cf Deut. 30:14; Prov. 3:1; 7:3 and many other places.

If this is the solution, what was the problem as Jeremiah perceived it? In spite of the fact that we may correctly assume that Jeremiah's perception was colored by his own contemporary difficulties, his problem with the old covenant is remarkably like Paul's own. The trouble, for both of them, with the covenant given at Sinai is its *exteriority,* symbolized by its inscription on the stone tablets borne down the mountain by Moses. The stones are, of course, only symbolic of the difficulty, which is drawn out both by Jeremiah and by Paul into a nuanced critique of the deficiency of a former conceptualization of the Lord's relationship with his people. Paul's focus on the stone tablets as the epitome of the negative extrinsic character of the law of the old covenant is entirely faithful to the thought of the prophet Jeremiah, who is the source of his imagery and of the contrast that he draws.

The pivotal focus of "writing" in the contrasts of II Corinthians 3:1-6 follows exactly the point of comparison drawn between the old and the new covenants by Jeremiah himself (Jer. 38:33 LXX). So, while the failure to remain in the covenant surely is a failure of the people to whom it was given, Jeremiah 38:33-34 (LXX) and Paul in II Cor. 3:2-6 are remarkable for their similar focus on the extrinsic legal expression of the covenant itself as the ultimate source of and solution to the problem.[39] Paul's appropriation of Jeremiah is a faithful extension of the prophet's thought.

In sum, then, Paul is aware of the fundamental reference of Jeremiah's promise of a new covenant to the story of the earlier covenant-making contained in the Book of Exodus. Furthermore, he is in very substantial agreement with the prophet's view of those stories. In the previous chapter of this study we have seen Paul go even farther than Jeremiah had gone in his critique of the Mosaic covenant and his definition of the characteristics of the now realized new covenant. He has done this by combining numerous prophetic passages and contrasting them with texts drawn from the prophet's own source, the Book of Exodus. There is no reason for surprise, therefore, when Paul goes on to cite another Exodus text as he continues to refine his readers' understanding of the reality of the new covenant in contrast to the old.

---

[39] It cannot be denied, of course, that in the majority of the prophecies of Jeremiah, it is the moral failure of the people which is deplored and blamed for the oncoming disaster. Nevertheless in this particular case, the covenant itself is what is improved, for the sake of Israel.

Exegetical evidence

As I have said above, I have displayed two more verses of Exodus 34 (Exod. 34:27-28) than are generally regarded as the subject of the Pauline midrash in verses 7-18. The role that these two additional verses play in Paul's composition is to provide the exegetical connection between Exodus 34:29-35 and the scriptural background of II Cor. 3:1-6 elucidated in Chapter One of this study. The reason that this connection is not usually seen is twofold. First, the scriptural background of the first six verses themselves has not heretofore been properly appreciated. Second, the exegetical techniques constitutive of the structure of that background, and of Paul's text as well, have not been fully utilized to explain that structure. Furthermore, scholars who choose Exodus 31:18 as the primary referent of "πλάκες λίθιναι" have led themselves into the wrong section of the Book of Exodus and have thereby been hampered from seeing the easy transition between II Cor. 3:6 and 7. If Paul has been in dialogue with Exod. 34:1-4 and 27-28 in II Cor. 3:2-3 and 6, why should he not go on to discuss the very next section of that Exodus passage?

For the early Jewish or Christian interpreter, as much as for the modern critical biblical scholar, a conclusive exegetical link must consist of a verbal correspondence between two texts. In this case, such primary exegetical links between Exodus 34:27-35 and the Jeremiah/Ezekiel text complex are found in Exod. 34:27 and 28. They do not exist, however, between Exodus 34:29-35 and the Prophetic texts Paul used in the first six verses. Exodus 34:27-28 can be linked verbally to Paul's scriptural background through διαθήκη and through γράφω, the two primary concepts with which Paul has been concerned in II Cor. 3:1-6 and the two major themes of Jeremiah's rethinking of Israel's relationship with the Lord. Through those two verses, therefore, Exodus 34:29-35 *as their continuation* is also exegetically linked to the rest of Paul's scriptural background. II Cor. 3:7-18 no longer need appear as an incongruous interruption of foreign material into the Pauline text.

These additional verses of Exodus 34 can now be added to the diagram of Paul's scriptural background begun in Chapter One of this study. Figure 4 describes these verbal connections spatially.

Figure 4

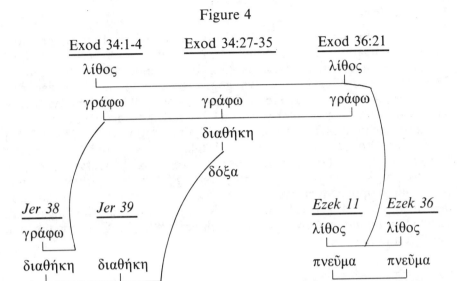

Covenant, διαφήκη, is a solid exegetical link between the two parts of Paul's scriptural background in II Cor. 3:1-18, that from the Prophets and that from the Pentateuch. As such, it is the most important thematic link between the two parts of his text, verses 1-6 and verses 7-18. If its scriptural background is as important to Paul's argument as I have shown it to be, and if it is used with integrity, then the most important concept within that background is the most fundamental level in Paul's own argument. Therefore, I must conclude that the most basic issue for II Cor. 3:1-18 as a whole is a comparison of covenants — an old, Mosaic covenant which prefigures a new covenant promised by Jeremiah and realized by Christ. In this unified argument, however, these two covenants are typified and expressed by their ministers, Moses and Paul.[40]

---

[40] The majority of commentators, on II Corinthians as well as on the Pauline literature in general, would reject this opinion. This has been noted in my Introduction. C. E. B. CRANFIELD, for example, in a brief treatment of II Cor. 3 contained in an essay which concludes his Romans commentary, argues very strongly that from II Cor. 3:7 on, Paul compares the *ministry* of Moses and the *ministry* of Paul from the point of view of their respective relationships to the *ministry* of Jesus Christ, "Concluding Remarks on Some Aspects of the Theology of Romans," in *Romans* II, The International Critical Commentary (Edinburgh: T. & T. Clark, 1979) p. 855. This is true as far as it goes, but CRANFIELD's remarks are illustrative of the danger of "running through" II Cor. 3 too

Historical factors

Scholarship on the liturgical use of scripture within Judaism provides another indication that Exodus 34:27-35 may have been combined regularly with Jeremiah 31:32-39 (38, LXX) and even with Jeremiah 32:40-41 (39, LXX) in the synagogue reading cycle as Seder and Haftarah. According to Jacob Mann, Seder 70 of the Palestinian Triennial cycle began at Exodus 34:27 and was accompanied by a Haftarah commencing at Jeremiah 31:32 and continued to v. 39.[41] Most of chapter 32 of Jeremiah was omitted. Only verses 40 and 41 of chapter 32 were added to fill out the customary ten verses of the Haftarah reading and to provide the desired "happy ending" for the reading.[42] These particular prophetic texts were chosen because of the verbal links already described. It is a general thesis of Mann's work that readings were selected and combined by means of such verbal "tallying" particularly in the Palestinian cycle.[43]

---

quickly. He does not get into the text deeply enough to realize the degree to which Paul's remarks in II Cor. 3:7-18 are determined by characteristics of the Jeremiah/Ezekiel covenant. Therefore, although it is true that the *problem* in II Cor. 3:7-18 is ministry, that problem is resolved on the basis of covenant and covenant is the most basic issue at stake in the text. Cranfield's concern is to defend the enduring value of the law for Paul, which is so clearly in evidence in Romans, from attack on the basis of II Cor. 3, which appears to be so negative with regard to it. The fact is, however, that Paul is only negative toward the old covenant in II Cor. 3 to the extent that it has been replaced by a new covenant and from that viewpoint. If the covenant brought by Moses is unaffected by the advent of Christ and Paul's ministry of him, then there is no reason to call Moses' ministry into question either. If the old covenant relationship between Israel and its Lord stands unchanged by Christ, then Moses, and not Christ, remains the ultimate authority for Israel. This is precisely the position which Paul is arguing against in II Cor. 3. It is because the new covenant promised by the prophets and inaugurated by Christ puts Israel into a different sort of covenantal relationship with God that the ministry of Moses must take second place to the apostolic ministry of Christ.

[41] *The Bible as Read and Preached in the Old Synagogue*, Vol. I: The Palestinian Triennial Cycle: Genesis and Exodus (New York: KTAV Publishing House, 1971) pp. 530-533; cf. Earl RICHARD, "Polemics," p. 347. MANN's work has been seriously criticized. In a "Prolegomenon" to the 1971 edition of his work, originally published in 1940, by Ben Zion WACHOLDER, the author admits that MANN failed to prove his hypothesis that "the weekly Prophetic portions were of greater significance for the development of the sermon than were the readings of the Torah," p. xii. The work of Earl RICHARD seems to have been influenced by this hypothesis, "Polemics," p. 352. However, WACHOLDER points out that this and other criticisms do not completely invalidate MANN's ground-breaking work and that many criticisms can only be made on the basis of tools supplied by that work itself (p. xiii). It seems to me to be permissible, therefore, to use MANN's work at least provisionally.

[42] MANN, *The Bible as Read*, p. 530.

[43] MANN, *The Bible as Read*, p. 11; WACHOLDER, "Prolegomenon," p. xxxi.

As Mann himself admits, there is considerable confusion in the Sedarim in this section of Exodus.[44] Various lists present different divisions within both Exodus and Jeremiah.[45] In addition there is the problem of the late dating of the witnesses to the synagogue readings cycle and the paucity of evidence regarding synagogue practices in the early first century. Nevertheless, I think the appearance of Exodus 34:27ff. in conjunction with Jeremiah 31:32ff., 32:40f. in even some later witnesses, when coupled with Paul's own implicit use of the combination, argues strongly for a pre-Christian combination of these texts. It argues that Paul is probably not innovative here, that part of his silence regarding his methods and his sources may have been due to their familiarity to his audience stemming from a common liturgical form.

In conclusion then, thematic and verbal links, as well as some slight historical information, indicate that Paul's use of Exodus 34:27-35 in combination with Jeremiah 38:31-34 (LXX) would have been an expected one for readers familiar with the Old Testament itself, with ancient exegesis of it and with Jewish liturgical use of these particular texts. The argument of II Cor. 3:1-6 does lead naturally to a discussion of Exodus 34:29-35. In the following section I will begin my discussion of Paul's interpretation of this new scriptural background by briefly introducing the exetical procedures he has used to pursue it and by locating them in II Cor. 3:7-18.

Introduction to the Exegetical Methodology of II Corinthians 3:7-18

Kal Va-Homer, Verses 7-11

There are two primary exegetical techniques present in the text of II Cor. 3:7-18 and both of these have been noted in previous analyses of the passage.[46] The first is the *kal va-homer* argument. This type of argument

---

[44] MANN, *The Bible as Read*, p. 530.

[45] A probable cause for this disturbance is the extreme sensitivity to the golden calf episode within Judaism and various viewpoints regarding its worthiness to be read and, if not, where to begin again. See SMOLAR/ABERBACH, "The Golden Calf," pp. 91, 96.

[46] All serious commentators since WINDISCH have noted the presence of a series of three *kal va-homer* inferences in II Cor. 3:7-11. The *pesher* in verse 17 is less frequently noticed, and treated with considerably less emphasis. Before the work of DUNN, " 'The Lord is the Spirit,' " in 1970, treatments of verse 17 were often theological and done in tandem with the investigation of verse 6. See for example, ALLO, *Seconde epître*, pp. 94-96, 107-111, which contains a good review of the history of interpretation of this point, as does COLLANGE, *Enigmes*, pp. 107-112, and the works of PRÜMM, SCHNEIDER and other literature cited in the Introduction to this study. Especially since DUNN, however, recent commentary has increasingly emphasized the exegetical nature of verses 16-17. See BARRETT, *Second Epistle*, p. 123; RICHARD, "Polemics," pp. 355-359 and, earlier, VAN UNNIK, "With Unveiled Face," p. 165.

functions according to the pattern: if A, which lacks y, has x, then B, which has y, certainly must have x as well.[47] If the inferior member of a pair possesses a characteristic, then its superior partner must necessarily possess it as well. A glance at verses 7-8, 9 and 11 of II Corinthians 3 reveals a set of three such arguments, each beginning with an "εἰ" statement and ending with the "πῶς" or "παλλῷ μᾶλλον" conclusion which is standard for the exegetical form in Greek. When the series of verses, omitting the parenthetical verse 10, is set in parallel with explanatory material removed, the presence of the standard form becomes more obvious. It is clear when the pattern is highlighted in this way, as it is in Figure 5, that this exegetical methodology is determinative for the structure of the text in verses 7-11.

Figure 5

I vv.7-8

| Εἰ δὲ | ἡ διακονία | τοῦ θανάτου... | ἐγενήθη ἐν δόξῃ |
| τῶς οὐχὶ μᾶλλον | ἡ διακονία | τοῦ πνεύματος | ἔσται ἐν δόξῃ |

II v. 9

| Εἰ γὰρ | τῇ διακονίᾳ | τῆς κατακρίσεως | δόξα |
| πολλῷ μᾶλλον | ἡ διακονία | τῆς δικαιοσύνης | περισσεύει δόξῃ |

III v. 11

Εἰ γὰρ	τὸ καταργούμενον		διὰ δόξης
πολλῷ μᾶλλον	τὸ μένον		εν δόξῃ
		(μένει)	

When the exegetical structure of verses 7-11 is appreciated and the proper parallelism of the verses is created through its form, Paul's identification of two covenant ministries can be more clearly seen. The inferior member of the pair is identified as ἡ διακονία τοῦ θανάτου (v. 7), τῇ διακονίᾳ τῆς κατακρίσεως (v. 9), and τὸ καταργούμενον (v. 11). On the contrary, the superior member of the pair is characterized as ἡ διακονία τοῦ πνεύματος (v. 8), ἡ διακονία τῆς δικαιοσύνης (v. 9), and τὸ μένον (v. 11). The source of these identifications is not to be found in the text of Exodus 34:29-35, nor is it explicit in this section of II Corinthians 3. Instead, the two ministries, inferior and superior, are defined using the covenant characteristics described in Chapter One of this study on the

---

[47] See Introduction, pp. 43-44 and notes.

basis of II Cor. 3:1-6 and its scriptural background. A complete analysis of this dependence of II Cor. 3:7-11 on the previous section may be put aside for a later section of this chapter.

The point for the moment is rather that the function of the exegetical arguments present in verses 7, 8, 9 and 11 is to predicate δόξα of the superior member of the pair on the basis of its presence in the inferior. It is with the word "δόξα" that each statement in the parallel structure concludes. Δόξα is known to be a characteristic of the inferior Mosaic ministry on the explicit evidence of Exodus 34:29-35. Moses' face was glorified as he came down the mountain. Exodus 34:29-35 is similarly the basis for the predication of δόξα to the superior Pauline ministry via the exegetical method of *kal va-homer*. The reliability of the Old Testament text, coupled with the reliability of the exegetical procedure applied to it, really provided an assurance to Paul that glory must indeed be a characteristic of his superior ministry. If Moses as minister of the old covenant had glory, then Paul, as minister of the superior new covenant, must also have glory.

It is not the superiority or inferiority of the terms themselves that is proven by these arguments. Only the transference of characteristics is effected. The identification of the ministries compared are presupposed, not proven, in the series of *kal va-homer* arguments. Moses' ministry is presupposed to be the inferior member of the pair. Paul's ministry is presumed to be the superior ministry, or else the arguments will not work. These presuppositions are justified by the arguments presented in the preceding verses, II Cor. 3:1-6. As I have said so often, they rest on the superiority of the new covenant.

Pesher, Verses 16-17

As I have said previously in this chapter, II Cor. 3:16 is a near quotation of Exodus 34:34. The uncommon construction "ἡνίκα δὲ ἐὰν" with which the verse begins occurs in the New Testament only here, and in a partial form in v. 15, and signals the assimilated text from Exodus. Within eschatological groups defining themselves over against the main body of Judaism, such as the monks of Qumran, it was common practice in interpreting texts of the Old Testament to do so verse by verse with a direct application and explanation of each verse following immediately. Such interpretations often identified characters or circumstances from the older text with persons or events within the interpreter's contemporary experience. At Qumran the form such exegesis most commonly took was the citation of a brief segment of text followed by the word, "*peser*" (interpretation), followed by a direct application to the current situation.[48]

---

[48] See Introduction, pp. 45-46 and notes, esprecially Maurya HORGAN, *Pesharim*, pp. 239-241.

In II Cor. 3:16 Paul's brief citation of Exod. 34:34 introduces such a *pesher* exegesis, although the formula itself is lacking. In verse 17 Paul does, however, provide an exegetical identification of one of the characters in the text he has cited in v. 16. The brief "ὁ δὲ κύριος τὸ πνεῦά ἐστιν" of verse 17a identifies the "κύριος" of the quoted text of v. 16 with a reality of Paul's Christian life, the spirit. As I have noted in my Introduction, the exegetical nature of the passage as a whole, as well as the nature of verse 16 as a nearly perfect quotation of Exodus 34:34, and the implications of this for the Pauline use of "κύριος," clearly indicate that this is simply the plain sense of the text.[49]

In his citation of Exodus 34:34, moreover, Paul has performed another exegetical operation typical of "pesher" exegesis. Paul's version of that Exodus verse in II Cor. 3:16 contains several variations, not known as Septuagintal variants, which serve to interpret and contemporize its meaning. The verb "ἐπιστρέφω," used by Paul to describe the action of Moses in which the veil is removed, is not the verb of Exodus 34:34 (LXX), which is "εἰσπορεύομαι." Paul's verb, "ἐπιστρεφω," is used commonly both in the Septuagint and in the New Testament to denote the act of turning to God in repentance or conversion.[50] The substitution of this verb interprets Moses' "going in to the Lord" as prototypical of the conversion, in Paul's own day, of those who turn toward the Lord through the spirit.

Paul returns to near correspondence with the present Septuagint text of Exodus with "περιαιρεῖται τὸ κάλυμμα." Here, however, he alters the verb form to the present indicative passive from the imperfect passive of Exodus.[51] This grammatical variation once again signals an interpretative step. The tense change indicates the bridging of the temporal gap between the Exodus story and the situation in which Paul and his Christian fellows find themselves. The veil is taken away *in Paul's day* in conversion to Christ.[52] Verse 17 completes this contemporization by identifying its agency in Paul's own time. It is the spirit who converts. It is the spirit who removes the veil.

---

[49] See Introduction, pp. 14-17 and notes, especially DUNN, "'The Lord is the Spirit,'" to which I will have occasion to refer more extensively below.

[50] BERTRAM, "ἐπιστρέφω," *TDNT* VII, pp. 723-724; COLLANGE, *Enigmes*, p. 103; RICHARD, "Polemics," p. 356.

[51] The form could be read as either middle or passive. BARRETT and RICHARD, as already noted, read it as middle. I have translated it as passive, as do COLLANGE, *Enigmes*, p. 101 and PRÜMM, *Diakonia Pneumatos*, p. 149. I do not think that it makes much difference, however. In either case, it is through the agency of the "Lord" that the veil is removed. The important thing about the change of verb is the clear tense change to the present.

[52] This change into the present tense is parallel to Paul's repeated use of καταργέω in the present in II Cor. 3:7, 11, 13 and 14 with the phrase "ἄχρι ... σήμερον ἡμέρας" in v. 14 and "ἕως σήμερον" in v. 15.

In these few remarks, I have pointed out the two major exegetical methods employed in this section of II Corinthians 3, briefly located the evidence for their use and described their functions. As I have said, this section is divided into two parts, verses 7-11 and verses 13-18, with verse 12-13a as a bridge between them. Each of these parts is thematically and structurally determined primarily by the exegetical procedure most prominent within it. The remainder of this chapter will pursue a more thorough analysis of each section.

The *Kal Va-Homer* Method in II Corinthians 3:7-11

I have already described the structure of these verses as a series of three *kal va-homer* arguments. In this section I would like to examine this form in verses 7-11 to show the combination of the Jeremiah/Ezekiel text complex with the story of Moses' glorification which is effected in it. This analysis will show that, although Exodus 34:29-35 sets the scene, the section is conceptually determined by the Jeremiah/Ezekiel covenant complex and implications drawn from it.

II Cor 3:7-8

Verses 7 and 8 of II Corinthians 3 contain the first of the three explicit *kal va-homer* arguments outlined above. The *kal va-homer* argument in II Cor. 3:7-8 transfers a single characteristic, glory (δόξα), from one ministry to the other. The elaboration of the basic form in verse 7: ...ἐν γράμμασιν ἐντετυπωμένη λίθοις ἐγενήθη ἐν δόξῃ, ὥστε μὴ δύνασθαι ἀτενίσαι τοὺς υἱοὺς Ἰσραὴλ εἰς τὸ πρόσωπον Μωϋσέως διὰ τὴν δόξαν τοῦ προσώπου αὐτοῦ... identifies the reference to Exod. 34:29-30 which introduces the concept of glory into Paul's composition. The witness of Exod. 34:29 assures Paul that the beginning of Moses' ministry of the "second" Sinai covenant was attended with glory. As a minister of that covenant, Moses possessed δόξα.

But, Moses' ministry is characterized as "ἡ διακονία τοῦ θανάτου" in II Cor. 3:7. This identification is not drawn from the text of Exodus 34. First, Moses is not called a διάκονος in Exod. 34:27-35. Second, it is certainly contradictory to the viewpoint not only of Exodus 34, but of the Book of Exodus as a whole, to call Moses' mediation in Exod. 34:29-35 a "ministry of death." Instead, the section of II Corinthians 3 which immediately precedes verse 7 supplies the information which explains these peculiarities.

In II Cor. 3:3 Paul has used the verb "διακονέω" to describe his own activity, that of "delivering," or converting, the letter which is the

Corinthian church. In II Cor. 3:6, Paul describes himself as a "διάκονος" of the new covenant. Indeed διακονέω/διακονία/διάκονος became in the New Testament and in the period shortly thereafter a word-group regularly used to describe specifically Christian service or ministry.[53] The title and function of "deacon" persist even today as a duly constituted Christian ministry. Paul has, therefore, described Moses' function and role with a term which originally better described his own role in emerging Christianity.

More important than that simple matter of terminology, however, is Paul's description of Moses' service as a "διακονία τοῦ θανάτου". The close connection between II Cor. 3:6 and 7 has already been described, and it is responsible for this shockingly negative assessment. The qualification, "τοῦ θανάτου," stems directly from the "ἀποκτέννω" of II Cor. 3:6c. Death is characteristic of the ministry of Moses because he ministered the written covenant (Exod. 34:27-29) which kills. Chapter One of this study has explained how Paul arrived at that conclusion regarding Moses' covenant. Here in II Cor. 3:7-11 the negative assessment of the Mosaic covenant made in II Cor. 3:2-6 is extended to include the Mosaic ministry as well.

The arguments and contrasts of II Cor. 3:2-6, therefore, are the hidden premise of all three of the *kal va-homer* inferences contained in verses 7-11. The Mosaic covenant has been judged inferior to the new covenant. The negativity of that ancient covenant has been transferred to Moses' ministry of it as well. Paul's final editorial addition to the verse — τὴν καταργουμένην — indicates this clearly. Therefore, the Mosaic ministry is known to be the *inferior* member of the pair of ministries which the *kal va-homer* arguments themselves explicitly compare. All such *kal va-komer* arguments operate on the basis of such deliberate presuppositions, since the function of the inference is not to *prove* the inferiority or superiority of the terms, but only to *transfer* characteristics from the inferior to the superior. In this case, the inferior Mosaic ministry possessed the quality of glory in spite of its inferiority.

Paul's ministry of the superior new covenant is the superior member of the *kal va-homer* comparison. It is called "ἡ διακονία τοῦ πνεύματος." This is a description drawn directly from the pool of covenant characteristics described in Chapter One of this study. The new covenant is a spiritual one and bestows the gift of the spirit. It is also directly tied to II Cor. 3:6bc, as is the description of its inferior counterpart. The spirit as a covenant characteristic is derived from Ezekiel 11 and 36 in combination with Jeremiah 38 (LXX) as has been shown previously.

---

[53] H. BEYER, "διακονέω," *TDNT* II, pp. 84-89; C. E. B. CRANFIELD, *A Commentary on Romans 12-13*, Scottish Journal of Theology Occasional Papers 12 (1965) p. 31.

Chapter One has also shown that the "τὸ δὲ πνεῦμα ζῳοποιεῖ" of 3:6c is
a conclusion based on the literary context of one of those Ezekiel texts,
Ezekiel 37:1-14. In II Cor. 3:8 Paul recals this description of the spiritual
nature of the new covenant, opposing it to the deathly character of the
old covenant. In II Cor. 3:7-8, however, the deathly character of the old
is represented by its minister, Moses, as the spiritual nature of the new is
represented by the ministry of Paul.

Having thus explained the terms of the *kal va-homer* inference in II
Cor. 3:7-8, we can see quite clearly how that inference itself works. The
inferior ministry of Moses began in glory, according to Exodus 34:29-30.
Moses' face shone with it as he came down from the mountain carrying
the two stone tablets. If this inferior ministry of an inferior covenant
possessed such glory, then surely the superior Pauline ministry of the
spiritual covenant must also possess glory. It's as simple as that, if you
will grant Paul his premises.

Paul wants to predicate glory of himself as the minister of a new
covenant. He does not simply wish to assert it, nor, apparently, was it
self-evident. Instead, Paul argues that his ministry possesses such glory on
the basis of the report of Moses' glorification in Exodus 34:29-35. His
desire to argue in this way reveals his deep concern with his relationship
to Moses and the model of ministry that he provided. Indeed, it depends
upon it. This concern has already been discovered in II Cor. 3:1-6 and
described in Chapter One of this study. Here we have seen Moses as a
model move into this new section of Paul's argument. In fact, the
argumentation of II Cor. 3:1-6 can now be viewed as the establishment of
the necessary presuppositions for the continuation contained in verses
7-18. II Cor. 3:5-6 established the parallel between Paul and Moses. II
Cor. 3:2-6 established as well the superiority of the new covenant, and
Paul's ministry of it, over the written covenant, and Moses' ministry of it.
In II Cor. 3:7ff. Paul goes on to acquire something that he apparently
lacks which can be provided to him by the interpretation of Exod.
34:29-30 just described. Just like Moses, the minister of the new covenant
is glorified. The ministry of the new, like the ministry of the old, must be
characterized by δόξα.[54]

---

[54] A subsequent study will be devoted to a discussion of the meaning of δόξα and
related concepts in relation to Paul's Christology. At this time, however, it is important to
notice that the δόξα which shone on Moses' face was evidence of his converse with God
(CHILDS, *Exodus*, pp. 618-619) and functioned as a guarantee of the divine origin of the
words of the covenant he brought to Israel and so of their effectiveness and reality. In
asserting that he himself possesses a similar glory, Paul is not so much laying claim to a
similar physical manifestation as he is to a similar divine origin for his own covenant and
gospel. This is not to say that Paul either denied the reality of Moses' physical
glorification or interpreted it allegorically. On the contrary, in accenting its physical
reality for Moses, he is able to reinterpret it for his own day according to its true meaning.

My effort in this section has been to unpack the terminology of Paul's argument and to describe its logic. This logic prevails as well in the two succeeding *kal va-homer* forms. The conclusion reached is also the same — the transference of glory to the Christian ministry from the Mosaic ministry. Only δόξα is taken from Exodus 34 in this series of inferences. None of the descriptions of the inferior or the superior ministries are drawn from Exodus. All prove to be derived either positively or negatively from the pool of covenant characteristics described on the basis of II Cor. 3:1-6 and its scriptural background.

II Cor. 3:9-11

The second *kal va-homer* argument is less elaborated and is fully contained in verse 9, the third in verse 11. The form is followed faithfully, and the arguments function identically to the first one in verses 7-8. The inferior and superior members of the comparison are identified in v. 9 as the "διακονία τῆς κατακρίσεως" and the "διακονία τῆς δικαιοσύνης." In v. 11 they are "τὸ καταργούμενον" and "τὸ μένον." There is nothing in Exodus 34:29-35 which explains these designations. Instead, the arguments and background of verses 1-6 again provide the immediate source for the characterizations. The positive characteristics of the superior new covenant and ministry are drawn directly from explicit statements in the scripture texts which have promised it. The negative characteristics of the inferior old covenant and ministry must be inferred in opposition to its replacement. It is easier, therefore, to treat the positive characteristics of the superior members of the comparisons first in the *kal va-homer* forms in verses 9 and 11.

In II Cor. 3:9, the Pauline ministry is called "διακονία τῆς δικαιοσύνης." Righteousness, δικαιοσύνη, in a very complicated concept in the Old Testament and so in the New Testament as well. In general, and from the human point of view, it is the existence of the individual in a right and pleasing relationship to God, however that relationship is established or retained. In the case of Israel, that right relationship is established and maintained in and through the covenant.[55]

The δόξα which Paul possesses therefore guarantees the reality and effectiveness of his ministry far better than a letter of recommendation could, because it is of divine, not merely human, origin. The problem is, then, to understand just what this glory is and how it *is* manifested in Paul. These questions, however, must await their answers in a later volume.

[55] See the article "δικαιοσύνη" in *TDNT* II, pp. 192-210 by G. SCHRENK, with caution, because of the very strong polemic overtones the discussion of the term has acquired in the Post-Reformation history of Christian thought; David HILL, *Greek Words and Hebrew Meanings* (Cambridge: The University Press, 1967) pp. 82-162, and J. A. ZIESLER, *The Meaning of Righteousness in Paul* (Cambridge: The University Press, 1972) with the bibliographies provided. None of these works, however, draws the connection

The word "δικαιοσύνη" does not occur in the Prophetic texts used in Chapter One of this study to form the covenant conceptual pool, but the ideas of forgiveness of sin and of the reestablishment of the proper moral and covenantal relationship between Israel and the Lord are explicit in Jeremiah 38:34; 39:39-40 (LXX) and Ezekiel 11:20; 36:25, 27, 31 — all of the Prophetic texts already seen to underlie II Cor. 3:1-6. It is very likely, therefore, that the idea that the new covenant will entail forgiveness and the reestablishment of the right covenantal relationship between Israel and its God stems directly from the prophets cited.

If, however, the new covenant brings forgiveness, mercy and therefore righteousness, it can be inferred that the old covenant which it supersedes entailed just the opposite — judgment and condemnation, the κατάκρισις of II Cor. 3:9a. It is not at all apparent from Exodus 34, nor is it explicit in Jeremiah and Ezekiel that κατάκρισις is a characteristic result of the old covenant. Yet it is clear from Jeremiah 38:32; 39:37, 40, 42 (LXX); Ezekiel 11:15, 18, 20, 21; 36:25, 27, 29, 31-32 and 37:11 that sin and judgment have been frequent under the old covenant. Furthermore, the same logical process which produced the "τὸ γὰρ γράμμα ἀποκτέννει" of II Cor. 3:6c, if applied to righteousness as a new covenant characteristic, would produce its opposite, judgment, as a characteristic of the old covenant, So, in this second kal va-homer argument, just as in the first, it is not material from Exodus 34 which defines the terms used, but concepts taken or derived from the Prophetic promises of a new covenant. As was the case with the kal va-homer inference in verses 7-8, the working of the argument itself is simple. If Moses' ministry of the old covenant, which brought only judgment or condemnation as the prophets testify, had glory as Exodus 34:29ff. testifies, then certainly Paul's ministry of the new covenant, which brings righteousness and restores man's right relationship with God, must also have glory.

Verse 10 elaborates on one word of verse 9, the verb "περισσεύω." According to II Cor. 3:9 the ministry of the new covenant abounds in glory. That is, its glory is superior to the glory which attended the inferior Mosaic ministry. This expansion of his meaning is dependent upon the form of argumentation Paul is using and clarifies it for his reader. The "how much more (πῶς or πολλῷ μᾶλλον)" of the second term of a kal va-homer inference always indicates that the superior term possesses the transferred quality to an even greater degree than the inferior term does,

that should be drawn between the righteousness that was established in the old covenant and the righteousness that was extended to Gentiles in the new covenant. If this parallel is not seen, and if a caricature of Judaism in the early Christian period which sees its righteousness as self-righteousness is accepted, then a vital link between Judaism and Christianity is severed.

on the basis of its very superiority.[56] The parenthetical remark of v. 10 insures that the reader does indeed understand the force of Paul's arguments.[57]

The third *kal va-homer* form occurs in verse 11. The expected word, "διακονία" is absent here. It is replaced by two participles, "τὸ καταργούμενον" and "τὸ μένον," in agreement with the participle, "τὸ δεδοξασμένον," of verse 10. The ambiguity of these participial forms provides another opportunity through which to explore the underlying presuppositions upon which the surface arguments have been built.

The phrase "τὸ καταργούμενον" has occurred before in this section of II Cor. 3. It concludes Paul's additions to Exodus 34:29 in II Cor. 3:7. In II Cor. 3:7 the form of the participle is singular *feminine* present passive. In verse 11 it is a singular *neuter* present passive. Therefore, in verse 7 it must refer to a feminine noun, while in verse 11 its referent must be a neuter noun or a general concept. The neuter participial form is sometimes deliberately ambiguous, signifying "*the thing* that is being brought to an end," or whatever, without being any more specific.[58] This ambiguity in verse 11 allows Paul to shift his reference or to refer to more than one reality at a time without grammatical contradiction.

In verse 7, the expected feminine referent of τὴν καταργουμένον is τὴν δόξαν. Paul seems to interpret Exodus 34 to mean that the glory of Moses' face was fading. There is no justification for this interpretation in Exodus 34:29-35, although neither does the text explicitly state that Moses' glory did not fade between the times when Moses was in the presence of the Lord. It is, however, certainly the clear implication of

---

[56] M. MIELZINER, *Introduction*, pp. 130-132.

[57] E. HILL has put forward a unique argument regarding the meaning of "τὸ δεδοξασμένον" in verse 10. He asks whether against the overwhelming majority of scholarly opinion, "τὸ δεδοξασμένον" could not refer to something in the new covenant, rather than to something in the old, "The Construction of Three Passages from St. Paul," *CBQ* 23 (1961) p. 299. He concludes that v. 10 is "an explanatory aside" (p. 301) which serves to explain just why Paul's face gives no evidence of the radiance that the logic of his own argument in verses 7-8 has just proved that he should have. To justify this conclusion HILL takes "ἐν τούτῳ τῷ μέρει" to refer to the "ἡ διακονία τῆς δικαιοσύνης" of v. 9 and "καὶ γὰρ" as the customary introduction to "an aside, an illustration, a further point" the function of which is to answer to a supposed but unstated objection" (p. 300). The objection in this case is that, unlike Moses', Paul's face displays no radiance. HILL translates Paul's rebuttal as: "Though in fact [καὶ γὰρ] the thing glorified in the (latter) case [Paul's ministry] has not been (manifestly) glorified, because its glory is so overwhelming" (p. 300). It is the addition of the parenthetical "manifestly" that destroys HILL's case, since it is being read into the Greek. Nevertheless, he was right in suggesting that "a question which has never been asked cannot really be said to have been answered ..." (p. 299) and he has provided an insight into the text regarding the objection to which Paul's arguments would have immediately been subject which cannot be lightly dismissed.

[58] MOULTON, *Grammar*, III, p. 21.

Exodus 34:35 that the glory of Moses' face was constantly renewed. Subsequent Jewish legend held that his glory remained until his death, and even asserted that it would still be visible if his tomb was found and opened.[59] Paul, however, is not in contradiction either with the plain sense of the text or with his general religious tradition in the interpretative phrase "τὴν καταργουμένον." The participle is in the present tense. Paul does indeed interpret the glory of Moses as a transient, fading glory. That glory ended when the covenant with which it was associated came to an end. That was, however, *not* during the wilderness period in Moses' day, but in Paul's own day with the inauguration of the new covenant in Christ and through Paul. Therefore, understood as a past event in the life of Moses himself, Moses' glory did not fade, nor does Paul assert that it did. However, read in the light of a future event, Moses' glory is eclipsed by the brilliance of Christ. II Cor. 3:7 is an interpretation of Exodus 34:29-35 for a new day.[60]

---

[59] GINZBERG, *Legends* III, pp. 93, 441, 473 and VI, note 953, p. 164; *The Biblical Antiquities of Philo* XIX, 16, ed. M. R. JAMES (New York: KTAV Publishing House, 1971) p. 132; Targum Onkelos on Deuteronomy 34:7, *The Targums of Onkelos and Jonathon Ben Uzziel on the Pentateuch*, Ed. J. W. ETHERIDGE (New York: KTAV Publishing House, 1968) p. 556. This legend is also mentioned by van UNNIK, "'With Unveiled Face,'" p. 157; HOOKER, "Beyond the Things That are Written?," p. 300 and many others. Jewish tradition is unanimous in stressing the lasting character of Moses' glorification.

[60] Against all commentators on this passage with the exception of Anthony Tyrell HANSON in *Jesus Christ in the Old Testament* (London: SPCK, 1965) p. 27, therefore, I must deny that Paul asserted that Moses' glory faded *during the wilderness period*. On the contrary Paul was at one with his tradition in believing that Moses' glory lasted until his death and even after, *until Paul's own day* in fact. Then, however, because the glory of Christ which so far surpassed it had entered the world, Moses' glory as well as his ministry and his covenant came to an end. At this point Paul would come into conflict with the Moses traditions of his time. COLLANGE's treatment might allow this interpretation, but he does not explicitly contradict the received scholarly opinion that Paul has somehow "misunderstood" or "misinterpreted" Exod. 34 by saying that the Exodus text itself asserts that Moses' glory was ending. But this is precisely what Paul is not doing. A modern critic who said Exod. 34 reports that Moses' glory ended would be wrong, because he would be concerned *only* with what Exod. 34:29ff. says about the events that transpired during Moses' lifetime. If he went on to assert that Moses' glory ended at any future date, his opinion would have nothing to do with the biblical text. But, when Paul says that Moses' glory "is fading" he is not making a historical statement about Exod. 34:29-30, but a hermeneutical one. He is telling his readers what the Exodus text means *in his own day*. As such, his statement cannot be ruled a "misinterpretation" from his point of view, nor can it contradict the text of Exodus. Rather, it is a contemporary interpretation of Exodus *based on the present day experience of Christ*. Commentators are once again unanimous in their appreciation of Paul's Christological perspective. Our point of disagreement lies in the exegetical focus of Paul's statements and their relationship to his opinion of the historical validity of the story of Moses' shining face in Exodus 34. See note 3 of this chapter on the present force of the verb "καταργέω."

This interpretation illustrates once again how completely Paul's use of Exodus 34 is determined by the previously discussed scriptural understanding of the new covenant. Paul's idea that the glory of Moses' face was fading or ending is not derived from Exodus nor retrojected into it, but stems from Paul's immediate conviction that the old covenant, and therefore the ministry of that old covenant, had been in his own time superseded by the superior new covenant. Because of this conviction, and in spite of the fact that it is on the basis of the past glory of Moses' ministry that glory is predicated of the present Christian ministry and covenant in verses 7-11, Paul cannot admit that Moses' glory remained in his own day to rival the glory of the Christian dispensation. God may not contradict himself.

This is not to say, however, that from his own point of view, Paul thought that he was "reading into" the text of Exodus a perspective of his own, however justified that accusation may seem from our modern conception of exegesis. On the contrary, the Prophetic promises of the new spiritual covenant had allowed him to find the *correct* interpretation of Moses' glory, and his veiling of it. Everyone will agree that is the cardinal principle of Jewish exegesis of this period, and of subsequent periods to our own day, that scripture interprets scripture. If a text is difficult or seems contradictory, the proper way to approach it is to find a text, or texts, in which the meaning is more clear and then to use the additional material to clarify that obscure passage.[61]

This is what Paul has done in II Corinthians 3 as a whole. The clear promises of the prophets about the coming of the new covenant have made it plain to him that Moses' glory must necessarily have faded for the promised new covenant and the necessary new ministry to have begun. Moses' glory was a witness to the divine participation in the old covenant. The odd feature of Exodus 34, Moses' veiling of his glorious face, receives therefore the most emphasis and is similarly explained for Paul by the advent of the superior promised covenant and his own enactment of its ministry. Moses' veiling himself had to do with the eventual ending of his own service and the passing away of the covenant he brought in the inauguration of that which replaced and surpassed it. This point of view is expressed especially in the "τὴν καταργουμένον" of

---

Contra ZERWICK, *Biblical Greek* (Rome: Scripta Pontificii Instituti Biblici, 1963) 371-372, p. 129 and with MOULTON, *Grammar* III, p. 79 I see the participle here denoting real present time, with additional support offered by the phrases "ἄχρι... σήμερον ἡμέρας" and "ἕως σήμερον" in verses 14 and 15 as evidence of Paul's intention to interpret Exod. 34 for his own time.

[61] Renée BLOCH, "Midrash," pp. 31-33; BOWKER, *Targums* pp. 5-14; NEUSNER, *Midrash*, pp. xix-xx, 1-2. NEUSNER's work gets at the heart of what I tried to express above about the historical reference of Paul's interpretation of Exod. 34, but from a theological perspective.

verse 7 and in the parenthetical verse 10, and is very explicit in verse 13 to which I will turn later in this chapter.

I have already said that the "οὐ δεδόξασται τὸ δεδοξασμένον" of II Cor. 3:10 reflects the passive "δεδόξασται" of Exod. 34:29 and 35. The verb in Exodus 34 refers to Moses' face. In II Cor. 3:10 the participle is neuter in implied agreement with τὸ πρόσωπον as well as in the general sense offered by the ambiguous neuter form. The sense of the verse is in exact agreement with the interpretation of Paul's perspective just given. That which was glorified has no glory *now* in view of a glory that surpasses it. Although once certainly glorious, it is eclipsed by a superior light which has come. Knowledge of the superior thing, most basically the new covenant, has come from the scriptural background described in Chapter One of this study. The knowledge that it is glorious has come from the *kal va-homer* arguments based on this background and Exodus 34.

To return, then, to a discussion of the third *kal va-homer* argument occurring in verse 11, instead of the expected "ἡ διακονία τοῦ," the neuter participle "τὸ καταργούμενον" appears. Having understood Paul's exegetical viewpoint on Exodus 34 from verses 7 and 10, we can see that his reference here is once again to the ending of the old in favor of the new. But if he refers simply to the δόξα of Moses' face again here, the participle should be feminine as it is in verse 7. If the reference were simply to ἡ διακονία or even ἡ διαθήκη, the participle should still be feminine. However, as I have said, in Greek it is possible to indicate an emphasis on a general quality rather than an individual reality through use of the neuter gender. Paul's use of the neuter participle in verse 11a, then, indicates an emphasis on the characteristic of "coming to an end" that Paul sees in his day as *common* to the glory of Moses' face, the ministry of the old covenant and that old covenant itself. Δόξα cannot even be the primary referent of τὸ καταργούμενον in verse 11a if the parallelism with v. 7a and v. 9a is to be maintained, as the coincidence of the *kal va-homer* form indicates that it should be. Διακονία is therefore implied as the primary reality standing behind the general participial form. A general reference to ἡ διακονία is also indicated by the dependence of the *kal va-homer* form on the presupposed superiority and inferiority of the covenants ministered.

Another participle, "τὸ μένον" replaces the expected "ἡ διακονία τοῦ." The characteristic of "remaining" can be directly inferred for the new covenant from Jeremiah 38:32 (LXX) as well as from Jeremiah 39:40 (LXX). Unlike the covenant with the fathers, the superior new covenant will remain (Jer. 38:32 LXX). It will be eternal (Jer. 39:40 LXX). In contrast, and of necessity, the old covenant will end. The force of the argument is identical to those of verses 7-8 and 9. Exodus 34:29-35 tells us that the old covenant was inaugurated in glory through the glory of its minister's face, even though it was destined to end. So, the new covenant, so much superior to the old in that it is destined to last forever, must be inaugurated in glory through its ministers. The new covenant is of the same divine origin as was the old.

Summary

The analysis of the *kal va-homer* arguments in verses 7-11 is now completed. Paul's utilization of the method has been limited to the appropriation of δόξα from the story of Moses' glorification preserved in Exod. 34:29-35 to his own ministry of the new covenant. The exegetical form does determine the logical structure of Paul's text. The concept of glory is derived from Exod. 34:29ff. Nevertheless, Paul's use of Exodus 34:29-35 itself has so far proved to be very slight. On the other hand, the influence of the new covenant conceptual pool on the terminology of the *kal va-homer* inferences and upon Paul's interpretation of Exod. 34:29-35 has proved to be immense. What is really interesting in verses 7-11 is Paul's constant reference to words and concepts drawn from Jeremiah and Ezekiel in the context of his interpretation of Exodus 34. As was the case in II Cor. 3:2-6, the promises of the prophets are the interpretative key to the Pentateuchal narrative.

Secondly, the ambivalence of Paul's relationship to Moses has become even more clear in this section than it was in II Cor. 3:1-6. The thrust of the inferences of verses 7-11 is that Paul is like Moses in glory. The importance of the issue of resemblance to a Mosaic pattern cannot be denied. But, Paul is not content to be only the equal of Moses in glory. He must be his superior. That is the full force of the exegetical methodology that he has chosen to employ. So, Paul is not like Moses. He is even better than Moses. Paul's covenant gives the spirit, while that of Moses brought death. Paul's covenant gives righteousness, while Moses' covenant brought judgment. Paul's covenant will last, while Moses' covenant is ending. As the covenants are, so are the ministries and the ministers. Paul possesses the everlasting glory of the minister of the spiritual covenant of righteousness. Moses possessed the transient glory of the minister of the written covenant of judgment. This is Paul's interpretation of Exodus 34:29-35. Its details will become even more clear as Paul begins to discuss Moses' veil in verses 13-18. His basic viewpoint, however, is immediately made clear in verse 12-13a, which functions as a summary of what has gone before and as an introduction to what will follow.

The "Pesher" Approach in II Corinthians 3:13-18

Verse 12-13a as Bridge

The second subdivision within II Cor. 3:7-18, verses 13-18, is preceded by the structurally pivotal verse 12 and 13a: ἔχοντες οὖν τοιαύτην ἐλπίδα πολλῇ παρρησίᾳ χρώμεθα, καὶ οὐ καθάπερ Μωϋσῆς ... The phrase "ἔχοντες οὖν τοιαύτην ἐλπίδα" serves to summarize and conclude the preceding discussion. What follows, "πολλῇ παρρησίᾳ χρώμεθα, καὶ οὐ καθάπερ Μωϋσῆς ..," introduces a new topic. How and why is Paul *not* like Moses?

In II Cor. 3:1-11 the new Christian covenant has been described, via the scriptual background presumed by the text, and judged to be superior to the Mosaic covenant. On the basis of the *kal va-homer* arguments in verses 7-11, the Pauline ministry of that Christian covenant has been proven to be superior to the Mosaic ministry of the Sinai covenant with respect to the glory which attaches to them both in that Paul's glory is eternal. In all of this discussion the issue in dispute seems to have been whether or not Paul is similar to Moses and, if so, how.[62] The answer has been a resounding "yes." Paul is like Moses in his status as a covenant minister (II Cor. 3:4-6) and in the glory that such a ministry entails. Indeed, Paul is even superior to Moses in glory because his covenant is superior to that of Moses in many ways (II Cor. 3:2, 3, 6, 8-11). The issue of conformance to a Mosaic model of apostleship has been met and solved on the level of covenant. Paul is like Moses, and not only like him but superior to him.

This superiority implies difference as well as similarity. In II Cor. 3:13-18 Paul begins to explore this *difference* between himself and Moses by making use of the veil of Moses as a metaphor representing the distinction between them. I do not suggest that Paul thought of the veil as a metaphor *in Exodus 34:29-35*. On the contrary, for Paul Moses' veiling himself is a *reality* of the history of Israel faithfully reported in Exodus. But, it is a reality whose meaning is completely clear only in light of Paul's own later interpretation and which he uses metaphorically to express that interpretation. II Cor. 3:13-18 is devoted exclusively to the explanation of the mysterious reality of Moses' veil.

---

[62] Or, conversely, what is the role of Moses vis-a-vis the ministry of the new covenant? In my opinion, commentators have paid far too little attention to the role that Moses plays in Paul's own argument. The otherwise excellent treatment by COLLANGE, for example, is so preoccupied by a refutation of GEORGI's hypothesis of opponents who use Moses as a model, that he fails to discuss verses 7-11 in a positive way (*Enigmes*, pp. 67-84).

It is surprising in itself that Paul chooses to talk about the veil at all, since it was almost completely ignored in Jewish legend and exegesis. That he does choose to discuss it at such length indicates Paul's emphasis on an aspect of the figure of Moses of little interest to his contemporaries and, possibly, in sharp distinction to other depictions of him. Paul's emphasis on Moses' veil signals his reinterpretation of the Mosaic pattern of ministry in terms of a prophetic model of service present in earliest Christianity as a depiction of Jesus Christ's own identity and also closer to Paul's personal experience — the humble and suffering prophet.

Verse 12a summarizes the discussion which immediately precedes and identifies a specific link between that argument and the issue of Moses' veil. The "οὖν" indicates this logical connection with verse 11. Because Paul has "such a hope," he will go on to deny his need for a veil and to contrast his behavior as a minister to that of Moses. It is plain the "hope" of v. 12a is defined by the final phrase of verse 11b: τὸ μένον μένει ἐν δόξῃ. The hope which Paul has as a minister of the Christian covenant is the hope that his covenant will remain and that, therefore, his glory as minister will remain with it.[63] Attention to the prepositions with which the conclusions to verse 11a and 11b are formed shows that while the glory of the old covenant was there only at its beginning (it is *through* [διὰ] glory), the glory of the new covenant is a constant and enduring quality (it *remains* [μένει] *in* [ἐν] glory). Paul, therefore, has the hope that the glory that he possesses as a minister of this enduring new covenant will never end.

This is in direct distinction to Moses' glory, according to II Cor. 3:7 (... διὰ τὴν δόξαν τοῦ προσώπου αὐτοῦ τὴν καταργουμένην), and even in distinction to Moses' *perception* of his glory, according to II Cor. 3:13 (... ἐτίθει κάλυμμα ἐπὶ τὸ πρόσωπον αὐτοῦ, *πρὸς τὸ μὴ ἀτενίσαι τοὺς υἱοὺς Ἰσραὴλ εἰς τὸ τέλος τοῦ καταργουμένου*). The consciousness of hope issues in boldness or confidence on Paul's part — πολλῇ παρρησία χρώμεθα — II Cor. 3:12b. Paul's hope arises ultimately from his knowledge of the superiority of the covenant which he ministers. Paul knows that the new covenant will never end. Conversely, the humility and reticence which stems from Moses' knowledge of the inferiority and transience of the covenant which he ministers issues in a quite different action and attitude on his part. Moses knows the "end" (τέλος, v. 13) of his glory and his covenant, and so he veils his face.[64] This is unabashed

---

[63] So also PLUMMER, BULTMANN, ALLO, PRÜMM, COLLANGE, BARRETT, and especially VAN UNNIK, "With Unveiled Face," pp. 158-159.

[64] In his article "'With Unveiled Face,'" W.C. VAN UNNIK has argued that Paul makes a "daring jump" (p. 159) in verses 12-13 by connecting Moses' veil with his own freedom of speech. With BARRETT (*Second Epistle*, pp. 118-119), I think that the jump is not all that daring, in view of the considerable parallel between verses 13 and 18, but

interpretation of Exodus 34:29ff. by Paul. There is absolutely no way to justify such a conclusion about Moses' veil from the text of Exodus 34:29-35 alone, but II Cor. 3:13a states Paul's viewpoint very clearly. Paul's interpretation of Exodus 34:33-34 is guided by a simple presupposition — we are not like Moses.

II Corinthians 3:13bc as the Epitome of Mosaic Ministry

Verse 13bc describes the single most important way in which "we" are not like Moses. Moses put a veil on his face. As I have said, "Μωϋσῆς ἐτίθει κάλυμμα ἐπὶ τὸ πρόσωπον αὐτοῦ" is a direct reference to Exodus 34:33. The following clause, "πρὸς τὸ μὴ ἀτενίσαι τοὺς υἱοὺς Ἰσραὴλ εἰς τὸ τέλος τοῦ καταργουμένου," presents Paul's interpretation of Moses' motivation for this veiling and its immediate effect upon his audience, the sons of Israel. These narrative details are lacking in the story as it is reported in Exodus, and Paul supplies them.[65]

Grammatically, "πρὸς τὸ μὴ ἀτενίσαι" is an infinitive phrase indicating intention. It is properly translated "so that (the sons of Israel) might not gaze upon ..."[66] The reality which the sons of Israel were thus

---

VAN UNNIK's observations about the rite of covering the head in Judaism are most interesting. His criticisms of WINDISCH (pp. 159-160) are also well taken. VAN UNNIK himself argues that in Aramaic the phrase "to cover the face or the head" expressed "shame and mourning" whereas "with uncovered head" meant "in freedom." He notes that in verse 18 Paul offers the literal translation of "with unveiled face" into Greek—"ἀνακεκαλυμμένῳ προσώπῳ." Therefore, what Moses did was in Paul's symbolic language a sign of shame and bondage, whereas Paul's contrasting action expressed confidence and freedom (p. 161). This is enlightening information about the symbolic language of the time, but it does not solve the structural problems that VAN UNNIK proposes it to solve. The break in the text at verse 12 that he sees as a problem is really only so on the hypothesis of WINDISCH that Paul's discussion of the veil is "a loosely connected digression" (VAN UNNIK, p. 154; WINDISCH, p. 117) that VAN UNNIK sets out to defeat. In light of Paul's extensive exegesis of Jer. 38 (LXX) and Exod. 34, however, the break is not really serious, and VAN UNNIK's treatment of the text is unnecessarily skewed by responding to WINDISCH. On the rite of covering the head, see also S. KRAUSS, "The Jewish Rite of Covering the Head," *HUCA* 19 (1945-1946) pp. 121-168, who also concludes that it is primarily a sign of mourning.

[65] For GEORGI, the pre-Pauline midrash contained the Exodus citation and read "καὶ Μωϋσῆς ἐτίθει κάλυμμα ἐπὶ πρόσωπον αὐτοῦ, πρὸς τὸ μὴ ἀτενίσαι τοὺς υἱοὺς Ἰσραὴλ εἰς τὸ τέλος." Paul's interpretation is limited to "οὐ καθάπερ" and "τοῦ καταργουμένου" (*Die Gegner*, p. 282, which contains a diagram of GEORGI's division of II Cor. 3:7-18 based on the argument of pp. 274-282 and SCHULZ's previous analysis). This theory has the effect of denying any importance to Moses or Exodus 34 for Paul himself and of making Paul's assessment of Moses entirely negative. It has not been unaffected by the Post-Reformation law/gospel debates.

[66] A number of commentators assume that Paul assigns different motives to Moses in verses 7 and 13. In verse 7, Moses tries to protect the sons of Israel from the brilliance of his face, which they fear. This is close to the text of Exod. 34:30-33. Their fear is

not permitted to continue looking at was the *end*, τὸ τέλος, of the thing which was and is now being brought to a close, "τοῦ καταργουμένου." Here is the third instance of this participial form of καταργέω in this seven-verse section. Its reference is very likely to be the same as that of the ambiguous neuter form which occurs in verse 11. Paul's intention again is to expand, via the use of the neuter gender in correspondence with verse 11, the more limited statement of verse 7 that Moses' glory was ending in order to emphasize that the general characteristic of "ending" belonged not only to Moses' glory but to the covenant and ministry of Moses as well.

    So, it is clear that Moses' action in veiling himself is, according to Paul, a deliberate one, aimed at concealing not only the glory of his face but the *end* of that glory, his ministry and his covenant. The "πρὸς ... μὴ" makes this explicit. Moses did not want the sons of Israel to see all the way up to that end. The term "τὸ τέλος" is an ambiguous one, like so much of Paul's terminology in this section. It denotes "end," both positively and negatively. If used negatively, τέλος means simply the end as temporal stop. If used positively, τέλος means, in addition to that, the end as completion or fulfillment.[67] Paul's use of the word in this or other genuine letters is not decisive in explaining his meaning here,[68] nor do

---

sometimes associated in Jewish tradition with their guilt over the incident of the golden calf, as well as with the natural awe and terror inspired by any theophanic appearance (GINZBERG, *Legends* III, pp. 143-144; PROVENCE, "'Who is Sufficient'?," notes this on p. 71). In verse 13, however, Paul says Moses veils his face for a different reason; i.e., to *prevent* the sons of Israel from seeing his face (SCHULZ, "Die Decke," pp. 8-9; FITZMYER, "Glory Reflected on the Face of Christ," p. 639; HOOKER, "Beyond the Things that are Written?," p. 298; RICHARD, "Polemics," does not seem to propose this distinction). I am not sure that I am in agreement with this received interpretation. Although verse 13 explains Moses' motivation more fully, it is possible that Paul had the same motivation in mind in verse 7, especially since the participle "καταργουμένην" occurs there, as "καταργουμένου" does in verse 13. In both cases Moses is said to have veiled his face so that Israel could not see his glory. I do not see sufficient cause to propose a radical difference between the verses. On the contrary, the two verses are complementary. For Paul it was the overwhelming τέλος of Moses' glory that made Moses' glory too brilliant to gaze upon and required his veil.

[67] ARNDT/GINGRICH, *Lexicon*, p. 689; G. DELLING, "τέλος," *TDNT* VIII, pp. 49-57 which bears witness to the ambiguity of the term even in its earliest usage.

[68] In the letters commonly considered to be genuine, Paul leans toward the sense of "goal, reward, or fulfillment" in his use of τέλος, certainly in Rom. 6:21,22; Phil. 3:19, and probably in Rom. 10:4 and II Cor. 11:15. He refers to the end-*time* with τέλος in I Cor. 1:8; 10:11; 15:24, in parallel with the use of the term in Jewish apocalyptic (DELLING, "τέλος," p. 53). In the unique case of Rom. 13:7, τέλος is used to mean payment or tribute, as it sometimes is in the LXX and secular Greek usage (DELLING, "τέλος," pp. 51, 52). It is difficult to determine his precise meaning in the only other use of τέλος in II Corinthians, II Cor. 1:13. Paul's use of τέλος in Rom. 10:4, "τέλος γὰρ νόμου Χριστὸς ..." is clearly the closest parallel to II Cor. 3:13, but the same ambiguity also exists there. Earlier critical opinion held that Rom. 10:4 referred primarily to Christ as the

commentators agree on its proper interpretation.[69] The wisest course is simply to admit that when Paul uses an ambiguous term or form, he means to play upon that very ambiguity.[70] We must allow him to do so.

The fact that verse 13 is Paul's definitive characterization of the Mosaic covenant ministry can be seen through a parallel characterization of the Christian ministry in verse 18 with which this subsection of II Corinthians 3 concludes. II Cor. 3:13 and 18 are significantly parallel descriptions of the activity of Moses as it is reported in Exodus 34:33 and the activity of Paul as he himself reports it.[71] Figure 6 illustrates the correspondence between the two verses.

----

temporal end of the law, but the dominant opinion today holds that Paul's emphasis is on Christ as the fulfillment of the law in a positive sense, W. SANDAY and A. HEADLAM, *A Critical and Exegetical Commentary on the Epistle to the Romans*, The International Critical Commentary, Fifth Ed. (Edinburgh: T. & T. Clark, 1902) p. 284; C. E. B. CRANFIELD, *Romans* II, pp. 515-520. It appears that there is no clear-cut instance in Paul's letters of his use of τέλος in an entirely negative sense or to mean simply "temporal stop" and only that, unless it be II Cor. 3:13. There is not sufficient reason to make II Cor. 3:13 such a unique case.

[69] PLUMMER, *II Corinthians*, pp. 97-98 decides unambiguously for "temporal stop" and sees the referent of "τοῦ καταργουμένου" as Moses' glory only, as do WINDISCH, *Der zweite Korintherbrief*, p. 120; BARRETT, *Second Epistle*, p. 118; HUGHES, *Second Epistle*, pp. 109-110. PRÜMM, in a lengthy discussion of the matter (*Diakonia Pneumatos*, pp. 137-140), decides on a temporal meaning for τέλος as "end" (p. 139) but refers "τοῦ καταργουμένου" to the Mosaic covenant (p. 137). His treatment of the whole passage views Paul's use of Exod. 34 as typological in the technical sense and so sees this temporal translation of τέλος as part of a larger, "ironic" treatment of Moses (p. 139). COLLANGE also translates "*fin*, or *terminus*," but his discussion is focused on Paul's polemic against opponents (*Enigmes*, p. 96). ALLO presents a brief review of the history of the interpretation of verse 13, and takes a more nuanced view of the ambiguous meaning of τέλος (*Seconde Epître*, pp. 90-91). FEUILLET says that τέλος has a double sense (*Le Christ, Sagesse de Dieu d'après les Epîtres pauliniennes*, p. 117). According to BARRETT *Second Epistle*, p. 120) both HÉRING and Ragnar BRING argue for the meaning "goal" or "climax" for τέλος in II Cor. 3:13. Even PLUMMER (*II Corinthians*, p. 97) must admit that ancient exegesis often referred τέλος in II Cor. 3:13 to Christ himself. FITZMYER, "Glory Reflected on the Face of Christ," p. 637 leaves the question open, as I prefer to do for the moment.

[70] Paul's use of the verbs "κατοπτρίζω" and "καταργέω" in this section are good examples of this ambiguous use of vocabulary.

[71] BARRETT, *Second Epistle*, p. 119 seems to imply this parallelism, but his treatment of v. 18 is disappointing. My interpretation assumes that Paul (and any other Christians he includes with himself; see Note 10 above) are to be compared with Moses and contrasted with the sons of Israel, but that the primary parallel is with Moses himself. Cf. BULTMANN, *Zweiter Korintherbrief*, p. 94. Whereas there were two groups in the OT text—Moses alone, who received a special revelation of divine glory, and Israel, who did not—there is one group in Christ to whom the glory of God has been fully revealed. See PLUMMER, *II Corinthians*, p. 105, LAMBRECHT, "Structure and Line of Thought," pp. 350, 357-362.

Figure 6
II Cor. 3:13 and 3:18

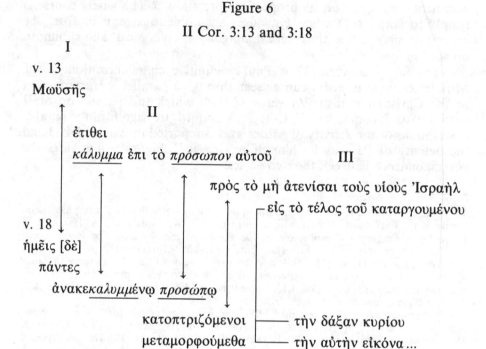

This diagram is divided into three sections, numbered I, II, III. Section I defines the actors who are compared — Moses and the ambiguous group "we all" which certainly includes Paul. Section II describes the action or condition of each group. Moses puts a veil on his face, while "we all" have unveiled faces. Section III details the results of the contrasted veiled or unveiled condition of the actors. As a result of Moses' veiled condition, the sons of Israel were unable to see his glory or its end. As a result of Paul's (et al.) unveiled condition, "we all" are seeing and/or reflecting the glory of the Lord and are even being transformed into that same image. The vocabulary and grammar of these two verses are not always strictly parallel. Where a verbal correspondence exists between them, it has been underlined. Nevertheless, the thematic similarity of these two verses is striking. They propose some surprising parallels in Section III. The contrast between the unenlightened condition of Israel following Moses' veiling, and "our" unveiled and glorified state is startling.

It is not possible to answer all of the questions posed by this parallelism between verses 13 and 18 at one time. Specifically, the proper identification of "τὸ τέλος" in verse 13 and an explanation of the alternate use of "τὴν δόξαν κυρίου" and "τὴν αὐτὴν εἰκόνα" in verse 18 must await a future treatment, even though these issues reach to the very heart of Paul's interpretation of Moses' veil. For now, however, the recognition of the thematic parallelism of these verses will allow us to begin to follow the use Paul has made of Moses' veil as a symbol of the difference between them.

These two summaries form a frame within which the temporal gap between the two ministries, that of Moses and that of Paul, is bridged through the rhetorical device of the movement of Moses' veil through space and time. This movement proceeds under the influence of additional scriptural texts, which are exegetically hooked into the already existing scriptural matrix of Paul's argument. For the remainder of this chapter, we will follow this movement of the veil to discover what it is that Moses' veil covers, if it does not cover Paul.

I undertake this investigation under the subtitle "The 'Pesher' Approach in II Corinthians 3:13-18" in order to highlight the specific pesher exegesis of verses 16-17 as the culmination of a development leading from verse 13, through verses 14-15, and concluding in verse 18, which is determined by the very same principles under which pesher interpretation itself is undertaken. The exegesis represented by the Qumran pesharim had to do above all with history, i.e., the past history represented by the text and the present-day history of the interpreter.[72] For an interpreter of this sort, the meaning of his own experience was hidden within the biblical text. His effort was to discover and expound this meaning as the fulfillment of the text itself in his own day and so to directly apply that text to his own experience.[73] The performance of such an exegetical operation is the equivalent of bridging the temporal gap between the biblical text and its contemporary readers. In fact, it is the annihilation or denial of that temporal gap.

Paul must somehow bridge the gap between the narrative "then" of the story of Moses' veiling and the temporal "now" in which he and his followers no longer wear veils, either physically or metaphorically. Furthermore, he must explain both how and why he has done so. By the time he says "ὁ δὲ κύριος τὸ πνεῦμά ἐστιν" in II Cor. 3:17, Paul has wiped away the gulf between Moses and the sons of Israel and himself and his fellow-Christians. He has done so as his contemporary, the exegete at Qumran, would have done, and as the later rabbinic exegete would continue to do. He has applied the text of Exodus directly to his own situation, and he has sought additional scripture texts to tell him more clearly just how the veil of Moses was intended to move through history into his own time. His problem is to explain his παρρησία in contrast to Moses' humility. Paul looks to scripture for its solution.

---

[72] HORGAN, *Pesharim*, p. 248.
[73] ELLIS, *Paul's Use*, p. 141.

II Cor. 3:14-18 as *Pesher*

J. D. G. Dunn on II Cor. 3:16-17

In 1970 an article entitled "2 Corinthians III. 17- 'The Lord is the Spirit.'" appeared in the *Journal of Theological Studies* which summarized what I believe to be the conclusive arguments proving that II Corinthians 3:16-17a is a specific *"pesher"* exegesis of Exodus 34:34.[74] In that article, J. D. G. Dunn argues that II Cor. 3:16 is a citation of the Septuagint form of Exodus 34:34 with only those variations which could be expected within the *pesher* form as it is elsewhere to be found in the New Testament.[75] He concludes that, because II Cor. 3:16 is the citation of a specific Old Testament text in which the title, "κύριος," refers to Yahweh and because in the context of such citations Paul's use of the title follows this common Septuagintal usage, the "κύριος" of II Cor. 3:17a refers, not to Christ as is usual in Paul, but to Yahweh, the Lord of the Old Testament passage with which Paul is working.[76] Dunn's argument rests, as a whole, on his recognition that all of II Cor. 3:7-18 is a "midrash or interpretative homily on Exodus xxxiv. 29-35."[77] The article is a pointed rebuttal of the majority opinion earlier in this century and specifically of Ingo Hermann's *Kyrios und Pneuma* which had argued very strongly for the *experiential* identification of Christ and the spirit.[78]

As I have said in my Introduction, I regard the question as closed by the work of Dunn and his predecessors. II Cor. 3:16 is certainly a citation of Exod. 34:34. The "κύριος" of II Cor. 3:17 must therefore be the κύριος of Exod. 34:34. The "πνεῦμα" is identified with the Lord of the Old Testament and not with Jesus Christ. Furthermore, this identification is not a dogmatic statement. It is an exegetical one, because of the exegetical nature of the argument in which Paul is engaged. That is not to say, however, that I agree completely with everything Dunn has had to say concerning the passage or that I feel that he has said everything that can be said about it. Specifically, I do not agree that Paul has used "the Exodus passage as an allegory" as Dunn asserts on p. 311 of this text and goes on to argue in the following pages. "Glory" does not represent or stand for anything else, outside of the real glory which was evident on Moses' face and is now present in Paul, in the argument in II Cor. 3:7-18.

---

[74] DUNN, "'The Lord is the Spirit,'" *JThS* 21 (1970) pp. 309-320. The article begins with several good bibliographical notes on both sides of the question.

[75] DUNN, "'The Lord is the Spirit,'" pp. 312-317.

[76] DUNN, "'The Lord is the Spirit,'" pp. 317-318.

[77] DUNN, "'The Lord is the Spirit,'" p. 311. He is indebted for this insight not only to WINDISCH, whom he cites, but to many others, among them and also very early, J. GOETTSBERGER, "Die Hülle des Mose," whom he does not.

[78] Ingo HERMANN, *Kyrios und Pneuma* (Munich: Kösel-Verlag, 1961).

It is accepted realistically and transferred to Paul, as I have argued above. "Veil" is used metaphorically to express Israel's blindness to Moses and misunderstanding of Paul's message, but that does not make Paul's use of Exodus 34 allegorical.

Furthermore, I think that because of the necessary brevity of his argument and his focus on verses 16-17 alone, Dunn has not carried his own basic insight into the text as far as it can go. Although he acknowledges the variations which II Cor. 3:16 has introduced into its citation of Exodus 34:34, he does not do all that can be done to explain them.[79] Although he says, "In verse 14 Paul extends his interpretation to his own time ...," he does not really explain how Paul does so.[80] He is absolutely right. The major thrust of all *pesher* or "*pesher*-like" exegesis *is* to extend the interpretation of a text into the interpreter's own time. In II Cor. 3:14-18 Paul is engaged in doing just that. We need to see, however, not only *that* he does so, but *how* he does so. In the next few pages, I would like to build upon this very fruitful insight, contained in, but not sufficiently expanded by, Dunn's work and discuss the way in which Paul has made the story of the veil of Moses contemporary in II Cor. 3:14-18.

Instructions for removing the veil

Both Exodus 34:34 and II Cor. 3:16 have to do with the way in which Moses' veil can be removed. The Exodus verse itself reports that Moses took the veil off his face whenever he went into the Tent of Meeting to speak to the Lord and left it off until he had communicated the Lord's commandments to the sons of Israel and allowed them to view his own continuing or renewed glorification. II Cor. 3:16 echoes this report but does not specify Moses as the one from whom the veil is removed by turning toward the Lord. Dropping "Μωϋσῆς" from its citation of Exod. 34:34 in this way is a major alteration and has the effect of extending the application of the verse from its original referent, Moses, to *anyone* who turns toward the Lord as Moses did when he entered the Tent of Meeting. Now, according to Exodus 34, no one but Moses had such a privilege at that time. Since the Tent of Meeting was no longer in existence when Paul cited Exod. 34:34 in II Cor. 3:16, he can hardly have intended a widespread literal imitation of Moses. On the contrary, he intended a contemporary application of the example Moses provided in Exod. 34:34. He supplies this application in II Cor. 3:17. As Dunn, and others, have argued, Paul substitutes a reality of his own Christian experience for the Lord who was available only to Moses according to

---

[79] DUNN, "'The Lord is the Spirit,'" pp. 314-315.
[80] DUNN, "'The Lord is the Spirit,'" p. 311.

Exodus 34, but was no longer available in the same way to his own contemporaries.[81]

On the basis of my earlier discussion of the new covenant in this and the preceding chapter, Paul's substitution is not difficult to understand. Paul knows that the new covenant has been given. The spirit is the gift and sign of that new covenant, just as the presence of the Lord in the Tent of Meeting was the gift and sign of God's covenant through Moses.[82] Under the new covenant, the spirit of the Lord is not only *with* God's people, but *in* God's people, according to Ezekiel 11:19, 36:26 and especially Ezekiel 37:6 and 14. Even Paul's remarkable equation of the Lord of the Old Testament with the spirit in II Cor. 3:17 is less startling if it is read in the context of Ezekiel 37:1-14. There, it is specifically *"my* spirit" which the Lord promises, that is, the spirit which Paul knows has been given is the Lord's own spirit (cf. II Cor. 3:17b). Under this new covenant, the Lord's spirit is not available to only one, or even to a few. It is available to all, to anyone who turns toward the Lord (cf. II Cor. 3:2; 4:2).

The meaning of II Cor. 3:16-17 is this: whenever anyone turns to the spirit, the veil is removed from him. That is, whenever anyone is converted to Christ through the spirit, he is no longer veiled, nor is anything veiled from him.[83] So Dunn correctly concludes.[84] But the argument presented for II Cor. 3:16-17 alone does not support this conclusion in its entirety. Two important problems remain to be dealt with, and they are the following: 1) How does the notion of conversion enter into Paul's interpreatation of Exodus 34:34? 2) How can Paul see the veil of Moses as a reality which extends into his own contemporary situation and so still needs to be removed through this conversion? We

---

[81] DUNN, " 'The Lord is the Spirit,' " p. 313 and the authors cited in Note 2 on the same page.

[82] The Tent of Meeting is a continuing sign of the divine presence at Sinai in Exod. 33:7-11. The Lord promises in Exod. 33:17 that he will maintain that presence and go with Moses and Israel into the promised land, although previously, in Exod. 33:3, he had denied that he would go with them because of the sin of the golden calf. The redaction of Exodus is obviously complicated at this point.

[83] SCHMITHALS, who argued that v. 17 and v. 18b are a non-Pauline (Gnostic) gloss and should be exercised to facilitate the interpretation of the midrash in II Cor. 3:7-18 is quite wrong. His argument is based on the difficulty introduced into the text by these verses and the admirable clarity afforded by their excision. He also offers a hypothesis regarding the original unity of the gloss as perfectly expressing the Corinthians' gnostic theology in poetic form. As usual, SCHMITHALS' argument is so entertaining that it is quite seductive. However, that is no warrant for the removal of sections of the Pauline text just because they are difficult, when there is no text-critical basis for doing so. In fact, SCHMITHALS would have us excise the precise exegetical conclusion Paul made with his citation of Exod. 34:34 ("Two Gnostic Glosses in II Corinthians" in *Gnosticism in Corinth*, pp. 315-325).

[84] DUNN, " 'The Lord is the Spirit,' " p. 313.

are not entitled to *assume* answers to these questions. Instead, their answers lie in II Cor. 3:13c-15 and the scripture texts which underlie them. These further background texts also explain the variations in Paul's citation of Exodus 34:34 which Dunn's fine treatment of verses 16-17 has left unexplained.

II Cor. 3:14-15 and the unbelief of Israel

According to II Cor. 3:16, Moses' veil is a reality, originating in the events of the life of Moses, which still has an enduring reality and significance within Paul's own experience. The veil does not rest on the face of Moses any longer, since Moses died in the wilderness. II Cor. 3:18 tells us that the veil does not lie on Paul's face as a minister of the new covenant. II Cor. 3:14 tells us where Moses' veil lay in Paul's day: ... ἄχρι... τῆς σήμερον ἡμέρας τὸ αὐτὸ κάλυμμα ἐπὶ τῇ ἀναγνώσει τῆς παλαιᾶς διαθήκης μένει. Until this very day, Paul says, the same veil lies on the reading, or understanding, of the old covenant. Dunn is quite right to point out the importance of the phrase, "τὸ αὐτὸ κάλυμμα." [85] It is the *same veil* that covered Moses which has travelled through history to cover something else. This phrase alone is the major indication of the "*pesher* approach" which Paul has taken to the interpretation of Exodus 34.

II Cor. 3:15 offers another explanation of the veil's location that is, in fact, only a refinement of his first statement in verse 14. Paul says: "...ἕως σήμερον ἡνίκα ἂν ἀναγινώσκηται Μωϋσῆς κάλυμμα ἐπὶ τὴν καρδίαν αὐτῶν κεῖται." Until today, he says, whenever Moses is read a veil lies on "their" heart. Who are "they?" The referent of "αὐτῶν" in verse 15 can only be the same as that of the "αὐτῶν" of verse 14, namely, the sons of Israel from verse 13c.[86] It was the sons of Israel who were prevented from seeing by Moses' veil originally, and it is still the sons of Israel who are affected by that same veil in Paul's own day.

It may be legitimately asked, however, how Paul knows that this is the case. He cannot possibly know it from Exodus 34:29-35, even if he does use the picture of Israel as sinful, fearful and reluctant to see drawn in that text as typical of Israel in all ages. He may be reflecting his personal experience of rejection by his own people which is amply attested in such passages as Romans 9:1-3 and Galatians 5:11-12. Indeed, the Gospels and the Acts of the Apostles paint a picture of rejection, misunderstanding and hostility on the part of the Jews toward Jesus and

---

[85] DUNN, "'The Lord is the Spirit,'" p. 312.

[86] COLLANGE, *Enigmes*, pp. 91-92. I would agree with PLUMMER, *II Corinthians*, p. 98 that Paul is thinking of *both* the sons of Israel in Moses' time *and* the Jews of his own time, not "without distinction of time" but *in continuity through* time.

his disciples that has become only too familiar to modern Christian readers. But we should not assume too quickly that these documents are an unbiased mirror of early Christian experience and *only* that. In this investigation, good results were obtained earlier through an analysis of Paul's vocabulary which led ultimately to a network of scripture texts which explained much of his thought in II Cor. 3:1-6. Since this is the case, such an analysis may again prove fruitful in providing a more concrete background for Paul's assumption that the veil of Moses covered Israel's heart in his own day and that the books of Moses (the old covenant, or Torah) were therefore veiled against them.[87]

Unfortunately, the key noun in the section, "κάλυμμα," does not occur in the Septuagint in any other relevant passages.[88] II Cor. 3:14-15 provides no other unique verbal links to known Septuagint texts. Nevertheless, the vocabulary of these verses as well as II Cor. 3:16, does show the influence of two texts from the prophet Isaiah. Paul's vocabulary does not lead directly to these Isaianic texts, however, but it does direct us to two parallel New Testament texts, John 12:39-41 and Romans 11:7-8. Analysis of those New Testament texts immediately reveals their dependence on Isaiah 6:9-10 and 29:10-12. A comparison of the Septuagint versions of these Isaianic texts with II Cor. 3:14-16 shows

---

[87] David DAUBE, in *The New Testament and Rabbinic Judaism* (London: The Athlone Press, 1956), understands II Cor. 3:14-15 as the most obvious case in Paul's own writings which provides validation for the picture drawn in Acts of the Apostle accusing the Jews of not understanding their own scriptures (pp. 434-435). He goes on to suggest that in I Corinthians Paul had already made a distinction between mere reading and real understanding of a "particularly secret or dangerous meaning beneath a text" (p. 435), and that II Cor. 3:14, along with several other NT texts, "tends in this direction" as well (p. 436). The secret meaning that the Jews do not understand, however, is a secret only to them, according to Paul in II Cor. 3:14-18. Christ has brought the old covenant to an end and inaugurated the new covenant, and the spirit has freed everyone from obligation to the old by revealing that it has been fulfilled in Christ — all in Paul's own day.

[88] Isaiah 25:7 refers, in the Hebrew, to the "covering that is cast over all peoples, the veil that is spread over all nations" (Translation of the Masoretic text by the Jewish Publication Society of America). This text in Hebrew certainly bears witness to the fact that the prophet Isaiah saw not only Israel, but the Gentiles as well, covered over in shame and mourning. It provides scriptural validation for VAN UNNIK's theory about the symbolic meaning of veiling in Judaism (" 'With Unveiled Face,' " pp. 160-161). C. F. D. MOULE notes a possible influence of this Isaianic text on II Cor. 3:14-15 ("2 Cor. 3,18b," p. 234). The context of II Cor. 3 in the letter as a whole very strikingly indicates Paul's awareness of this passage from Isaiah. II Corinthians 5:4 concludes — "so that the mortal may be swallowed up by life." This is not the place for an examination of the function of this phrase within the argument it follows. In fact, it appears abruptly without discernible warning in Chapter 5, and PLUMMER, for example, regards a reference to Isa.25:8 as quite likely but inexplicable (*II Corinthians.* p. 149). It could be explained, however, by the presence of Isaiah 25:7-8 in Paul's mind during the composition of a large section of II Corinthians through the presence of the hook, veil, in the Hebrew text. Without thorough investigation of a larger portion of II Corinthians, however, no certain conclusion can be drawn.

their considerable influence on it as well. Therefore, despite the lack of unique hook-words to make the relationship of II Cor. 3:14-16 with its scripural background obvious, Isaiah 6 and 29 are a part of the complex substructure of Paul's argument. They can be associated with the other texts in that background in retrospect through non-unique, but still significant, verbal correspondences. The single word in II Corinthians 3:14 which leads to the discovery of this new background is the verb, πωρόω.

Isaiah 6:9-10 and context

To anyone familiar with New Testament thought and its repeated apologetic use of certain Old Testament texts, II Cor. 3:14 is reminiscent of Isaiah 6:9-10. One has the feeling that Paul could be referring to this familiar explanation for the unbelief of the Jews.[89] Commentators on II Corinthians sometimes note this but do not go far in explaning or working through what strikes them as a casual similarity.[90] In fact, however, Paul is referring specifically to Isaiah 6, and not to Isaiah 6 alone, but the road to this discovery is more complex than the simple verbal clues which led, in my discussion of II Cor. 3:1-6, to Jeremiah 38 or Ezekiel 11. This road leads through the Gospel of John.

The verb Paul uses for "harden" in II Cor. 3:14 is πωρόω, a verb which does not occur at all in any version of the Septuagint still extant. It is, therefore, not the verb for "to harden" in the Septuagint version of Isaiah 6:10 as we know it. The verb, πωρόω, *is,* however, used very occasionally in the New Testament.[91] A glance at these uses reveals that in each case a situation of unbelief or misunderstanding is involved, an obtuseness toward God's revelation in Christ. In one case, a quotation of Isaiah 6:9-10 is clear. The author of John 12:39-41 apparently intends to quote Isaiah 6:10 in verse 40, and he does so with the verb "πωρόω." John's setting is the familiar one, the unbelief with which the Jews received the ministry of Jesus, their hardness of heart. The quotation here is universally accepted as stemming from Isaiah 6:9-10.[92] According to Barrett, John is translating a Hebrew version of Isaiah, rather than reflecting a variety of the Septuagint unknown to us.[93] However this may

---

[89] Isaiah 6:9-10 is cited apologetically in Mark 4:10-13; Mt. 13:14-15; John 12:39-41; Acts 28:25-27. See DODD, *According to the Scriptures*, pp. 36-39 and LINDARS, *New Testament Apologetic, pp. 159-167.*

[90] BARRETT, *Second Epistle*, p. 120; possibly HOOKER, "Beyond the Things that are Written?," p. 300; PROVENCE, "'Who is Sufficient?," notes a parallel with Romans 9-11 and Deuteronomy 29:3, but does not see behind those texts (pp. 78-79).

[91] Mk. 6:52; 8:17; Jn. 12:40; Rom. 11:7; II Cor. 3:14.

[92] C. K. BARRETT, *The Gospel According to St. John* (London: SPCK, 1962) pp. 359-360; Raymond BROWN, *The Gospel According to John i-xii*, The Anchor Bible (Garden City, New York: Doubleday & Co., 1966) pp. 484-487; DODD, *According to the Scriptures*, pp. 36-38; Lindars, *New Testament Apologetic*, pp. 159-160.

[93] BARRETT, *St. John*, p. 359.

be, the presence of a quotation of Isaiah 6:9-10 in John 12:40-41 which uses the verb "πωρόω" allows us to suppose that Paul may also, in using this verb in II Cor. 3:14, intend a reference to this key apologetic text. Whether both Paul and John are themselves identically translating the Hebrew text of the prophet, reflecting an unknown Greek text of Isaiah, or dependent on earlier Christian usage of Isaiah 6 in which this particular Greek translation of the Hebrew was made, makes little difference to my argument. What is important is whether or not Isaiah 6:9-10 is influential in II Corinthians 3:14-16 and, if so, how it is useful in explaining it. This indirect verbal evidence of the presence of Isaiah 6:9-10 behind II Corinthians 3:14-16 indicates that Paul has drawn his idea that the sons of Israel are still blinded by the veil of Moses and so ignorant of the full glory of his revelation partially from the words of the prophet concerning Israel's continuing ignorance and hardness of heart.

As with the background texts in Chapter One of this study, I will display a Septuagint version of Isaiah 6:1-11, John's quotation in its context, here so that the reader can judge the proposed influence of this text on II Cor. 3 in Greek and see the numerous, but not unique, verbal links with the scriptural background previously assembled.

Isaiah 6:1-11 [94]

1) Καὶ ἐγένετο τοῦ ἐνιαυτοῦ, οὗ ἀπέθανεν Ὀζίας ὁ βασιλεύς, εἶδον τὸν κύριον καθήμενον ἐπὶ θρόνου ὑψηλοῦ καὶ ἐπηρμένου, καὶ πλήρης ὁ οἶκος τῆς δόξης αὐτοῦ. 2) καὶ σεραφιν εἱστήκεισαν κύκλῳ αὐτοῦ, ἓξ πτέρυγες τῷ ἑνὶ καὶ ἓξ πτέρυγες τῷ ἑνί, καὶ ταῖς μὲν δυσὶ κατεκάλυπτον τὸ πρόσωπον καὶ ταῖς δυσὶ κατεκάλυπτον τοὺς πόδας καὶ ταῖς δυσὶν ἐπέταντο. 3) καὶ ἐκέκραγον ἕτερος πρὸς τὸν ἕτερον καὶ ἔλεγον Ἅγιος ἅγιος ἅγιος κύριος σαβαωθ, πλήρης πᾶσα ἡ γῆ τῆς δόξης αὐτοῦ. 4) καὶ ἐπήρθη τὸ ὑπέρθυρον ἀπὸ τῆς φωνῆς, ἧς ἐκέκραγον, καὶ ὁ οἶκος ἐπλήσθη καπνοῦ. 5) καὶ εἶπα Ὦ τάλας ἐγώ, ὅτι κατανένυγμαι, ὅτι ἄνθρωπος ὢν καὶ ἀκάθαρτα χείλη ἔχων ἐν μέσῳ λαοῦ ἀκάθαρτα χείλη ἔχοντος ἐγὼ οἰκῶ καὶ τὸν βασιλέα κύριον σαβαωθ εἶδον τοῖς ὀφθαλμοῖς μου. 6) καὶ ἀπεστάλη πρός με ἓν τῶν σεραφιν, καὶ ἐν τῇ χειρὶ εἶχεν ἄνθρακα, ὃν τῇ λαβίδι ἔλαβεν ἀπὸ τοῦ θυσιαστηρίου, 7) καὶ ἥψατο τοῦ στόματός μου καὶ εἶπεν Ἰδοὺ ἥψατο τοῦτο τῶν χειλέων σου καὶ ἀφελεῖ τὰς ἀνομίας σου καὶ τὰς ἁμαρτίας σου περικαθαριεῖ. 8) καὶ ἤκουσα τῆς φωνῆς κυρίου λέγοντος Τίνα ἀποστείλω, καὶ τίς πορεύσεται πρὸς τὸν λαὸν τοῦτον; καὶ εἶπα Ἰδού εἰμι ἐγώ· ἀπόστειλόν με. 9) καὶ εἶπε Πορεύθητι καὶ εἶπον τῷ λαῷ τούτῳ Ἀκοῇ ἀκούσετε καὶ οὐ μὴ συνῆτε

---

[94] The Septuagint text of Isaiah 6:1-11 displayed here is taken from the critical Göttingen edition, as are all the other texts from the prophet Isaiah used in this study, *Septuaginta* XIV. Isaias, ed. Joseph ZIEGLER (Göttingen: Vandenhoeck & Ruprecht, 1967). The translation below, as was the case with the other texts cited so far, is drawn from the Bagster edition of the Septuagint.

καὶ βλέποντες βλέψτε καὶ οὐ μὴ ἴδητε· 10) ἐπαχύνθη γὰρ ἡ καρδία τοῦ
λαοῦ τούτου, καὶ τοῖς ὠσὶν αὐτῶν βαρέως ἤκουσαν καὶ τοὺς ὀφθαλμοὺς
αὐτῶν ἐκάμμυσαν, μήποτε ἴδωσι τοῖς ὀφθαλμοῖς καὶ τοῖς ὠσὶν ἀκούσωσι
καὶ τῇ καρδίᾳ συνῶσι καὶ ἐπιστρέψωσι καὶ ἰάσομαι αὐτούς. 11) καὶ εἶπα
Ἕως πότε, κύριε; καὶ εἶπεν Ἕως ἂν ἐρημωθῶσι πόλεις παρὰ τὸ μὴ
κατοικεῖσθαι καὶ οἶκοι παρὰ τὸ μὴ εἶναι ἀνθρώπους καὶ ἡ γῆ κατα-
λειφθήσεται ἔρημος.

1) And it came to pass in the year in which king Ozias died, that I saw the
Lord sitting on a high and exalted throne and the house was full of his
glory. 2) And seraphs stood round about him, each one had six wings and
with two they covered their face and with two they covered their feet and
with two they flew. 3) And one cried to the other and they said, Holy,
holy, holy is the Lord of hosts; the whole earth is full of his glory. 4) And
the lintel shook at the voice they uttered, and the house was filled with
smoke. 5) And I said, woe is me, for I am pricked to the heart, for being a
man and having unclean lips. I dwell in the midst of a people having
unclean lips, and I have seen with mine eyes the King, the Lord of hosts. 6)
And there was sent to me one of the seraphs, and he had in his hand a
coal, which he had taken off the altar with the tongs; 7) and he touched my
mouth, and said, Behold, this has touched thy lips, and will take away
thine iniquities, and will purge off thy sins. 8) And I heard the voice of the
Lord saying Whom shall I send, and who will go to this people? And I
said, Behold I am here, send me. 9) And he said, Go and say to this people,
Ye shall hear indeed, but ye shall not understand, and ye shall see indeed,
but ye shall not perceive: 10) For the heart of this people has become
gross, and their ears are dull of hearing and their eyes have they closed, lest
they should see with their eyes and hear with their ears, and understand
with their heart, and be converted, and I should heal them. 11) And I said,
How long, O Lord? And he said, Until the cities be deserted by reason of
their not being inhabited, and the houses by reason of there being no men,
and the land shall be left desolate.

Apart from providing the theme of the "hardening" of Israel
expressed by the verb "πωρόω" in II Cor. 3:14, Isaiah 6:10 can also be
used to explain a variation in the text of Exodus 34:34 as it is quoted by
Paul in II Cor. 3:16. As I have said earlier, "ἐπιστρέφω" is not a known
Septuagint variant for the verb in Exodus 34:34. It is, however, the
characteristic Septuagint and New Testament word for the "turning" of
conversion. Paul has altered his citation of Exodus 34 by using ἐπιστρέφω,
and Isaiah 6:10 is a likely proximate source for this variation.[95]

---

[95] Two other significant explanations have been offered for this variation. PLUMMER
suggested that Paul modified his citation of Exod. 34:34 on the basis of Exod. 34:31—καὶ
ἐπεστράφησαν πρὸς αὐτὸν [Moses]—*II Corinthians*, p. 102. This is certainly possible, but
the occurrence of "ἐπιστρέφω" in Exod. 34:31 also makes Isaiah 6 an even more likely
candidate for its interpretation because of the presence of the same verb in verse 10. LE

The oracle in Isaiah 6:9-10 concludes, in the Septuagint, "μήποτε ἴδωσι τοῖς ὀφθαλμοῖς ... καὶ τῇ καρδίᾳ συνῶσι καὶ ἐπιστρέψωσι καὶ ἰάσομαι αὐτούς." You will notice that the translation of the Septuagint version provided above acknowledges the common connotation of the verb "ἐπιστρέφω" by translating it "be converted." For Isaiah the heart of Israel is "hardened" lest [96] they understand and *turn* and so be healed. The verb "ἐπιστρέφω" is a key word in Isaiah 6:10. It is used in its characteristic Septuagint sense, that is, to turn in repentance and conversion. By altering his text of Exodus with this key verb, then, Paul has appropriated a second major theme of this classic apologetic text from Isaiah and used it to interpret Exodus 34. The "turning toward the Lord" which one can perform to remove Moses' veil is the "turning" of repentance and conversion. But it is a "turning" which at least some of the sons of Israel will not perform, according to the prophet.

The incidental verbal correspondences between the Greek text of Isa. 6:1-11 and the other scripture texts in Paul's background are several. Isaiah 6:1-11 contains the key words δόξα (verses 1 and 3), κύριος (verses 1, 3, 5, 8 and 11), and καρδία (verse 10). We have already seen the importance of the concept of glory in Paul's argument in II Cor. 3:7-11 and 18. As is well known, glory is also significant in the whole of the Gospel of John. In John 12:41 glory is used in a very specific sense with reference to the prophecy of Isaiah. John 12:41 reads "ταῦτα εἶπεν Ἡσαΐας, ὅτι εἶδεν τὴν δόξαν αὐτοῦ καὶ ἐλάλησεν περὶ αὐτοῦ." The first half of this verse asserts that Isaiah spoke the prophecy just quoted because the prophet saw either God's or Jesus' glory. The general reference is clearly to Isaiah's vision as reported in Isaiah 6:1-5. Isaiah did view the Lord and his glory (δόξα in the LXX) according to the text. Does John mean that Isaiah saw the glory of God, or that he saw Jesus'

DÉAUT has argued that II Cor. 3:16 shows the influence of the Targum of Exod. 33-34 in the variant "ἐπιστρέφω," "Traditions targumiques dans le corpus paulinien?," *Biblica* 42 (1961) pp. 43-47. He points out that Exod. 33:7-10 reports that the sons of Israel stood and looked toward the Tent of Meeting whenever Moses went in to consult the Lord. This installation of the Tent of Meeting outside of the camp follows the incident of the golden calf, and at that time the people were out of favor with the Lord and wore mourning apparel as a sign of penitence and grief (Exod. 33:3-6). LE DÉAUT proposes that, in view of Israel's situation, the Targums interpreted this turning toward the Tent of Meeting as "une véritable *conversion du coeur*" (p. 46), and that Paul reflects this understanding of the parallel interaction between Moses, Israel and the Lord in Exod. 34:29-35 by the use of the common Septuagint verb for conversion in II Cor. 3:16. His argument is difficult to substantiate because of the uncertainty of any particular targumic interpretation and the language difference between the Targums and Paul's text. Nevertheless, if he is correct, such an understanding of Exod. 34 mediated through the Targums doesn't preclude its interpretation by Isa. 6:9-10 in II Cor. 3:14-16. It makes it all the more likely.

[96] Cf. my translation of II Cor. 3:14, and Note 8 of the present chapter.

or Christ's glory in particular during his vision? John 12:36-39 has just applied the prophecy to Jesus. It is the Jews' disbelief in *Jesus* which the prophet is made to condemn. The conclusion to be drawn seems obvious: Jesus is associated by John with the glory viewed by Isaiah and about which he spoke.[97] The referent of the double "αὐτοῦ" of Jn. 12:41 must be the same as that of the "αὐτόν" of Jn. 12:42 and 12:37, Jesus himself. The issue of John's interpretation of Isaiah 6:1-5 is too complicated to be thoroughly analyzed here, where it is something of a digression. But John's apparent association of the Lord Jesus Christ with the Lord and his glory viewed by Isaiah in his inaugural vision does anticipate similar exegetical presuppositions with regard to glory and Moses' vision apparently present also in the conclusion of Paul's argument, II Cor. 4:1-6. Here, however, it is only important to see the link in John 12:36-43 and II Cor. 3:7-15 between glory and the disbelief of the Jews. It was the glory of the old covenant that the sons of Israel could not see. It is the glory of Jesus (John 12) or of the new covenant (II Cor. 3) to which they are still blind.[98]

[97] According to BARRETT, *St. John*, p. 360, John surely refers to Isaiah's vision, and probably meant that Isaiah saw the glory of Christ, although for "most of the New Testament writers, including John, the whole Old Testament spoke of Christ." BROWN, *John*, pp. 486-487, is in agreement and notes that Jn. 12:41 should possibly be interpreted in light of Jn. 1:14, where "Jesus is the shekinah of God" (p. 487). John 12:41 presupposes a text of Isaiah 6 which said that Isaiah saw God's *glory*, whereas the canonical text of Isaiah says that Isaiah saw the Lord himself. The Targum of Isaiah 6:1 reads, "... I saw the glory of the Lord sitting upon a throne ...," according to the edition and translation of J. F. STENNING, *The Targum of Isaiah* (Oxford: Clarendon Press, 1949) p. 20, and verse 5 reads, "... the glory of the Shekinah of the King of ages, the Lord of hosts, have mine eyes seen," (p. 22). The identification of the Christ with the shekinah is intriguing, but it is not always accepted as easily as BROWN accepts it. At any rate, John's statement in 12:41 must mean either that Jesus Christ was present and active in the vision of Isaiah or that Isaiah looked into the future and saw the life and glory of Jesus. On the basis of similar statements in I Cor. 10:4, for example, I would choose the former explanation. See A. T. HANSON's *Jesus Christ in the Old Testament* (London: SPCK, 1965) on the real presence of Jesus Christ in events of the Old Testament period.

[98] Before leaving John's witness to the early Christian use of Isaiah 6, it is important to point out the odd coincidence of theme between this section of John's gospel and Paul's letter to Corinth. In John 12:35-36 and again at 12:46 Jesus is light. In II Cor. 4:4 and 6 the theme of light is the dominant one associated with the Christ. John 12:43 discusses the problem of appearances before men. This theme is extremely significant in II Corinthians as a whole, but especially at II Cor. 3:1; 5:12 and all of Chapters 10-13. Finally, in John 12:49 the phrase "ὅτι ἐγὼ ἐξ ἐμαυτοῦ οὐκ ἐλάλησα." is quite reminiscent of Paul's οὐχ ὅτι ἀφ' ἑαυτῶν ἱκανοί ἐσμεν λογίσασθαί τι ὡς ἐξ ἑαυτῶν..." in II Cor. 3:5. What relationship exists which accounts for these similarities? I suggest that it is not a relationship between Paul and John, but a common background drawn originally from a catena of scripture texts which formed a matrix and pattern for early Christian thought and early Christian texts. I consider my own work on II Cor. 3 as a contribution to the discovery of such a network of concrete background texts and the analysis of its probable structure. DODD and LINDARS have attempted such reconstructions but on such a wide scale and with such broad strokes that the value of their endeavor is somewhat

The allusions to Isaiah 6:10 in verse 14 and 16 clearly indicate Paul's appropriation of the theme of the hardening of Israel and its resulting unbelief and ignorance of God's plan. There is no possibility that Paul has originated such a usage. In the case of Isaiah 6 it is more reasonable to suppose that here we can again see Paul in touch with very early Christian tradition, using a common apologetic argument to augment his own metaphor of the veil, dictated by the text of Exodus 34, in order to explain Israel's current state of unbelief and to support his assertion that the veil now resides in Israel itself.

It more than augments his theme; it refocuses it. In Exodus 34, as it is cited in II Cor. 3:13, it is Moses' action in veiling himself which is squarely responsible for "unseeing" Israel. The sons of Israel *can't* see because something obscures their vision, and Moses is its agent. The contemporary form of this "blinded" condition with which Paul must deal is apparently, on the basis of John 12:36-43 and other early Christian use of Isa. 6:9-10, Israel's failure to accept Christ. The introduction of the theme of "hardening" from Isaiah 6 so defines it but also tends to shift attention as well as responsibility for Israel's lack of vision away from Moses. This, as well as the fact of the veil's movements from verse 13 to verse 15 (from Moses' face to Israel's heart), indicates that Paul did not wish to carry *Moses'* responsibility for Israel's misunderstanding into the present day. By using what amounted to a "stock" argument for explaining Israel's rejection of Jesus and the gospel of Christ, Paul expresses his preference for an explanation which will leave Moses' responsibility for Israel's blindness in the past history of the Exodus text. Just as his veil moves from him onto Israel, so does the responsibility for it.[99] Isaiah 6 provides the major enabling factor for this shift of responsibility within Paul's argument in II Cor. 3:13-15.

Isaiah 29:10-12 and context

Unbelief, or better, lack of vision, as a thematic becomes even more clear in Paul's conclusion at II Cor. 4:3-4 where it is defined as rejection

---

compromised. In fact, such study must be conducted in the most minute detail, and without the presupposition that we possess all the pieces of the puzzle in the relatively few canonical documents that remain to us.

[99] Cf., from a different methodological standpoint, LAMBRECHT, "Structure and Line of Thought," p. 359. Exactly where this responsibility does lie remains as much a problem for us as it did for Paul. Isaiah 6:9-10 assigns this responsibility to God himself, or to the sinfulness and obduracy of Israel. It is a commonplace of apocalyptic thought that the divine plan controls belief as well as unbelief until the catastrophic end which makes everything clear, doing away with both. It is most probable that Paul shared this viewpoint, cf. Rom. 11. See RUSSELL, *Between the Testaments*, pp. 97-98, 104-111 and Paul D. HANSON, *The Dawn of Apocalyptic* (Philadelphia: Fortress Press, 1975) to get a feel for the way in which such "apocalyptic ideas" were rooted in and arose as interpretations of real historical event and experience.

of Paul's own gospel. It is also more specifically defined in II Cor. 3:14-15, however, and on the basis of another associated text from Isaiah. It is not simply unbelief or ignorance in general with which Paul is concerned. According to II Cor. 3:14-15, Paul intends a particular sort of veiling or blindness — the inability to understand God's word in scripture. The justification for this definition of Israel's unbelief also comes to Paul from scripture, from Isaiah 29:10-12. Once again, however, the road into this background is not a direct one, but leads through another New Testament text, Romans 11.[100] Again the trail begins at the word "πωρόω" in II Cor. 3:14. One of the few New Testament uses of the term has already been discussed and has led unambiguously to Isaiah 6. Yet, Paul's use of πωρόω in Romans 11:7 introduces, surprisingly, a citation of Isaiah 29:10, "ἔδωκεν αὐτοῖς ὁ θεὸς πνεῦμα κατανύξεως," in correspondence with the Septuagint version of Isaiah. However, it is not a simple quotation in several respects. First of all, the resemblance to Isaiah 29 ends with the quoted section. Secondly, the verb "πωρόω" does not occur in Isaiah 29:10 or its immediate context, even though it is used to introduce a citation of verse 10, and neither is the idea of hardening or any reasonable synonym for "πωρόω" found in either the Hebrew or Greek versions. Why then has Paul used this signal word as introduction?

The answer lies in the fact that Romans 11:7-8 is a "composite quotation," i.e., the citation of more than one text within a single formula.[101] The verse continues, following "πνεῦμα κατανύξεως," with "ὀφθαλμοὺς τοῦ μὴ βλέπειν καὶ ὦτα τοῦ μὴ ἀκούειν..." There is a reference to "covered eyes" in Isa. 29:10, but nothing about ears or hearing. A secondary reference to Isaiah 6:10 is obvious. Such a reference explains the presence of πωρόω in Paul's introductory formula. As I have argued previously, Paul appears to have possessed a version of Isaiah 6 which contained this word or to have so rendered the Hebrew text himself. Therefore, Romans 11:7-8 bears witness to a Pauline, and most probably a pre-Pauline, combination of Isaiah 6:9-10 and 29:10-12.

Romans 11:8 closes with the phrase "ἕως τῆς σήμερον ἡμέρας," which is not to be found in either text from Isaiah. It may be an answer to the question posed at the beginning of Isaiah 6:11 — "ἕως πότε, κύριε;". The model for Paul's expression, however, is found by most commentators on Romans in Deuteronomy 29:4.[102] Although the Greek

---

[100] Van Unnik saw the relevance of Isaiah 29:10 to II Cor. 3:14 and 15 and expressed surprise that it is not noted in the commentaries ("'With Unveiled Face,'" p. 162). He also came to the text through Romans 11:8 and its use of πωρόω.

[101] Sanday-Headlam, *Epistle to the Romans*, pp. 314-315; Cranfield, *Romans*, II, pp. 549-551 sees the quotation as basically Deut. 29:4 and concentrates most of his discussion on the etymology of the terms used rather than on the citations themselves.

[102] Cranfield, *Romans*, II, pp. 550-551; Sanday-Headlam, *Epistle to the Romans*,

expression "ἕως τῆς ἡμέρας ταύτης" is by no means unique to Deuteronomy 29 and is not an exact match for Paul's expression in Rom. 11:8, this passage is chosen because of the close similarity in structure between it and Isaiah 6:10.

Deuteronomy 29:1-4 [103]

> 1) οὗτοι οἱ λόγοι τῆς διαθήκης, οὓς ἐνετείλατο κύριος Μωυσῇ στῆσαι τοῖς υἱοῖς Ἰσραὴλ ἐν γῇ Μωάβ, πλὴν τῆς διαθήκης, ἧς διέθετο αὐτοῖς ἐν Χωρήβ. 2) καὶ ἐκάλεσεν Μωυσῆς πάντας τοὺς υἱοὺς Ἰσραὴλ καὶ εἶπεν πρὸς αὐτούς Ὑμεῖς ἑωράκατε πάντα. ὅσα ἐποίησεν κύριος ἐν γῇ Αἰγύπτῳ ἐνώπιον ὑμῶν Φαραὼ καὶ τοῖς θεράπουσιν αὐτοῦ καὶ πάσῃ τῇ γῇ αὐτοῦ, 3) τοὺς πειρασμοὺς τοὺς μεγάλους, οὓς ἑωράκασιν οἱ ὀφθαλμοί σου, τὰ σημεῖα καὶ τὰ τέρατα τὰ μεγάλα ἐκεῖνα· 4) καὶ οὐκ ἔδωκεν κύριος ὁ θεὸς ὑμῖν καρδίαν εἰδέναι καὶ ὀφθαλμοὺς βλέπειν καὶ ὦτα ἀκούειν ἕως τῆς ἡμέρας ταύτης.

> 1) These are the words of the covenant, which the Lord commanded Moses to make with the children of Israel in the land of Moab, besides the covenant which he made with them in Choreb. 2) And Moses called all the sons of Israel and said to them, Ye have seen all things that the Lord did in the land of Egypt before you to Pharao and his servants and all his land: 3) the great temptations which thine eyes have seen, the signs and those great wonders. 4) Yet the Lord God has not given you a heart to know, and eyes to see and ears to hear, until this day.

It is easily recognized how Deuteronomy 29:4 might have influenced the text of Romans 11:8. The expression of Rom. 11:8c "ἕως τῆς σήμερον ἡμέρας" is in partial correspondence with the close of Deut. 29:4.

Without going into the importance of this composite quotation in Romans itself, or into the possible compositional dependence of any of the Old Testament texts on the other, it is important to notice that the three texts (Isaiah 6, Isaiah 29 and Deuteronomy 29) are easily associated

---

p. 314; C. K. BARRETT, *A Commentary on the Epistle to the Romans* (New York: Harper & Brothers, Publishers, 1957) p. 210; Ernst KÄSEMANN, *Commentary on Romans*, trans. Geoffrey W. Bromiley (Grand Rapids, Michigan: William B. Eerdmans Publishing Co., 1980) p. 301. All of these authors in fact assume that Deut. 29:4 is the primary text cited "loosely" or "freely." Although I have not done a thorough analysis of Chapters 9-11 of Romans, as they have, I cannot agree with their choice. The text as cited seems closer to Isa. 6:9, and a combination of Isa. 6 with Isa. 29 is likely once one recognizes that πωρόω was part of the text of Isa. 6 that Paul and John apparently knew. It is true, however, that Deut. 29:4 is a clear parallel to Isa. 6:9-10 and the expression "ἕως τῆς σήμερον ἡμέρας" does suggest the version in Deuteronomy 29.

[103] This text of Deuteronomy 29:1-4 is taken from the critical Göttingen edition, *Septuaginta*, III 2. Deuteronomium. Edited by J. W. WEVERS (Göttingen: Vandenhoeck & Ruprecht, 1977). As with the other texts cited, the English translation is from the Bagster edition of the Septuagint.

verbally in various ways through καρδία, πνεῦμα, and ὀφθαλμός in a manner similar to that described for the Jeremiah, Ezekiel and Exodus texts in Chapter One of this study. Romans 11:7-8, therefore, provides an unexpected bit of evidence for the prevalence of such verbal associations of Prophetic and Pentateuchal texts. Furthermore, Deuteronomy 29 presents Moses recalling the words of the covenant and the events of the Exodus to the "sons of Israel" in a scene parallel to that reported in Exodus 34:29-35. Most importantly, however, an analysis of II Cor. 3:14-15 shows that it too reveals the influence of this same combination of texts. Evidence for the influence of Isaiah 6 has already been presented. Deuteronomy 29:4, if it is echoed in Romans 11:8, may be heard also in II Cor. 3:14 (ἄρχι γὰρ τῆς σήμερον ἡμέρας) and 15, (ἕως σήμερον) although exact verbal correspondence is lacking.[104] The idea that events originating in the past have prevailed or remained influential *until this very day* fits very well into the *pesher*-perspective directing Paul's argument there. In Deuteronomy 29 Moses himself provides a model for thinking that events experienced in one time may only be fully understood in a later day (Deut. 29:2-4). This is exactly Paul's point, but the "later day" is his own time.

If Isaiah 29 is drawn into the background of II Corinthians 3:14-15 in the association with Isaiah 6 visible from Romans, several elements which previously seemed gratuitous in Paul's line of thought can be explained. As I have said, in verse 14 Paul defines the unbelief of Israel as an inability to read or understand the "old covenant." In verse 15, in parallel to the "τὸ αὐτὸ κάλυμμα ἐπὶ τῇ ἀναγνώσει τῆς παλαιᾶς διαθήκης μένει," Paul repeats this idea in a slightly different form: ἡνίκα ἂν ἀναγινώσκηται Μωϋσῆς κάλυμμα ἐτὶ τὴν καρδίαν αὐτῶν κεῖται. Whenever "Moses" (as synonymous with the "old covenant") is read as a book by Israel, a veil lies on its heart and "Moses" is not understood. For this last metaphor (a veil lies on their heart) we must have recourse again to Isaiah 6:10, "καὶ τῇ καρδίᾳ συνῶσι..." It is the heart that understands or does not understand.[105] According to Jeremiah 38:33-34 (LXX) it is the heart which should have received the knowledge of the new covenant, but according to these Isaiah passages the heart of Israel, at least, has not.

---

[104] A number of texts, especially Ezekiel 2:3 and 20:29,31 provide a closer verbal parallel. The prophetic perspective is also clearer: Israel has provoked the Lord in the past and continues to do so today. The evidence of Romans, the close parallel between Isa. 6:9-10 and Deut. 29:4, and the connection of Deuteronomy 29 with Moses and the recitation of the old covenant are probably decisive for a source in Deuteronomy, however.

[105] PLUMMER, *II Corinthians*, p. 101 notes this familiar meaning of καρδία, especially in Paul. In contrast, ALLO does not and, in addition, denies the influence of Isa. 6:9 on the verse (*Seconde Epître*, p. 92.).

The rest of the significant features of Paul's argument here in verses 14-15 can be drawn from Isaiah 29. This text allows Paul to make his two most important inferences of this section. First, Isa. 29:10 seems to speak of "covering" the prophets, rulers and/or the seers of Israel, but only in the Hebrew.[106] Unfortunately, no certain verbal hooks can be drawn between the Hebrew text of Isaiah 29:10 and Exodus 34:33-35. The Septuagint version which we possess is a poor translation, replacing the Hebrew verb form meaning "to cover" with the substantive "covered things," and so offers no conceptual or verbal links to Exodus 34. Nevertheless, a thematic correspondence does exist in the Hebrew, through the idea of "covering," which might have led Paul to the Hebrew text of Isaiah 29 to explain his contemporization of Exodus 34. Furthermore, Paul may have been in possession of either a Hebrew text which could be verbally linked to Exodus 34:33-35 or a Greek version which correctly translated the Hebrew, and thus provided a verbal link with the Greek text of Exodus 34.

According to the Hebrew text of Isaiah 29:10a, Israel is asleep. Israel's eyes are closed and so cannot see. Isaiah 29:10b reports that a covering lies on the leaders among the sons of Israel, those who might have been expected to see visions or interpret texts for the community as Moses did during the exodus. Thus the sons of Israel, according to the prophetic word of Isaiah 29:10, are still prevented from understanding because of a veil of sorts, a lack of vision.

More important than this uncertain link to the Hebrew through "covering," however, is the fact that Isaiah 29:11-12 introduces the notion of reading in a book and Israel's inability to do so properly, a theme so important for Paul in II Cor. 3:14-15. The key word, "ἀναγινώσκω" repeated in II Cor. 3:14 and 15 is present in Isa. 29:11 and 12 (LXX) as well.

---

[106] Isaiah 29:10 is an exceptionally difficult verse in the Hebrew, with a complicated textual history in consequence. This difficult no doubt accounts for the LXX mistranslation. No definite conclusions regarding Paul's argument can be drawn on the basis of the Hebrew text. However, it is obvious that Isa. 29:10 might have been a Prophetic text with particular value for interpreting Moses' veil, if Paul's Hebrew version did read "God has covered the heads of the prophets and seers...," as it might well have done. The Targum of Isaiah here reads, "For the Lord hath cast among you the spirit of error, and hath hidden from you the prophets..." (STENNING, Targum of Isaiah, p. 92). Such a reading may be relevant, since for Paul Moses is still "hidden" from the sons of Israel.

Isaiah 29:10-15 (LXX)

10) ὅτι πεπότικεν ὑμᾶς κύριος πνεύματι κατανύξεως καὶ καμμύσει τοὺς ὀφθαλμοὺς αὐτῶν καὶ τῶν προφητῶν αὐτῶν τῶν ἀρχόντων αὐτῶν, οἱ ὁρῶντες τὰ κρυπτά. 11) καὶ ἔσονται ὑμῖν πάντα τὰ ῥήματα ταῦτα ὡς οἱ λόγοι τοῦ βιβλίου τοῦ ἐσφραγισμένου τούτου, ὃ ἐὰν δῶσιν αὐτὸ ἀνθρώπῳ ἐπισταμένῳ γράμματα λέγοντες Ἀνάγνωθι ταῦτα· καὶ ἐρεῖ Οὐ δύναμαι ἀναγνῶναι, ἐσφράγισται γάρ. 12) καὶ δοθήσεται τὸ βιβλίον τοῦτο εἰς χεῖρας ἀνθρώπου μὴ ἐπισταμένου γράμματα, καὶ ἐρεῖ αὐτῷ Ἀνάγνωθι τοῦτο· καὶ ἐρεῖ Οὐκ ἐπίσταμαι γράμματα. 13) καὶ εἶπε κύριος Ἐγγίζει μοι ὁ λαὸς οὗτος, τοῖς χείλεσιν αὐτῶν τιμῶσί με, ἡ δὲ καρδία αὐτῶν πόρρω ἀπέχει ἀπ' ἐμοῦ· μάτην δὲ σέβονταί με διδάσκοντες ἐντάλματα ἀνθρώπων καὶ διδασκαλίας. 14) διὰ τοῦτο ἰδοὺ προσθήσω τοῦ μεταθεῖναι τὸν λαὸν τοῦτον καὶ μεταθήσω αὐτοὺς καὶ ἀπολῶ τὴν σοφίαν τῶν σοφῶν καὶ τὴν σύνεσιν τῶν συνετῶν κρύψω. 15) οὐαὶ οἱ βαθέως βουλὴν ποιοῦντες καὶ οὐ διὰ κυρίου· οὐαὶ οἱ ἐν κρυφῇ βουλὴν ποιοῦντες καὶ ἔσται ἐν σκότει τὰ ἔργα αὐτῶν, καὶ ἐροῦσι Τίς ἡμᾶς ἑώρακε καὶ τὶς ἡμᾶς Γνώσεται ἢ ἃ ἡμεῖς ποιοῦμεν;

10) For the Lord has made you to drink a spirit of deep sleep; and he shall close their eyes and the eyes of their prophets and of their rulers who see secret things. 11) And all these things shall be to you as the words of this sealed book, which if they shall give to a learned man, saying, Read this, he shall then say, I cannot read it for it is sealed. 12) And this book shall be given into the hands of a man that is unlearned, and one shall say to him, Read this, and he shall say, I am not learned. 13) And the Lord has said, This people honor me with their lips, but their heart is far from me, but in vain do they worship me, teaching the commandments and doctrines of men. 14) Therefore behold I will proceed to remove this people, and I will remove them, and I will destroy the wisdom of the wise and will hide the understanding of the prudent. 15) Woe to them that deepen their counsel and not by the Lord. Woe to them that take secret counsel and whose works are in darkness and they say, Who has seen us? and who shall know us, or what we do?

For Isaiah 29:11-12, the phenomena of disbelief and ignorance are symbolized by Israel's inability, from the most learned to the more simple, to read the words of a book. This metaphor of Israel's disbelief is concretized by Paul in II Cor. 3:14-15 as their inability to read the "old covenant" or "the books of Moses," just as Isaiah had foretold.[107] This

---

[107] The interpretation, stemming from Origen, of II Cor. 3:16-17 as referring to a spiritual reading of scripture versus a literal reading, while not strictly to the point, has some relevance here. Paul *is* talking about two opposed ways of reading and understanding the scriptures of Israel. Paul's interpretation of the scriptures is "spiritual," if one means by the term an interpretation prompted by the spirit's revelation of their fulfillment in Christ. The "sons of Israel" in Paul's time have not "turned" toward this

ignorance has been represented for Paul, under the influence of Exodus 34 and in keeping with his ongoing effort to apply it to his contemporary experience of Israel, by the veil of Moses. The lack of vision characteristic of Israel at Sinai and caused by the veiling of Moses' face extends into Paul's own day. Evidence for this ignorance or misunderstanding has been found in Prophetic oracles which decry Israel's continuous resistance to the divine will and inability to understand the prophet's own message. It is described by Paul, who has combined the Pentateuchal and Prophetic reports, as a veil lying over Israel's reading of its own scripture and a hardening of its heart.

Summary

The discovery of the relevance of Isaiah 6:9-10, 29:10-12, and Deuteronomy 29:2-4 to II Corinthians 3:14-15 has clarified Paul's thought and its development in these verses in several ways. I will now summarize the meaning of this section beginning from verse 13 and taking into consideration the information which the additional scriptural background has provided. Several questions posed earlier in this section on the basis of Dunn's analysis of II Cor. 3:16-17 have now been answered more fully.

Many narrative elements from the original Exodus story have been drawn into Paul's contemporary scene. The "sons of Israel," actors in the original drama, are present to Paul as well (II Cor. 3:13, 14, 15 and 16). The nominal referent of the repeated use of "αὐτῶν" in these verses is always the "υἱοὺς Ἰσραὴλ" of II Cor. 3:13. Therefore, one set of actors from Exodus 34 is transferred directly into the interpreter's contemporary period, because Israel is not only present, but important to Paul. The other actor, Moses, is not so easily transferred, for obvious reasons. He is present in the contemporary scene, nevertheless, but as a book (II Cor. 3:15). This transference of the witness and authority of Moses himself to his books is a commonplace within the first-century Jewish and Christian communities.

One of the major props of the Exodus story, the veil of Moses, is drawn into the contemporary scene also. Since Moses, whom it originally covered, has become a book, logically the veil should now cover the books of Moses. Instead, it is the *reading* of the book by Israel that is veiled, and not the book itself, in II Cor. 3:14, and the *readers* of the book whose understanding is veiled in II Cor. 3:15. It is easy to imagine why

---

spirit, have not received this revelation and do not, therefore, read their own scriptures correctly. Their reading might be characterized as "literal," on the basis of II Cor. 3:6. While this is not what Origen meant by the opposition between literal and spiritual reading of scripture, his interpretation of the passage does not completely miss the mark.

Paul would want to make this shift. If the veil of Moses still lay upon his book, *no one* in the contemporary scene could see it properly, any more than the Israel of old could gaze upon the man Moses. Paul is quite confident, as his method of argument in II Corinthians 3 itself illustrates, that he and his associates are well able to read Moses' book. They have been enabled to do so by turning to the Lord in conversion as Paul's citation of Exodus 34:34 directs. Since they have done so, the spirit has removed the veil from their hearts and they can see Moses' glory and understand his books. The sons of Israel have not followed this instruction and so remain veiled.

It is this shift in the location of the veil that the scriptural background elucidated above can explain. The veil must move, but, since scripture is being interpreted, scripture itself must provide an explanation for its movement and information regarding its present location. It is axiomatic, especially for emerging rabbinic Judaism, that scripture can only be adequately interpreted by scripture. This viewpoint is completely congenial to the basic impulse of *pesher* exegesis outlined at the beginning of this section. Of course, it is Paul's own experience of the refusal of his Jewish listeners or opponents to accept his interpretations of the scriptures which prompts him to call upon texts as he does. But it is also and equally his conviction that scripture does indeed hold the key to explaining that experience. He is absolutely sincere in this outlook, which I have dubbed a *"pesher* perspective," and faithful to it in this section of his text.[108]

So, in searching the scripture for an explanation for the meaning of the veil, the problem of its current location and its contemporary meaning for Israel, Paul has found several texts which give him the clues that he wants. He probably found them in earlier Christian exegesis of Isaiah already established at the time he was writing, as the evidence from John and Romans indicates.[109] Isaiah 29:10 speaks of a covering, or veiling, of Israel. Both Isaiah 6 and Isaiah 29 lament the hardness of heart, unbelief and ignorance of Israel. Paul sees the situation described

---

[108] As Ragnar BRING has said in a 1971 article, "For him [Paul], as for the early Christians generally, the Old Testament was without any doubt God's own message, revealed by himself; the Old Testament was the Holy Scriptures which must first be understood and then obeyed." "Paul and the Old Testament," *Studia Theologica* 25 (1971) 22. In applying the Prophetic texts to elucidate the text of Exod. 34:29-35, Paul was trying to *understand* the Exodus text better. Having once discovered its meaning for his own time and situation, he understood himself and directed his actions according to the pattern it recommended. II Cor. 3:18 is a self-description based on Paul's exegesis of Exodus 34:29-35 and obedient to its word.

[109] Even though Romans was written at roughly the same time as II Corinthians, Paul's casual introduction in Rom. 11:7-8 of a composite citation involving a text also used in Mark and John indicates widespread and early exegetical work.

by the prophet as the continuation in history of the lack of vision Israel experienced as a result of Moses' veil. He has used Isaiah 6:9-10 and 29:10-12 to interpret and contemporize Exodus 34:33-35. From the time of the Exodus, Israel was hardened, ἐπωρώθη τὰ νοήματα αὐτῶν (II Cor. 3:14).

A closer look at these texts, especially at the immediate contexts in Isaiah 6 and 29, and even Deuteronomy 29, indicates that all contain sufficient verbal links with one another and with the scriptural background previously described in Chapter One of this study to be justifiably hooked into the developing scriptural matrix. Isaiah 6:1-10, taking into account the whole scene of Isaiah's vision, shares the important word "δόξα" with Exodus 34, the key word "καρδία" with the Prophetic text-complex and the word "ὀφθαλμός" with Deuteronomy 29:1-4 and Isaiah 29:10-13. Isaiah 29:9-15 shares the key word "πνεῦμα" with Ezekiel texts, "καρδία" with the whole Prophetic text-complex, and "ὀφθαλμός" with the other members of the set introduced in this chapter. Deuteronomy 29:1-4 can be tied to the Exodus and Jeremiah texts via "διαθήκη," to the Prophetic text-complex through "καρδία" and to its partners in this section through "ὀφθαλμός." Figure 7 expresses these relationships visually in a further elaboration of the text-diagram begun in Chapter One.

Figure 7

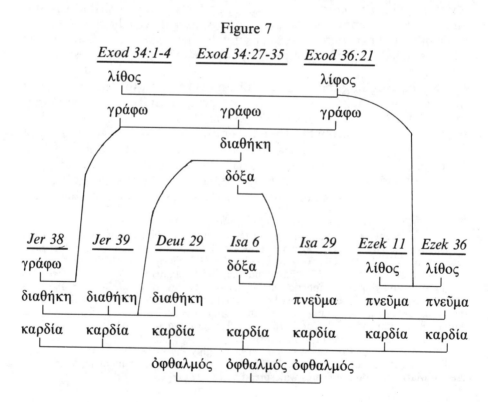

Once these connections have been established, just as in the case of the related texts in Chapter One, the transference of concepts from one to the other that is their mutual interpretation is free to begin. This is what Paul has done in II Cor. 3:14-16. He has used the Isaiah and Deuteronomy texts to interpret Exodus 34 in various ways. The fact that both verse 14 and verse 15 begin with the uncertain and transitional "ἀλλὰ" indicates this interpretative reformulation. These beginning conjunctions might be translated "but scripture also says..." in order to express Paul's intention.

The facet of Exodus 34 which Paul intends Isaiah 6 and 29 to clarify is, as I have said, the veil. On the basis of Isaiah 6:10 and 29:10, Paul asserts in verses 14 and 15 that the veil is now on Israel. On the basis of Isaiah 29:11 alone Paul can assert, as he does in verse 14, that the veil lies on the reading of the old covenant. Finally, on the basis of the conceptual combination of Isaiah 29:11 and 6:10, Paul can assert that the veil lies on the hearts of the Jews.

According to Isaiah 29:11-12 Israel cannot understand the events of its own experience. Israel is in a state of ignorance like that of a man who cannot read when he is confronted with the words of a book or like that of a man told to get his information from a book which is closed and sealed against him. In Isaiah 6:10 this lack of understanding is expressed differently. Israel is like a man whose heart, the seat of his faculty of knowing, is immobilized or stultified. II Cor. 3:15 is a combination of both of these ideas with the metaphor of the veil. Whenever the sons of Israel read the books of Moses, the veil from Exodus 34:34-35 lies on their hearts. The result is the same as the basic notion expressed in Isaiah 6 and 29: Israel does not understand. Israel cannot read its own books; Israel's heart is veiled. Israel's heart is hardened. True to the interpretative impulse of the specific *pesher* which follows in v. 16, the loose adoption in verses 14 and 15 of the idiom "ἕως τῆς ἡμέρας ταύτης" from Deuteronomy 29:4, via its previous association with Isaiah 6 and 29, brings this definition of Israel's condition into Paul's own day.

Exodus 34:34 has given quite specific directions by which this veil can be removed from Israel's heart and verse 16 cites them explicitly, with the interpretative modification that the turning required is conversion. Verse 17a, as has already been argued, draws these directions into the present by substituting a present-day actor, the spirit, for the character of the Exodus story, Yahweh, "the Lord," by whose agency the veil is removed. Thus, the transfer from Exodus to the contemporary scene is completed in verse 17a. Israel is certainly there. The veil has arrived, via Isaiah, and Paul knows where it lies. Moses is there in the form of the books of the old covenant. The means for removing the veil is there via the *pesher* citation and interpretation itself. In verse 18 Paul identifies himself and his allies as "sons of Israel" who have availed themselves of the prescribed means for the veil's removal and goes on to describe their condition as a result. The glory of Moses is there on their faces. In the conclusion of the argument in II Cor. 4:3-4, he also describes the condition of those who have not taken advantage of the spirit's removal of the veil. They are blinded and are being utterly destroyed.

II Cor. 3:18 — A Summary of Paul's Use of Exodus 34:29-35

Verse 18 concludes the preceding argument by drawing a deliberate comparison between Moses' condition and behavior as it is reported in Exodus 34:34-35 and Paul's condition and behavior. This comparison is introduced in verse 17b by the bridging statement "οὖ δὲ τὸ πνεῦμα κυρίου, ἐλευθερία," which, like verse 12 which asserts hope and boldness to be characteristically Christian attitudes, asserts that freedom is similarly a Christian prerogative under the new covenant. This is in direct contrast to Moses' behavior under the old covenant which was characterized by the humility and restraint expressed by his veil.[110]

Paul's ministry, according to verse 18a, again in contrast to that of Moses, is a ministry carried on with an unveiled face. This unveiled condition has two parallel effects in Paul described in verse 18b. The first of these effects is that his face is allowed to reflect the glory of the Lord.[111] This is precisely what Moses' face in Exod. 34:34 was not allowed to do for very long. It is only in contrast to Moses that this reflection takes on its full significance. Paul can and is allowed to do what Moses could not. This must be, if the parallel with Moses is to be sustained, because Paul has availed himself of the same method that Moses had for removing the veil, the method offered in Exodus 34:34, as interpreted by Isaiah 6:10. He has turned to the Lord who is the spirit, as Moses turned to the Lord.

This conclusion is indicated also by the cryptic "καθάπερ ἀπὸ κυρίου πνεύματος" with which the verse, as well as the section, ends. The phrase is grammatically workable, but lacks specific meaning as it

---

[110] VAN UNNIK, "'With Unveiled Face,'" pp. 165-166.

[111] With DUPONT, therefore, I take κατοπτρίζω to mean primarily "to reflect as a mirror does." "Le Chrétien, miroir de la gloire divine d'après II Cor., III, 18," pp. 397, 402, passim, against HUGEDE, La métaphore du miroir, p. 24. The parallelism with Moses in "ἀνακεκαλυμμένῳ προσώπῳ," is determinative for Paul's intention in using the verb. However, this does not at all deny that both Moses and Paul, and all Christians, are also able to see the glory of God as if in a mirror, that mirror being Christ, the image of God (cf. II Cor. 3:18; 4:4,6; HUGEDE, La métaphore du miroir, p. 35). See for a very recent treatment of the same issue, J. LAMBRECHT, "Transformation," pp. 246-251, although I cannot agree that the "contextual arguments decidedly favor the meaning of 'beholding'," p. 248.

stands.[112] It appears to be a shorthand notation of the full expression of his thought which the author has not seen fit to provide. The best way to deal with it, therefore, is to have recourse to the two other instances in this same section of II Corinthians 3, verses 13 and 17, where the same words occur and to decipher from them what Paul's intended meaning in verse 18c might possibly be.[113]

Verse 13 asserts, using the word "καθάπερ," that Paul and his fellows are not like Moses when he veiled his face. This thought is repeated in verse 18a. The appearance of "καθάπερ" in the positive expression of what Paul *is* like is not surprising, but it should be followed once again by "Moses" if the comparison being drawn is to be completed. We are not like Moses when he veiled his face, but we are like Moses. This is the pivotal comparison between verses 13 and 18. When then are we like Moses? Obviously we are like Moses *when he did not veil his face*. We are like Moses when he was in the presence of the Lord (who is also the spirit) and his veil was removed, as Paul has just finished explaining in verses 16-17. Then Moses was free, and bold, and reflected divine glory.[114] The ambiguous "κυρίου" and "πνεύματος" of verse 18c point unmistakably to verse 17 for their explanation if indeed one exists at all in Paul's text. The otherwise superfluous "δὲ" from the beginning of verse 18 further indicates direct reference to what precedes. Taking verse 17a as the model for the conjunction of κύριος and πνεῦμα in 18c then, the best grammatical choice would be that the genitive "πνεύματος" is in apposition to κυρίου on the basis of the identity established in verse 17a. The expression then reads in English "from the Lord who is the spirit."

Paul's intended *meaning* in verse 18 with the addition of "καθάπερ ἀπὸ κυρίου πνεύματος" thus interpreted can, on the basis of this analysis, be presented as something like this — "we all, with an unveiled face, *unlike* Moses when he faced the sons of Israel, reflect the glory of the Lord and are being transfigured into that same image gradually (or on the basis of its brilliance)[115] *like* Moses was when he turned to the Lord, just as we have now done. We, like Moses, derive our glory from the

---

[112] The most distinguished English commentary on the passage, that of PLUMMER, asserts that it is "impossible to decide with certainty what the words mean," *II Corinthians*, p. 108. On the contrary, I think we can attain reasonable certainty by considering the phrase in context.

[113] This is the approach suggested by MOULE, "2 Cor. 3,18b" and DUNN, " 'The Lord is the Spirit.' "

[114] VAN UNNIK, " 'With Unveiled Face,' " p. 167; DUPONT, "Le Chrétien, miroir de la gloire divine," pp. 399, 402.

[115] Recall Note 12 on the translation of II Cor. 3:18 for the alternatives offered here for "ἀπὸ δόξης εἰς δόξαν," both of which are probably intended.

Lord. For us, the Lord is a life-giving spirit." [116] Admittedly, this is an interpretation of the Greek of the text and not a simple translation of it. It is justified, I think, by the shorthand nature of the Greek, by its fidelity to expressions as they are used elsewhere in the section and to Paul's argument as expressed elsewhere, and by its rapport with the exegetical relationship with Exodus 34 of the passage as a whole.

By concluding in this fashion, Paul has brought into play yet another feature of the story in Exodus 34, which is implied in this concluding verse. Exodus 34:35 reports that the sons of Israel saw that Moses' face was glorified when he came out of the Tent of Meeting after talking with the Lord. This means that he was not only glorified on the mountain when he received the covenant, but derived glory from the Lord on a continuing basis. It is this continuing glorification of Moses in which Paul and others are enabled by the spirit to share, according to Paul's cryptic summary "καθάπερ ἀπὸ κυρίου πνεύματος."

Conclusions

My analysis of the explicit argumentation of II Corinthians 3:7-18, as well as of 3:1-6, is now complete. In the course of the present chapter, I have explored Paul's use of Exodus 34:29-35. His interpretation has been carried out using two exegetical methods: *kal va-homer* inference and *pesher* interpretation. We have seen that the terms of the *kal va-homer* inference have been heavily influenced by the new covenant conceptual pool that stands behind II Cor. 3:1-6. On the basis of this interpenetration of the two sections of Chapter 3, verses 1-6 and 7-11, there is no need for the hypothesis of an interpolated source beginning at verse 7. The terms drawn from the preceding section are more significant for our understanding of verses 7-11 than is the rather simple operation of the arguments themselves contained therein. The sole function of the *kal va-homer* inferences is to transfer δόξα from the first covenant minister, Moses, to his later counterpart, Paul.

We have also seen that the explicit *pesher* exegesis of II Cor. 3:16-17 is surrounded by a *"pesher-* like" contemporization of Exodus

---

[116] Such a paraphrase gains some support from Dunn, " 'The Lord is the Spirit,' " p. 314, where he asserts *that* but does not explain *how*, the "ἀπὸ κυρίου πνεύματος" of v. 18 "rounds off" Paul's exposition of and argumentation on Exodus 34. I found this a most fruitful suggestion and have developed my own interpretation as a result. This interpretation does no violence to the grammar of verse 18 and does exploit the clear parallelism between verses 13, 16 and 18 which is more clear on the level of vocabulary than it has been conceptually. I conclude therefore with Dunn and contra Plummer that it is possible to interpret verse 18 adequately.

34:29-35. This reinterpretation of Exodus 34 has been performed under the influence of a further scriptural background from the prophet Isaiah. This additional background describes Israel's chronic state of unbelief. Paul uses it to explain the enduring existence and effect of Moses' veil into his own day and to justify his assertion that Israel does not know how to read and understand its own scriptures. It is not only the veil of Moses which has moved through history into Paul's day. The glory which Moses reflected so briefly and so modestly according to Exodus 34:29-35 has moved through history as well. The glory that Moses revealed, however sparingly or mysteriously, is present in Paul's day on his own, unveiled face.

Throughout the preceding argument, the importance of Moses as counterpart, role model and foil for Paul has been both obvious and immense. The argument of II Corinthians 3 as a whole now appears to be based on Moses and several stories about his life and activity as prototypical for Christian life and the activity of the Christian minister or apostle. This Pentateuchal model is modified and amplified, however, through the use of Prophetic texts. These later oracles, understood to refer specifically to Paul's own time, enable him to adjust the basic prototype which Moses provides to fit his contemporary situation more exactly. For example, because the promised new covenant has arrived with its gift of the spirit, Paul no longer must display the humility of his predecessor Moses. Moses could not reveal everything. Paul may. Paul need not veil his face and may behave with the boldness and freedom characteristic of the full-fledged member of Greek society. Furthermore, Paul knows through the prophet Isaiah that the "sons of Israel" were not only hampered in their vision of the glory of the old covenant, but still possess hardened hearts which cannot understand the glory of the new. These "hardened minds" in Israel stand in direct contrast to the soft and fleshly hearts promised by Ezekiel and given to Paul, which are able to receive the spirit which unveils and reveals and enlivens. In Moses' day, according to II Cor. 3:14, it had not been revealed that *in Christ* the covenant, ministry and glory of Moses would be brought to an end (μὴ ἀνακαλυπτόμενον, ὅτι ἐν Χριστῷ καταργεῖται). This is what unbelieving, veiled Israel could not see in Moses' day and still cannot see in Paul's.

CHAPTER THREE

CONCLUSIONS, UNANSWERED QUESTIONS AND SUGGESTIONS FOR FURTHER RESEARCH

Introduction

Moses as Model

This final chapter of my study of II Corinthians 3:1-4:6 returns to the question of Paul's self-defense. Although II Cor. 3:1 protests against the making of a new beginning with the Corinthians by undertaking to recommend, or justify, himself, to them again, the argument of II Cor. 3:2-18 is the beginning of just such a renewed self-identification on Paul's part as an implicit defense of his conduct as an apostle. In II Cor. 4:1 Paul turns explicitly to a discussion of that conduct. Paul argues that his behavior is in complete conformance with the proper model of ministry.

In II Cor. 4:1-6, Moses is Paul's primary model for the proper conduct of a minister (διάκονος) or servant (δοῦλος) of God. Moses was an important model for various groups within Judaism at this time.[1] The figure of Moses was understood in several different ways, however, corresponding to the distinguishing characteristics of the groups themselves. For some he was the perfect philosopher, the ideal king and

---

[1] On the various roles assigned to Moses during this period, see J. JEREMIAS, "Μωϋσῆς, " *TDNT* IV, pp. 848-873; Renée BLOCH, "Quelques aspects de la figure de Moïse dans la tradition rabbinique" in *Moïse. L'homme de l'alliance* (Tournai: Desclee & Co., 1955) pp. 93-167; Bernard BOTTE, "La vie de Moïse par Philon" in *Moïse. L'homme de l'alliance,* pp. 55-62; P. DEMANN, "Moïse et la loi dans la pensée de Saint Paul" in *Moïse. L'homme de l'alliance,* pp. 189-242; A. DESCAMPS, "Moïse dans les Evangiles et dans la tradition apostolique" in *Moïse. L'homme de l'alliance,* pp. 171-187; Geza VERMES, "La figure de Moïse au tournant des deux Testaments" in *Moïse. L'homme de l'alliance,* pp. 55-62; Howard M. TEEPLE, *The Mosaic Eschatological Prophet.* Journal of Biblical Literature Monograph Series X (Philadelphia: Society of Biblical Literature, 1957) especially pp. 29-73, 100-115; C. K. BARRETT, *From First Adam to Last,* pp. 46-67; GEORGI, *Die Gegner,* especially pp. 145-167, 258-265; Wayne MEEKS, *The Prophet-King. Moses Traditions and the Johannine Christology.* Supplements to Novum Testamentum XIV (Leiden: E. J. BRILL, 1967) Chapters III, IV. VII; John G. GAGER, *Moses in Greco-Roman Paganism* (Nashville: Abingdon Press, 1972); David TIEDE, *The Charismatic Figure as Miracle Worker* pp. 101-240; Carl H. HOLLADAY, *Theios Aner in Hellenistic Judaism.* Chapters 2 and 3 passim; Mary Rose D'ANGELO, *Moses in the Letter to the Hebrews. SBL* Dissertation Series 42 (Missoula, Montana: Scholars Press, 1979), as well as the primary texts and older bibliography cited therein.

priest; for others, a visionary and wonder-worker;[2] for still others, the prophet par excellence. It is in this last group that Paul, and a significant segment of early Christianity and Judaism with him, belong. Of course, distinctions between these various views of Moses cannot be too sharply drawn. They tend to mix and are distinguishable only according to the dominant tone struck in each portrait. The biblical tradition in the Pentateuch itself provides justification for each picture.[3] In Exodus, Numbers and Deuteronomy, Moses means many things to Israel and performs many deeds in God's service. He is liberator,[4] miracle-worker,[5] mediator,[6] judge,[7] law-giver,[8] prophet[9] and priest.[10] Selection among the various facets of the elaborate portrait of Moses developed during the long composition, assembly and redaction of the Pentateuchal traditions is made according to the contemporary needs and concerns of any reader or interpreter. Paul's understanding of Moses was no doubt influenced by his concerns both as a Jew in the first century, Greco-Roman world and by his commitment to faith in Jesus Christ.

In a subsequent study I shall undertake to investigate the figure of Moses in the Intertestamental and New Testament periods as well as the Pauline appropriation of this paradigm in his authentic letters. For now, however, we shall focus only on Paul's use of the figure of Moses as model in the conclusion of the particular exegetical argument which has been the subject of the present study. Paul has nearly single-mindedly chosen the picture of Moses as prophet as his model of apostleship in II Corinthians, especially II Corinthians 3. His conformance to that model

----

[2] This aspect of the figure of Moses as it is presented in the ancient sources has been reviewed and emphasized in the work of GEORGI, GAGER, TIEDE and HOLLADAY, while the earlier work of French and Scandinavian scholars and more recent studies emerging out of Yale University in the United States stress his prophetic character.

[3] Albert GELIN, "Moïse dans l'Ancien Testament" in *Moïse. L'homme de l'alliance*, pp. 29-52.

[4] Exod. 3:10-12, 14:1-31; 17:8-13.

[5] Exod. 4:29-31; 9:8-12, 22-35; 10:12-29; 11:10; 17:4-7; Num. 20:6-13.

[6] Exod. 19:3-25; 20:18-22; 32:11-14, 30-34; Num. 14:10-20.

[7] Exod. 18:13-26.

[8] Exod. 24:3-4, 7; 34:27-35:1; Deut. 1:1-5; 4:44-45; 5:1-5; 31:9-13, etc.

[9] Deut. 18:15-18; 31:26-29; 34:10-12.

[10] Exod. 24:4b-8. Certainly, these differences in Moses' role in Israel sometimes reflect the various sources which have been brought together to produce the Pentateuchal narrative which we now possess (GELIN, "Moïse dans l'Ancien Testament," pp. 31-32). CHILDS' analysis of the Book of Exodus is done very much from the point of view of differences in the presentation of Moses' office (*Exodus*, p. 357 as an example of this general thesis). We cannot analyze these sources here, however, and this omission is, to a certain extent, justified by Paul himself. Paul would not have seen differing literary sources behind the tapestry of Moses' biblical portrait. He would have seen, more simply, a single man of vast blessing and power in his variety of functions — the greatest man of God presented by his biblical tradition.

is the backbone of his self-defense. Since the focus here will be on the conclusion to Paul's argument in II Cor. 3:1-18 which is contained in II Cor. 4:1-6, it is important to see the relationship between the conclusions drawn there by Paul and the argument which is summarized by them.

Chapter One of this study has elicited the scriptural background for Paul's statements in II Cor. 3:1-6 from Jeremiah 38:31-34 and 39:37-42 (LXX); Ezekiel 11:16-23, 36:24-32 and 37:1-14 as well as Exodus 4:10-12. Chapter Two analyzed Paul's explicit use of Exodus 34:27-35 in II Cor. 3:7-18 and described the influence of a further Prophetic background drawn from Isaiah 6:1-10 and 29:10-12 especially. In both of those chapters the task at hand was to enable the modern reader to see Paul the exegete at work. The probable exegetical structure of his scriptural materials and the certain exegetical structure of the arguments he presents in II Cor. 3:7-18 were used to provide a doorway through which the modern reader could enter into his thought-process itself.

Now we end with Paul the apostle defining and defending himself and his ministry in terms and patterns supplied to him by his scriptural background and his earlier arguments based upon it. We need to see how that foregoing material allows him to put together the defense which II Cor. 4:1-6 presents. Paul's defense is really a counter-offensive which makes use of the full force of the divine authority of the scriptural background which we can now see standing behind his words to Corinth. The task of this brief chapter, therefore, is to explore this counter-offensive as it is begun in II Cor. 4:1-6. Certainly, Paul's self-defense does not end at II Cor. 4:6. Most commentators would agree that it continues through Chapter 7 and is picked up again in Chapters 10-13 of II Corinthians. Therefore, in order to do justice to the question, in further investigations the analysis done on this single text should be validated in the literary unit of which it is now a part. If my arguments regarding II Cor. 3:1-4:6 really reach into and adequately represent Paul's own thought, then traces of his method as I have described it, and of his self-understanding as I will present it here should be found in the rest of II Corinthians, and in his other epistles as well. The outlines of the picture of Paul as the new Moses, minister of the new Christian covenant, which are available from II Cor. 3:1-4:6 alone, can be colored in through use of the larger field available to us when we take advantage of the traditional literary unit of which the smaller selection is part,[11] as well as the letter corpus within which II Corinthians stands.

---

[11] This line of argument would presume some sort of unity of the letter as it is received. Such a working assumption is valid on two grounds. First, the witness of the textual tradition of II Corinthians to the unity of the letter as we have it is really unassailable in the last analysis. Because of this tradition, the interpreter is entitled to work with the letter as a whole despite the conclusions of very recent scholarship on the

The Primary Text — II Corinthians 4:1-6

Therefore, having this ministry inasmuch as we have received mercy,[12] we do not lose heart. Instead, we renounce the hidden things of shame, neither walking in cunning [13] nor adulterating the word of God,[14] but by the clear display of the truth recommending ourselves to every conscience of men in the presence of God. And if indeed our gospel is veiled, it is veiled in those who are being destroyed, in whom the god of this age blinded the minds of the ones who do not believe,[15] so that they would not see the light of the

---

compilation of the Pauline corpus. Second, even a compiler, granted any intelligence and literary sensitivity at all, perceives or constructs a unity in the materials which he joins. Therefore, analysis of such redactional unity, parallel to that perceived and analyzed in gospel research, is a continuing possibility. On either level — compositional or redactional — the whole of II Corinthians should support the interpretation given for any single passage.

[12] Commentators agree that "καθὼς ἠλεήθημεν" should be read with what precedes. COLLANGE, *Enigmes*, p. 127; PLUMMER, *II Corinthians*, p. 110.

[13] The verb "περιπατέω" is used by Paul in the Old Testament sense as a synonym for "to live, to conduct one's life;" COLLANGE, *Enigmes*, p. 129.

[14] Paul's phrase "δολοῦντες τον λόγον τοῦ θεοῦ" is interesting in two ways. First, it is a good parallel for the expression "κατηλεύοντες τὸν λόγον τοῦ θεοῦ" in II Cor. 2:17. In both cases Paul is denying that he is a cheap and dishonest peddler, prone to diluting or tainting the wares he sells. Paul's denial that he in any sense "sells" his message is vehement elsewhere in the Corinthian letters (I Cor. 9:6-18; II Cor. 11:7-12; 12:13-18). Both verbs are used to refer especially to sellers of wine and incense, and the metaphor of incense does seem to be present in II Cor. 2:14-15. See BRUCE, *1 and 2 Corinthians*, pp. 187-189, 195; HUGHES, *Second Epistle*, pp. 77-80, 83 and note 22. Second, there is not unanimity in critical opinion about the meaning of the phrase "τὸν λόγον τοῦ θεοῦ." I understand it to mean the word of God in scripture, both here and in 2:17, with COLLANGE, *Enigmes*, p. 129 and STRACHAN and against PLUMMER, *II Corinthians*, p. 112, and HUGHES.

[15] The grammar of this verse is problematic. COLLANGE, *Enigmes*, p. 133, on "ἐν οἷς ... τῶν ἀπίστων," says simply that it is "incorrecte." Both PLUMMER, *II Corinthians*, p. 114 and ZERWICK, *Analysis* II, p. 541 dismiss the problem and translate "ἐν οἷς" as "in whose case." I do not think that a certain translation can be made. I would prefer to translate: "among whom (ἐν οἷς) the god of this age blinded the minds of the unbelievers," as a more literal reproduction of Paul's Greek. This translation presupposes, though, a larger group (τοῖς ἀπολλυμένοις, v. 3), those who are being destroyed (cf. II Cor. 2:15-16) and a more specific, smaller subset of those (τῶν ἀπίστων, v. 4), the unbelievers, i.e., those who do not believe in Jesus Christ as Lord. I do not think that this is wholly far-fetched since Paul argues elsewhere that all of sinful mankind is subject to the wrath of God (Rom. 1:18; 2:1-2, 9; 3:5-20) except those who believe in Jesus Christ (Rom. 3:21-26), and yet makes a considerable issue out of the relationship of Jew and Gentile within this situation. Therefore, following the context of such an argument in Romans 1-3, the larger group would be the whole of mankind which is perishing in sin. The Jews, however, while included within this larger group, can be further divided into those who believe in Jesus and those who do not. The term "ἄπιστος" is most properly applied to such an unbelieving Jew. Gentiles who do not believe in Jesus Christ will perish, but *Jews* who do not believe *have been blinded and will perish*, because they had a revelation of the Image of God in their scriptures but could not see him. This hypothesis

gospel of the glory of Christ who is the Image of God. For we do not proclaim ourselves, but Christ Jesus as Lord, and ourselves as your servants on account of Jesus,[16] since it is the God who says "Out of darkness light will shine," who shone into our hearts for the illumination of the knowledge of the glory of God in the face of Christ.[17]

II Corinthians 4:1-6 as Conclusion

Indications

The customary chapter division after II Corinthians 3:18 is widely recognized to be both mistaken and misleading.[18] II Cor. 3:18 is an exceptionally difficult verse. Its artificial isolation, created by this incorrect chapter break, contributes unnecessarily to its obscurity. While 3:18 is intended to conclude the explicit treatment of Exodus 34:27-35

---

cannot be substantiated out of II Cor. 3:1-4:6 alone, however, and so I have not reflected it in my translation. It is a topic for further research. The hypothesis is not without rapport with Paul's argument in II Cor. 3, however, since it does discuss contemporary "sons of Israel" in distinction to those who have the revelation of Christ and does so in the context of the Christological interpretation of their own scriptures.

[16] It is often held that Paul refers to the earthly Jesus when he uses the name "Jesus" alone as he does at the end of v. 5. GEORGI, *Die Gegner*, pp. 283, 286 and PLUMMER, *II Corinthians*, p. 119, for example. If this is true, I wonder whether there may be a part of the Jesus-tradition behind II Cor. 4:5. Paul seems to reflect an understanding of ministry similar to that contained in Mt. 20:24-28 par; 23:11-12 par, especially Mt. 20:26-27 / Mk. 10:43-44 —"... whoever would be great among you must be your servant (διάκονος) and whoever would be first among you must be your slave (δοῦλος)." The context of this saying in the gospels is the suffering and death of the Lord himself. It is of course equally true that Paul does not make an absolute disjunction between the human Jesus and the resurrected Lord. It is the same Jesus who lived, died and was raised (PLUMMER, *II Corinthians*, pp. 130-131; COLLANGE, *Enigmes*, p. 138). Nevertheless, I must agree with GEORGI that Paul sees the death and resurrection as a distinct change in the status of Jesus Christ, which Paul's opponents may not have recognized (*Die Gegner*, pp. 286-287, 292-293, 300). After his resurrection, Jesus was something that he was not during his earthly life — the glorified Lord. In this case, Paul might use the name "Jesus" alone to refer to something particularly characteristic of Jesus in his earthly ministry in Israel, his role as δοῦλος and his recommendation of the same pattern of service to his followers.

[17] According to COLLANGE, *Enigmes*, pp. 141-142 and JERVELL, *Imago Dei*, p. 197, Paul is reflecting traditional, and probably cultic, language in II Cor. 4:6, as well as in 3:18 and 4:4. Its original setting might have been an early baptismal hymn. A. BENOIT, *Le baptême chrétien au second siecle*, p. 85 is cited in support here by COLLANGE, while JERVELL simply refers to WINDISCH's commentary in general. I find this suggestion preferable to the more common view, that II Cor. 4:4 and 6 reflect Paul's conversion experience on the road to Damascus (see COLLANGE, *Enigmes*, p. 138).

[18] PLUMMER, *II Corinthians*, p. 109 who asserts that the first six verses of Chapter 4 are a series of 3 couplets — verses 1-2 on the glory of the new ministry, verses 3-4 on the condition of those who cannot see the glory of the gospel and verses 5-6 on the source of this glory. I cannot see his theme in verses 1-2, which seem to me to summarize and reject criticisms made against the new ministry rather than describe its glory.

which was begun in 3:7, it does not solve the difficulties over authority, legitimacy and acceptance with which Chapter 3 began. II Cor. 4:1-6, on the other hand, does provide this more general conclusion. In II Cor. 4:1-6 in response to a challenge to his authority and/or criticism of his conduct as a minister, Paul draws out of the scriptural texts assembled as the background for II Cor. 3:1-18, themes specifically related to the issues of enablement by God, proper conduct before men and the response to be expected by those who are sent by the Lord to Israel. These themes are then further elaborated in the rest of II Corinthians.

Numerous grammatical and lexical features indicate the unity of 4:1-6 with what precedes. The first verse of the section begins with the strong connective "διὰ τοῦτο," introducing the logical conclusion of what has gone before. Since Paul has just finished describing his own ministry in comparison and contrast to that of Moses in II Cor. 3:18, the "διακονίαν ταύτην" of 4:1 should logically refer to his reflection of the glory of the Lord described there, just as the connective indicates that it does.

The correspondences in theme and vocabulary between II Cor. 3:1-18 and II Cor. 4:1-6 reinforce this logical and grammatical connection. The reference to the "word of god" (τὴν λόγον τοῦ θεοῦ) in 4:2 corresponds to the "reading" (ἀναγινώσκω) of the "old covenant" and of "Moses" in 3:14 and 15. The "clear display of the truth" (τῇ φανερώσει τῆς ἀληθείας) in 4:2 corresponds to Paul's "unveiled face" (ἀνακεκαλυμμένῳ προσώπῳ) in 3:18, especially since it is joined to an explicit reference to veiling in 4:3 (κεκαλυμμένον τὸ εὐαγγέλιον ἡμῶν) which points directly back to the discussion of Moses' veil in 3:13-18. II Corinthians 4:2 repeats the verb "ασυνίστημι" with which the unit begins in 3:1. Finally, the repetition of the terms "εἰκών" and "δόξα" in 4:4 and 4:6 provide a thematic and verbal association with "τὴν δόξαν κυρίου κατοπτριζόμενοι τὴν αὐτὴν εἰκόνα μεταμορφούμεθα" of 3:18.

Chapter 4, verse 6, then, is the real conclusion of the argument begun in 3:1, A new topic is begun in 4:7 and carried on until 6:10 — the treasure hidden in earthen vessels. [19] This theme is not unrelated to the argument of 3:1-4:6, but it moves in the opposite direction. From II Cor. 4:7 on, Paul's emphasis is on the earthly side of his heavenly ministry. In the previous section he directed attention upward in describing the treasure itself, the shared glory of the Christ into whose image all Christians are gradually being transformed.

---

[19] PLUMMER, *Il Corinthians*, pp. 121-123.

Scriptural citations and allusions within the conclusion itself

Before discussing its appropriation or modification of the model of ministry provided by Moses, several peculiarities of the text of II Cor. 4:1-6 itself should be unravelled. In each case, an obscurity in II Cor. 4:1-6 leads to the recognition of a scriptural background informing Paul's argument. II Cor. 4:6 contains a composite quotation of Genesis 1:3 and Isaiah 9:2. II Cor. 4:4 reflects a further use of Isaiah 6:10 which corresponds to Paul's earlier reference to Isaiah 6 in II Cor. 3:14.

Genesis 1 and Isaiah 9

In spite of the fact that the whole unit, II Cor. 3:1-4:6, has been continuously occupied with an interpretation of Old Testament texts, II Corinthians 4:6 contains its only explicit quotation of a particular scripture text. At first glance, Paul's reference in II Cor. 4:6 seems to be to the creation of light (φῶς) in Genesis 1:3. Genesis 1:1-3 reads in the Septuagint: [20]

> 1) Ἐν ἀρχῇ ἐποίησεν ὁ θεὸς τὸν οὐρανὸν καὶ τὴν γῆν. 2) ἡ δὲ γῆ ἦν ἀόρατος καὶ ἀκατασκεύαστος, καὶ σκότος ἐπάνω τῆς ἀβύσσου, καὶ πνεῦμα θεοῦ ἐπεφέρετο ἐπάνω τοῦ ὕδατος. 3) καὶ εἶπεν ὁ θεός Γενηθήτω φῶς. καὶ ἐγένετο φῶς.

> In the beginning God made the heaven and the earth. But the earth was unsightly and unfurnished and darkness was over the deep and the Spirit of God moved over the water. And God said "Let there be light," and there was light.

The "ὁ θεὸς ὁ εἰπών" of II Cor. 4:6a mimics the "εἶπεν ὁ θεός" of Genesis 1:3.

There are, however, two difficulties with seeing Genesis 1:3 as Paul's sole source-text. The verb in Genesis 1:3 is γίνομαι not λάμπω, as in II Cor. 4:6. Furthermore, the terms "φῶς" and "σκότος" are not coupled in the creation formula in Genesis 1:3 as they are in II Cor. 4:6. A situation of darkness (σκότος) is presumed in Genesis from verse 2, but the terms are not set in parallel in God's creative word. These discrepancies suggest that we look elsewhere for a secondary scriptural influence on the form of the Pauline citation. [21]

---

[20] The Greek text of Genesis 1:1-3 is taken from the critical text of the Göttingen edition, *Septuaginta. Vetus Testamentum Graecum I. Genesis.* Edited by John W. WEVERS (Göttingen: Vandenhoeck & Ruprecht, 1974). As was the case with the texts of the Septuagint cited earlier in this study, the English translation is from the Bagster edition.

[21] COLLANGE, *Enigmes,* pp. 138-140 argues strongly that Paul's reference is to Isa. 9:1 (Hebrew text) *rather than* to Gen. 1:3. He is followed by RICHARD, "Polemics," pp. 359-361. I prefer, however, to see it as a composite quotation, a mutual interpretation of Genesis creation and Isaianic recreation, although I would not disagree with RICHARD's analysis of the structure of the verse ("Polemics," pp. 360-361). See also JERVELL, *Imago Dei,* p. 195.

Isaiah 9:2 offers the only instance in the Septuagint in which the terms "φῶς," "σκότος," and "λάμπω" are closely associated. Moreover, the form of the verb "λάμπω" in Isa. 9:2 (LXX) is identical to Paul's usage in II Cor. 4:6. The future "λάμψει" is used in both cases. Isaiah 9:2 reads in the Septuagint:

> 2) ὁ λαὸς ὁ πορευόμενος ἐν σκότει, ἴδετε φῶς μέγα· οἱ κατοικοῦντες ἐν χώρᾳ καὶ σκιᾷ θανάτου, φῶς λάμψει ἐφ' ὑμᾶς.

> 2) O people walking in darkness, behold a great light: ye that dwell in the region and shadow of death, a light shall shine upon you.[22]

It is extremely likely that Paul has amplified and altered his reference to Genesis 1:3 with the vocabulary of Isaiah 9:2 (LXX). Because he has done so, as I have argued before in Chapter One of this study, we can conclude that Paul understands Genesis 1:3 and Isaiah 9:2 (LXX) to be mutually interpreting. The two texts are easily associated verbally via both φῶς and σκότος. In their exegetical association, the creation of light is viewed as salvific, or redemptive, while the salvation promised by Isaiah is cast as creative, or re-creative.

Still, the correspondence between Paul's citation and these cited texts is not quite perfect. In Isaiah 9:2 (LXX) the verb "λάμπω" does not occur within a direct parallelism of σκότος and φῶς. A closer pairing of the two nouns occurs at Isaiah 58:10, although without the verb "λάμπω." Isaiah 58:10 reads in context:

> 8) τότε ῥαγήσεται πρόιμον τὸ φῶς σου, καὶ τὰ ἰάματά σου ταχὺ ἀνατελεῖ, καὶ προπορεύσεται ἔμπροσθέν σου ἡ δικαιοσύνη σου, καὶ ἡ δόξα τοῦ θεοῦ περιστελεῖ σε· 9) τότε βοήσῃ, καὶ ὁ θεὸς εἰσακούσεταί σου· ἔτι λαλοῦντός σου ἐρεῖ 'ἰδοὺ πάρειμι. ἐὰν ἀφέλῃς ἀπὸ σοῦ σύνδεσμον καὶ χειροτονίαν καὶ ῥῆμα γογγυσμοῦ 10) καὶ δῷς πεινῶντι τὸν ἄρτον ἐκ ψυχῆς σου καὶ ψυχὴν τεταπεινωμένην ἐμπλήσῃς, τότε ἀνατελεῖ ἐν τῷ σκότει τὸ φῶς σου, καὶ τὸ σκότος σου ὡς μεσημβρία. 11) καὶ ἔσται ὁ θεός σου μετὰ σοῦ διὰ παντός· καὶ ἐμπλησθήσῃ καθάπερ ἐπιθυμεῖ ἡ ψυχή σου, καὶ τὰ ὀστᾶ σου πιανθήσεται, καὶ ἔσται ὡς κῆπος μεθύων καὶ ὡς πηγὴ ἥν μὴ ἐξέλιπεν ὕδωρ.

> 8) Then shall thy light break forth as the morning, and thy health shall speedily spring forth; and thy righteousness shall go before thee. 9) Then shalt thou cry, and God shall hearken to thee; while thou art yet speaking he will say, "Behold, I am here." If thou remove from thee the band, and the stretching forth of the hands, and murmuring speech; 10) and if thou

---

[22] Like the selections taken from the Septuagint text of Isaiah in Chapter Two of this study, this and the following citation are drawn from the critical Göttingen text and the translation is once again from the Bagster edition.

give bread to the hungry from thy heart, and satisfy the afflicted soul; then shall thy light spring up in darkness, and thy darkness shall be as noon-day; 11) and thy God shall be with thee continually, and thou shalt be satisfied according as thy soul desires; and thy bones shall be made fat, and shall be as a well-watered garden, and as a fountain from which the water has failed.

The phrase "ἀνατελεῖ ἐν τῷ σκότει τὸ φῶς" brings the two nouns into a closer parallelism than that in which they stand in Isa. 9:2 (LXX). It is possible, then that Isa. 58:10 may also have influenced the phrasing of Paul's reference to the Genesis report of God's creation of the primal light. Isaiah 58:10 can similarly be verbally linked with the other two texts through φῶς and σκότος. If it is so linked, then Genesis 1:3, Isaiah 9:2 (LXX) and Isaiah 58:10 all stand together as mutually interpreting behind II Corinthians 4:6. This new Isaiah text adds the theme of righteous actions to that of salvific creation and re-creation presented by Genesis 1:3 and Isa. 9:2 (LXX). Light springs up in darkness because murmuring has ceased and the hungry are fed (v. 9). In addition, verse 8 promises that the glory of God (ἡ δόξα τοῦ θεοῦ) will encompass the righteous Israel. Δόξα provides another verbal link with Paul's earlier scriptural background and increases the likelihood that this text too is relevant to Paul's citation.

In conclusion, therefore, we can say that Paul's exegetical activity once again stands behind the deceptively simple phrase, "ὁ θεὸς ὁ εἰπών, Ἐχ σκότους φῶς λάμψει" of II Cor. 4:6. First, under the influence of Isaiah 9:2 (LXX), and possibly 58:10, Paul has altered the form in which he has cited Genesis 1:3, thus uniting the texts. The conceptual combination of the texts is the significant result of such exegesis. For Paul, Genesis 1 and these prophecies of Isaiah stand together. They are mutually explanatory. The interpretation of Pentateuchal texts on the basis of prophecy has been a basic feature of Paul's method of argument in II Cor. 3:1-18. It seems that this methodology continues in his conclusion. The composite citation in II Cor. 4:6 indicates, first, that the theme of creation is significant for Paul's argument.[23] The probable use of Isa. 9:2 (LXX) and 58:10 in conjunction with Genesis 1:3 indicates as well that a shift toward the prophecies of Isaiah as a hermeneutical key to understanding that theme may be underway in Paul's composition. II Cor. 4:4 also offers another evidence for the influence of Isaiah.

---

[23] I cannot agree with JERVELL, who says that II Cor. 3:18-4:6 is *primarily* an interpretation of Gen. 1 (*Imago Dei* pp. 173-176, 194-197). It is primarily a defense of Paul's apostolate according to a Mosaic pattern influenced by a Christology drawn in part from reflection on the Genesis stories about primeval events and realities, as reinterpreted by prophetic texts.

Isaiah 6

In Chapter Two of his study, I referred to John 12:40 in order to establish Paul's reference to Isaiah 6:10 in II Corinthians 3:14 with the verb "πωρόω." It is possible that Isa. 6:10 again provides an explanation for the presence of the verb "τυφλόω" in II Cor. 4:4.[24] As in Chapter Two, however, evidence for the influence of Isa. 6:10 in II Corinthians must be drawn indirectly through John 12.

Within his quotation of Isaiah 6:10 in 12:40, the author of John uses the expression "τετύφλωκεν αὐτῶν τοὺς ὀφθαλμούς." That he intends a quotation of Isaiah 6:10 cannot be doubted, since it is introduced in 12:39 with the formula "εἶπεν 'Ἠσαιάς." As was the case with the verb "πωρόω" which immediately follows in the Johannine citation, τυφλόω does not occur as a Septuagint variant of Isa. 6:10 today. Therefore, John is working with a Greek text of Isaiah of which we have no knowledge or he is translating a Hebrew text.

Whatever the case, in light of John 12:40 it appears that Paul may also bear witness to this form of citation of Isaiah 6:10 in II Cor. 3:14 with πωρόω and in II Cor. 4:4 with τυφλόω. In both cases the variant verbs with which John 12:40 cites Isaiah 6:10 are present in Paul's text. In both cases, while not citing the Isaiah text explicitly, Paul is arguing in a way that is parallel to common Christian apologetic use of the passage from Isaiah to explain the unbelief which greeted Jesus and the Christian message from the Jews. In II Cor. 3:14, Paul refers to a "hardening" that prevents understanding. In II Cor. 4:4, he speaks of a "blinding" that similarly prevents understanding. In II Cor. 3:14 the Israelites in Moses' time could not see the consummation of Moses' glory. In II Cor. 4:4 the Jews of Paul's own day cannot see the light of his own preaching of the glory of Christ. Because Paul's use of Isa 6:10 in II Cor. 3:14 is well indicated by the rarity of the verb, it is possible to conclude for II Cor. 4:4 as well, because of the verbal correspondence with John, that Paul intends a second reference to Isaiah. Paul's reflection of Isaiah 6:10 is, however, modified in two specific ways, both of which find some echo in John 12 and both of which indicate wider Christian interpretation of this classic prophecy than these two Pauline remnants of it encompass.

First, in II Cor. 3:14 and 4:4 the noun following πωρόω and τυφλόω is νόημα, from νοῦς, the verbal form of which is νοέω, to perceive. The nouns which are expected from Isaiah 6:10 are καρδία and οφθαλμός, and these are the nouns which John 12:40 contains. This variation between John and Paul seems to me to indicate that John 12:40 and II Cor. 3:14 and 4:4 reflect a difference in translation or interpretation of the Hebrew text of Isaiah 6:10, rather than a variant Greek text. In John

---

[24] So also B. LINDARS, *New Testament Apologetic*, pp. 162-163.

12:40 the wording "τετύφλωκεν αὐτῶν τοὺς ὀφθαλμοὺς καὶ ἐπώρωσεν αὐτῶν τὴν καρδίαν ..." is a fairly literal, though partial, translation of the wording of Isaiah 6:10. II Cor. 3:14, however, rather than citing the *words* of the prophecy, seems to translate its *meaning*, particularly in the Hebrew. Paul's "ἐπωρώθη τὰ νοήματα αὐτῶν" translates the Semitic idea that the heart is the seat of understanding and knowledge within the human person for the Greek, for whom the locus of knowledge is the mind, or νοῦς. Paul, therefore, has repeated the intention of the prophet's hebrew wording rather than its expression. John too goes on to reflect a similar understanding of this Hebrew meaning in 12:40b, with the verb "νοέω," in "ἵνα μὴ ... νοήσωσιν τῇ καρδίᾳ ..." The verb "νοέω" does not stem from the Septuagint of Isaiah 6. There the verb is "ἀσυνίημι." Therefore, both Paul and John have done their best to convey the sense of the Hebrew but in different forms. Paul conveys this sense in an allusion to the text rather than in a citation and therefore his expression of the main clause varies from that of John. In Paul's view, his hearers do not understand his message about Jesus Christ. They cannot see the light emanating from the glory of the object of his preaching, any more than Israel could in the case of Moses. He therefore repeats the νοήματα, which stems from 3:14, in 4:4 as the object of τυφλόω instead of "eyes." Here it is less appropriate than it was in II Cor. 3:14 where it replaced "hearts."

Paul's second variation from Isaiah 6:10 is in 4:4 only. He ascribes the "blinding" of the minds to the god of this age, "ὁ θεὸς τοῦ αἰῶνος τούτου." This unique expression seems to convey a common belief of the period that there was a power, or powers, not God ruling the visible cosmos which, if evil, was responsible for the human experience of evil.[25] In Jewish apocalyptic literature the hope that God himself would again exercise control over his creation, vanquish the power of evil and restore order and goodness at the end of this age and thus inaugurate the age to

---

[25] See E. R. Dodds' reference to Plato on the demonic (*Symposium* 202D 13-203A 6), although Dodds applies it to a somewhat later time. Plato says, "Everything that is daemonic ... is intermediate between God and mortal. Interpreting and conveying the wishes of men to gods and the will of gods to men, it stands between the two and fills the gap ..." Dodds says, "This precise definition of the vague terms 'daemon' and 'daemonios' was something of a novelty in Plato's day, but in the second century after Christ it was the expression of a truism. Virtually everyone, pagan, Jewish, Christian or Gnostic, believed in the existence of these beings and in their function as mediators, whether he called them daemons or angels or aions or simply 'spirits'. *Pagan and Christian in an Age of Anxiety* (New York: W. W. Norton & Co., 1970) pp. 37-38. See further, for example, Russell, *Between the Testaments*, p. 112; Joseph Bonsirven, *Palestinian Judaism in the Time of Jesus Christ*. Translated by W. Wolf (New York: Holt, Rinehart and Winston, 1964) pp. 33-41.

come had become a central belief.[26] The figure of a single, evil demi-god does not appear explicitly with much frequency in the New Testament, however, but interestingly, it does appear, under a very similar name, in John 12:31 "ὁ ἄρχων τοῦ κόσμου τούτου."[27] The appearance of this figure in the context of two separate discussions of Isaiah 6:10 may indicate a more general Christian tendency to use such a Satanic figure to explain the hardening and blindness which was perceived to have overtaken Israel just as Isaiah had predicted it would.

John 12 contains several other similarities to Paul's ongoing argument in II Corinthians 3-4. The themes, and the texts, which immediately precede and follow John's citation of Isa. 6:10 in 12:40 especially resemble II Cor. 4:3-6 and its background. John 12:38 contains a citation of Isaiah 53:1. The thematic importance of this text for John is the theme of unbelief which it explicitly presents. The citation of Isa. 6:10 follows immediately to explain this unbelief. However, no *verbal* hook connects the two citations. The two texts can only be linked verbally through δόξα, which occurs at Isa. 53:2 and 6:1. It becomes apparent that John appreciates this as the link between the two texts that he has cited in Jn. 12:41 — Isaiah said this (verses 38 and 40 / Isa. 53:1 and 6:10) because he saw his glory, δόξα. This vision has reference to both Isa. 6:1 and Isa. 53:2 and plays on their connection. Isaiah himself saw the glory of the Lord in his inaugural vision. Isaiah 53:2 can be taken to contrast with this vision. It refers to *not* seeing glory in the Lord's servant. John is able to develop, on the basis of this verbal and thematic combination of texts, the paradox of the reality of glory in Christ, hidden from the eyes of ordinary men, in 12:37, 42-43.

John 12, therefore, bears witness to the combination of at least Isaiah 6 and 53. The exegetical procedure used to connect them resembles that used by Paul extensively in II Cor. 3:1-6 and 4:6. John 12:46 offers a possibility for expanding this linkage to include either or both Isaiah 42:6 and 49:6.[28] "I have come as a light into the world" (Jn. 12: 46a, ἐγὼ φῶς εἰς τὸν κόσμον ἐλήλυθα) is quite close to an express fulfillment statement of "ἔδωκά σε... εἰς φῶς ἐθνῶν," (Isa. 42:6) and "τέθεικά σε... εἰς φῶς ἐθνῶν" (Isa. 49:6). The hook word to these texts would again be δόξα, glory. Isaiah 42 and 49 are one source for the important concept of light

---

[26] HANSON, *Dawn of Apocalyptic,* pp. 8, 11-12, 23-24, 26, 28; Donald E. GOWAN, *Bridge Between the Testaments,* (Pittsburgh: The Pickwick Press, 1976) pp. 456-458; RUSSELL, *Between the Testaments,* pp. 97-98.

[27] See A. F. SEGAL, "Ruler of this World: Attitudes About Mediator Figures and the Importance of Sociology for Self-Definiton" in *Jewish and Christian Self-Definition* II. Edited by E. P. SANDERS with A. I. BAUMGARTEN and A. MENDELSON (Philadelphia: Fortress Press, 1981) pp. 245-268 on the Johannine "ἄρχων τοῦ κοσμου τούτου".

[28] BROWN, *John* I, p. 479, mentions Isa. 49:5-6 thematically, but not exegetically.

(φῶς) with which John is involved in 12:35-36 and 46. The light of creation, with which Christ is identified in the Prologue, is interpreted as the salvific light promised by Isaiah as well.[29] Anyone who believes in Jesus does not remain in darkness, just as Isaiah 42:7 promises.[30] For Paul, anyone who does not believe in his gospel (II Cor. 4:4) is blind, and therefore in darkness. They cannot see the light which emanates from the face of Jesus Christ (II Cor. 4:6) which is mediated through that gospel. Paul and John are very similar in their characterization of those who do not receive their message about Jesus Christ, as opposed to those who do, just as they seem to be very similar in their exegetical sources and technique.

We have now seen, therefore, that John 12 not only leads to our perception of Paul's use of Isaiah 6:10 in II Cor. 3:14 and 4:4, but also suggests a traditional association of texts from the prophet Isaiah including at least Isaiah 6, 53, 42 and 49. John's use of this traditional exegesis highlights the hook words "glory" and "light" with which Paul is very concerned in II Corinthians 3-4 and gives us the benefit of two explicit citations of the texts with which he is working. John's use of these Prophetic texts may be a clue to their general importance for Paul as well, since Paul does use three texts from Isaiah in this section — Isa. 6:10, 9:2 and 58:10.[31]

II Corinthians 3-4 is very similar to John 12:37-50 thematically. For John 12:37-43 taken as a unit, the overriding concern is the fact of Jesus' rejection by some of the Jews in spite of his divine mission, even though it was authenticated by many signs. Because his glory was essentially hidden from the majority of men, although Isaiah saw it and presumably John did too, even those who believed in Jesus preferred the praise of their own fellows to the ostracism that would result from admitting to

---

[29] According to LINDARS in *The Gospel of John*. New Century Bible (London: Oliphants, 1972) p. 436, the references in 12:36b-50 to the Prologue "make an *inclusio*, bringing all the first twelve chapters under the heading of response to the light." He does not, however, pursue these allusions in detail here, nor does he seem to view them along exegetical lines.

[30] This argument for an exegetical linkage between Jn. 12:37-43 and verse 46 runs afoul of the tendency of modern commentary on the Gospel of John to split verses 44-50 off from the rest of the chapter as an unrelated discourse. See BROWN, *John* I, p. 490. I would not care to challenge the great Johannine scholars on this point. Possibly, however, the excesses to which redactional theories of this gospel have sometimes been extended are due to inattention to a unity constructed on an exegetical base, rather than on a geographical or temporal one.

[31] BROWN's remarks on the relevance of Deuteronomy 29:2-4 in Jn. 12:37 and 18:18-19 at Jn. 12:48-50 are also interesting in view of Paul's reflection of Deut. 29:1-4 in II Cor. 3:14-15 and his use of the figure of Moses in the whole unit (*John* I, pp. 485-486, 491-493). This is another indication of a similar exegetical background for the two texts (John 12 and II Cor. 3-4), buried deep in early Christian apologetic.

that belief. In II Corintians as a whole, Paul opposes the true glory of his authentic ministry stemming from Christ to the self-glorification and praise of men (II Cor. 3:1, 5:12; 10:12-13, 18; 12:19) preferred by his opponents. II Cor. 4:5, "... we do not proclaim ourselves, but Christ Jesus as Lord and ourselves as your servants on account of Jesus" bears a striking resemblance to Jesus' statement in Jn. 12:49, "...I have not spoken on my own authority; the Father who sent me has himself given me commandment what to say and what to speak." There is a relationship between Paul's argument in II Corinthians 4 and that contained in John 12. We have seen a few examples of it, but have not been able to investigate it any more fully. In his argument John leans heavily on the humble and despised position of the servant of the Lord which is described in Isa. 52:13-15; 53:1-6.[32] This section of the gospel is introduced in John 12:24-26, 32-33 with the theme of death, which occurs also at Isa. 53:7-12. As an argument concerning the *content* of Paul's self-defense can certainly show, Paul also adopts a similar theme of glorification only through death and suffering. The apologetic that John applies to Jesus, Paul constructs for himself. It is possible, therefore, that such an argument on Paul's part presupposes knowledge and use of similar exegetical groundwork from Isaiah. But this also is the subject of a future study.

The Structure and Intention of Paul's Conclusion

Introduction

As we have already seen, in II Cor. 3:1-6 Paul claimed the new covenant of Jeremiah as the object of his ministry. This appropriation to himself of a new covenant, superseding the Sinai covenant brought to Israel by Moses, set Paul as minister of that new covenant into a natural parallelism with Moses, the minister of the old covenant. That parallelism was made explicit in II Cor. 3:5-6 especially. In imitation of Exod. 4:10-12, Paul claimed his own divinely commissioned authority and competence to minister as the equal to and successor of Moses' own authority.

In II Cor. 3:7-18 Paul argued his way to a proper understanding of the figure and the actions of Moses as they are portrayed in Exodus 34:29-35 by specifically relating the mysterious phenomenon of Moses' veil to the advent of the new covenant in Christ. Because he received the revelation of Christ as the fulfillment of the old covenant and the giver of

---

[32] BROWN, *John* I, pp. 146, 478-479, 485 against Rudolf SCHNACKENBURG, *The Gospel According to St. John* II (New York: The Seabury Press, 1980) p. 414.

the new, Paul surpasses even Moses himself as a minister, on the basis of the superior and lasting quality of the object of his ministry. In his own defense, then, Paul draws in his conclusion in II Cor. 4:1-6 on this previous line of argument by describing his own behavior and his own situation in terms originally applicable to Moses. Paul appropriates to himself Moses' own role and authority toward Israel as well as his favored position before God in 4:1, 2, 3 and 6.

There is, however, a fly in this most felicitous of ointments. It has been evident since II Cor. 3:1 (as well as earlier in the Corinthian letters) that Paul's efforts and his message have not been universally well received. It is quite clear that this is so again in 4:1, 2 and 3. Paul's ministry and character are obviously subject to various accusations of error and even fraud. This is not the response which Moses' ministry of the old covenant received, at least not in that section of Exodus with which Paul has so far been concerned,[33] nor is it the reception which would be expected for Moses' successor, the glory of whose message far exceeds that of Moses and his covenant. All should be rosy and yet all is obviously not so.

Therefore, there is a need to explain the discrepancy between the expectations which this adoption and surpassing of the model of Moses' glorious ministry raise and the reality of criticism and rejection in which Paul was actually enmeshed. Paul has already used texts from the prophet Isaiah to interpret the persistence of disbelief and misunderstanding in spite of the presence of the full revelation of Christ which should have dispelled them. Although the glory of God was once hidden from Israel by Moses' veil, now it is revealed in unveiled faces. Nevertheless, many are still blind to it. On the basis of the concluding verses of II Corinthians 4 and of Chapters 5-7 and 10-13 of II Corinthians as well, it can be suggested that Paul finds further explanation for his own rejection, and for the rejection of Jesus as Lord, in the model of the suffering prophet, righteous man, or servant of the Lord present in the biblical tradition in the Servant Songs of Isaiah, the Wisdom of Solomon and numerous canonical psalms and other extracanonical books. The figure of Moses himself may have been associated with that of the righteous sufferer at this period and may even have been significant in its development.[34] It is

---

[33] Especially in the Book of Numbers, however (Num. 12:1-15; 14:1-10; 16:1-14, 41; 20:2-5; 21:4-9), as well in the book of Exodus itself (Exod. 16:2-3; 17:2-4), Moses himself suffers constant criticism and even attack as a weak and erring leader and as one who falsely "lords it over" Israel.

[34] This is the thesis of J. JEREMIAS in his article "Μωυσῆς" in TDNT IV, pp. 848-873; Aage BENTZEN, King and Messiah, pp. 52, 65-72; Renée BLOCH, "Quelques Aspects de la figure de Moïse," pp. 127-138 and Peter JONES, "L'Apôtre Paul: Un second Moïse pour la communauté de la nouvelle alliance: Une Etude sur l'autorité

certain that Moses is depicted as the greatest of the suffering prophets in the New Testament, in the Acts of the Apostles particularly. It is equally certain that Jesus himself was understood according to the pattern of the suffering servant of God or righteous one in the earliest strata of Christian literature.[35] Verification of Paul's own identification with this second biblical model must come from the larger literary context of II Corinthians. This shall be the subject of my next volume on II Corinthians. His conformance to the pattern of Mosaic service and authority, however, is clear from II Cor. 4:1-6 alone. Therefore, we will focus here on Paul as the "Moses" of his own day according to this single text.[36]

Paul the New Moses

Moses' mercy

According to II Cor 4:1, Paul received his ministry of mirroring the glory of God by being transformed into Christ, his Image, because he received mercy. This "καθὼς ἠλεήθημεν" is not simply a pious phrase, but another evocation of the positive comparison with Moses which was

apostlique paulinienne," *Foi et Vie* 75 (1976) p. 56. This idea is traceable in modern times to the work of Ernst Sellin, *Mose und seine Bedeutung für die israelitisch-jüdische Religionsgeschichte*, published in 1922, which held that the servant of the Isaianic servant songs was intended to be Moses himself *redivivus*. See Teeple, *The Mosaic Eschatological Prophet*, pp. 56-63 for a brief review of the history of this debate. Teeple himself rejects both the identification of the suffering servant of Isaiah with Moses himself and his identification with a new Moses for the biblical period, but admits that Moses was interpreted as a suffering figure in the rabbinic period and associated particularly with Isaiah 53, as the work of Renée Bloch has admirably established. Meeks also cautions against the exaggeration of the theme of suffering in the career of Moses at too early a period in *The Prophet-King*, pp. 203-204. In fact, in agreement with these last scholars it must be admitted that the thesis of Jeremias and Bentzen has scant evidence to support it earlier than the intertestamental and Christian period. Nevertheless, the general Mosaic/Exodus theme of Deutero-Isaiah can hardly be denied. Further study should concentrate on evidence from the centuries surrounding the birth of Christ, in the literature of which considerable evidence of the importance of suffering can be presented, and on the biblical text itself.

[35] Cullmann, *Christology*, pp. 51-82; Schweizer, *Lordship and Discipleship*, pp. 32-41, 49-55, 61-76; Dodd, *According to the Scriptures*, pp. 88-103; Lindars, *New Testament Apologetic*, pp. 75-137.

[36] Peter Jones has proposed and defended a Mosaic model of apostleship for Paul in his unpublished dissertation, "The Apostle Paul: A Second Moses According to II Corinthians 2:14-4:7," and in the article which is a partial summary of it with some additional material on the apostle as one who builds and plants the community, "L'Apôtre Paul: Un second Moïse pour la communauté de la nouvelle alliance: Une Etude sur l'autorité apostolique paulinienne." Like Teeple, Jones makes extensive use of Qumran material to clarify the picture of Moses on which this concept of apostleship is based. This study is content to reemphasize several of Jones' insights and to point out instances of the influence of Mosaic patterns which he has not noted.

struck in 3:6 and struck again, but superceded, in 3:7-18. In addition to being granted a vision of the divine glory prior to his reception of the second set of stone tablets, Moses was also permitted to hear the pronouncement of the divine name (Exod. 34:5-7). More than a mere appellation in the modern sense, Moses heard a summary of divine attributes, a verbal representation of the divinity itself, as names were commonly understood in the ancient Near East.[37]

The leading characteristic of the divine nature which was revealed to Moses was mercy. The promise of this favored revelation of the name to Moses appears in Exodus 33:19 and reads in part "ἐλεήσω ὃν ἂν ἐλεῶ...." This quality, the divine ability to be merciful according to his own will and pleasure, is repeated first in the course of the actual theophany of Exod. 34:6.[38] The fact that Moses receives a vision of divine glory and hears the divine name is in itself proof in Exodus that God has indeed had mercy on Moses, in granting his request, and on Israel, in forgiving the recent apostasy of the golden calf. It proves the value of Moses' intercession for Israel and guarantees the Lord's partial forgiveness of Israel's sin.

Romans 9:14-33 indicates that Paul was conscious of this aspect of Exod. 33:19 and did in fact apply it to explain Christian election in Gentile believers vis-a-vis the priority of the Jew. Exodus 33:19 is cited explicitly in Rom. 9:15. There follows to the end of the chapter a string of citations, including Isaiah 29:16, 45:9 and 64:8, structured around hook-words with the purpose of explaining the reception of the divine mercy by Gentiles and its withdrawal from the Jews of Paul's time.[39] In II Cor. 4:1 Paul probably relies on this general understanding of the acceptance of Christ on the part of the Gentiles rather than Jews as a divine mercy and, by extension, his ministry in the service of this Gentile

---

[37] PEDERSEN, *Israel* I-II, pp. 245-250; EICHRODT, *Theology of the Old Testament* II pp. 40-45.

[38] It is interesting to note that Jeremiah 38:29-30 (LXX), the introduction to the central promise of the new covenant, offers an improvement on this proclamation. Exod. 34:7 reads "[the Lord] ... will by no means clear the guilty, visiting the iniquity of the fathers upon the children and the children's children, to the third and fourth generation." In contrast, Jeremiah 38:29-30 (LXX) reads "In those days they shall no longer say: 'The fathers have eaten sour grapes, and the children's teeth are set on edge.' But every one shall die for his own sin. Each man who eats sour grapes, his teeth shall be set on edge." This contrast was probably not lost on early Christian exegesis.

[39] The discussion in Romans 9 is further related to II Cor. 4:3, 7 by its mention in verses 21-23 of vessels of dishonor made for destruction (ἀπώλεια) versus vessels of mercy made for glory (δόξα). Such a double coincidence of vocabulary and scriptural warrant may indicate a correspondence of underlying theme as well. In Romans 9, Paul is involved in a passionate attempt to understand God's apparent rejection of his people of promise in favor of the Gentiles who have accepted Paul's message about Christ. Possibly in II Corinthians a similar problem is present. Cf. note 15 above.

conversion as a divine mercy as well. Even more specifically, Paul appropriates to himself the Mosaic model of ministry, by placing himself vis-a-vis his own converts in the position Moses occupied toward Israel. Just as Moses received mercy in his reception of the vision of the Lord and the revelation of his name, so Paul receives his vision of the glorious Christ and knows his name — Jesus — as a mercy. Paul possesses Moses' mercy, as he had already appropriated Moses' authority (Exod. 4:10-12/II Cor. 3:5-6) and Moses' vision (Exod. 33:18-23; 34:5-8/II Cor. 3:18).[40]

Moses' veil

We have seen in Chapter Two of this study that the prophecies of Isaiah 6 and 29 have been used within a pesher-like exegesis to move Moses' veil into Paul's own time and to explain the lack of understanding which prevails among those of the old covenant who cannot see Christ as the organic and intended end of that covenant. In II Cor. 3:14 and 15, Moses' veil rests, no longer on his face, but on the reading of (14) or the understanding of (15) the written witness to Moses. This indicates that it is now precisely the reading of the scriptures which is veiled and so does not yield the proper view of Christ as their end. It is therefore a Christological exegesis of the books of the old covenant which Paul proposes but which some reject. In II Cor. 4:3 the metaphor of the veil appears again, repeating Paul's assertion of disbelief on the part of the sons of Israel, but with a different object. This time it is Paul's own

---

[40] One of the vexing problems in the interpretation of II Corinthians is the failure of the Thanksgiving section, 1:3-7, to specifically forecast and summarize the most important themes which will later emerge in the text. The key description of God, "the Father of mercies and God of all comfort," in II Cor. 1:3 does, however, mirror the beginning of the "naming" in Exod. 33:19 by using the same verbs, ἐλεέω and οἰκτίρω in their nominal form. This may indicate the considerable importance of the theophany to Moses to Paul's theology in II Corinthians. Coupled with these themes of mercy and compassion, is the theme of suffering, that of Jesus Christ and that of Paul himself. This theme stems, not only from Paul's personal experience, but from early Christian apologetic which made use of numerous canonical psalms, the Wisdom of Solomon and especially the servant songs of Deutero-Isaiah to interpret the sufferings of Jesus. The theology of the letter should then, according to the program established by the Thanksgiving section, revolve around the theophany of God's glory and the revelation of God's name in combination with the sufferings to be expected by God's servant. This chapter, in fact, hopes to suggest just this combination as the kernel of Paul's interpretation of Moses, of Christ and of himself with which he defends his actions and explains his situation. The Thanksgiving section of the letter may therefore be programmatic in a way seldom realized. See Peter T. O'BRIEN, *Introductory Thanksgivings in the Letters of Paul.* Supplements to Novum Testamentum 49 (Leiden: E.J. Brill, 1977) pp. 233-258. O'BRIEN treats the introduction to II Corinthians last, as an oddity, and prefers to call it a *Berakah,* probably correctly. He extends the form to verse 11 and argues briefly for an epistolary function in spite of its exceptional form and highly personal character.

gospel against which the understanding of the unbelievers is veiled. In addition to his covenant ministry, his vision of glory and his mercy, Paul has appropriated to himself Moses' veil.

In II Corinthians 4 it is no longer the face of Moses which is veiled, nor is it the books of Moses which the sons of Israel are prevented from understanding. It is the preaching of Paul which has supplanted both Moses and the books of the old covenant as a vehicle of revelaton and an object of misunderstanding. No physical veil covers his gospel, any more than a physical veil covered the books of the old covenant when they were being read in the liturgy of the synagogue. Like the books of the old covenant, Paul's gospel is veiled by the blindness of the minds of those who hear it but do not believe it.

Two things are striking about Paul's statement in 4:3-4. First, the adoption of the scriptural image of the veil in relation to his own ministry makes clear the degree to which Paul has identified himself with Moses as a model of ministry. In his own day, Paul is a replica of Moses, right down to the mysterious phenomenon of his veiling. Second, Paul has by implication placed his own preaching, his gospel, on a level comparable with that of Moses' books and Moses' message by claiming that his gospel is veiled in its hearers just as Moses' books are veiled in their readers.[41] This parallelism is the natural result of the correspondence between Moses and Paul as covenant ministers. Just as importantly, however, it also arises from the identity of object which the two ministries intend to convey. In II Cor. 4:4c Paul describes the "content" of his gospel. It is the gospel of the glory of Christ, the Image of God. Christian preaching and, inevitably, Christian literature as well are thereby set on the same level as the Old Testament scripture as revelations of the divine glory which came to full expression in Christ.

Paul as a Second Moses

Once we have become aware of the degree to which Paul has adopted for himself certain key aspects of Moses' Exodus ministry, it becomes increasingly clear that each facet of his behavior which has been mentioned in the whole section, II Cor. 3:1-46, is in fact a reflection of some aspect of Moses' actions in Exodus, particularly Exodus 33-34. We have already noted the most striking of these parallels, but a few more remain, recognizable as Mosaic reminiscences only in the larger context of the clear key correspondences.

In II Cor. 4:2 Paul maintains that he recommends himself to all men "by the clear display of the truth" (τῇ φανερώσει τῆς ἀληθείας). He does not "adulterate the word of God" (μηδὲ δολοῦντες τὴν λόγον τοῦ θεοῦ).

---

[41] JONES, "L'Apôtre Paul," p. 50.

He has a model for such open reporting of God's word in Exodus 34:32. When he came down from the mountain, Moses told the sons of Israel *all* that the Lord had commanded on the mountain (πάντα ὅσα ἐνετείλατο κύριος πρὸς αὐτὸν ἐν τῷ ὄρει Σινά). Furthermore, while he did so, a reflection of the divine glory, later to arrive fully in Christ, was clearly visible to Israel on his face. Moses provides no model for deception, and Paul imitates his open communication of the divine word.

Though no model for secretiveness, Moses is a model for humility and self-effacement.[42] Numbers 12:3 tells us "... Moses was a very humble man, more humble than anyone else on the face of the earth." The veil with which he covered his reflection of the divine glory in Exod. 34:33 was one symbol of that humility. This aspect of Moses' ministry had rightly been discarded by Paul, but had been incorrectly, and under the influence of the "god of this age," adopted by Israel itself. But Moses was a model of humility in other ways as well. We have seen one other instance of this humility which Paul did adopt — Moses' insistence in Exodus 4:10-12 that he was neither worthy of nor competent for the ministry for which the Lord designated him. The Lord must put the words in his mouth and the power in his hands. This aspect of Moses' humility is accepted by Paul as his own, in II Cor. 3:5-6 and again at 4:5.[43] II Cor. 4:5 begins "... it is not ourselves we preach ...." What Paul and those who conduct themselves in a similar way preach is Jesus Christ as Lord and themselves as servants only. In this conception of ministry, the minister is only a vehicle for the communication of God's message, in Paul's case a message about the Lordship of Christ who is the glorious divine Image.

Moses, too, in his ministry was simply a conveyor of God's own words for Israel and a doer of God's own actions for Israel.[44] In Exodus 34:32 and 34, Moses is reported to be and do just that. He hears and he speaks the Lord's commandments. He does not make the law, he merely repeats God's law to Israel. He does not "preach himself," but communicates the Lord's will for Israel.[45] In II Cor. 4:5 Paul firmly

---

[42] BLOCH, "Quelques Aspects de la figure de Moïse," pp. 119, 133; TEEPLE, *The Mosaic Eschatological Prophet*, p. 39.

[43] JONES, "L'Apôtre Paul," p. 47.

[44] BLOCH, "Quelques Aspects de la figure de Moïse," pp. 120-121.

[45] It is the general thesis of the work of Renee BLOCH in "Quelques Aspects de la figure de Moïse" that within the living tradition of Judaism the dominant characterization of Moses was as the self-effacing servant of God, the savior of Israel and its mediator before its Lord, who suffered with and for Israel in the days of the exodus and the wilderness. She feels that the modern (Christian) "authoritarian" perception of Moses is misguided and fails to appreciate the love and esteem in which he was and still is held within Judaism. Her article, although somewhat old now, is still particularly rich in the citation of primary rabbinic sources not elsewhere easily available to support the views proposed.

insists that he acts in imitation of this Mosaic model, only Paul preaches the Lord Jesus Christ openly rather than the old covenant in which he was veiled.

In II Cor. 4:6 Paul returns to a consideration of Moses' vision of the divine glory, which he has already appropriated to himself in 3:18. He modifies it a bit in its adoption here in order to conform to the ministry of a new covenant. According to II Cor. 4:6b, the God who created light, emphasizing the reference of the quotation to Genesis 1:3 for a moment, has shone into Paul's heart. That same God shone on Moses, as is promised in Exodus 33:17-23 and presumed from Exodus 34:6 and 29. Moses' reflection of this divine radiance, however, was located on his face (Exod. 34:29), not in his heart. It was a visible reminder and proof of his communion with God. Paul tells us that his own reception of the divine light, however, was in his heart, not on his face. Two important conclusions may immediately be drawn from his statement.

First, such an interior illumination would have no visible effects. it would offer no external validation of the vision that Paul claims. Unlike Moses, Paul must defend the reality of his divine favor without external verification. Just as he lacks the stone tablets that Moses had for the old covenant as proof of his possession of that covenant for Israel, so Paul also lacks the external radiance as proof of his communion with the divine glory which Moses possessed.

This, however, brings us to the second relevant observation to be made on Paul's statement in II Cor. 4:6. It is entirely typical of the new covenant which Paul ministers, the new covenant of Jeremiah 38:31-34 (LXX), to be interior, to be in the heart.[46] According to Jer. 38:33 (LXX) and II Cor. 3:2-3, the new covenant itself will be, and is written in the heart. If the evidence of the new covenant is interior, so is the vision which creates and inaugurates it. Its light is in Paul's heart. However, it is not only God the creator who has shone into Paul's heart. It is, therefore, not only the divine glory as indistinctly revealed in creation, or as partially revealed to Moses as he viewed the back of the human form in which the divine glory passed by him, which dwells in Paul's heart. It is the divine glory as fully revealed in the face, not the back, of Christ, who is the glorious Image of God himself, which Paul knows (cf. Exod. 33:20-23 and II Cor 4:6).

It is well known and has been mentioned before in this study that in the mentality of the Old Testament the heart is the locus of knowing. Since Paul's vision, as just described under the twin influences of Exodus 33-34 and Jeremiah 38 (LXX), is in the heart, the effect of this vision upon him within that biblical persepective is not sight, but knowledge.

---

[46] JONES, "L'Apôtre Paul," p. 48.

The divine illumination gives him *knowledge* of the glory of Christ. Similarly, lacking external glorification because of the interiority of his vision of the glorious Christ, Paul, unlike Moses, can only *offer* knowledge of the glorious face of Christ, not its physical reflection.[47] Paul's own glorification on the model of the divine Image (II Cor. 3:18) is an interior, invisible thing, at least for the time being. II Cor. 4:16, 18 and 5:12, 17 also bear witness to the interiority of the transformation of the Christian, as well as to the difficulties this invisible glorification might cause. It is on these difficulties that the full force of Paul's exegetical argument is brought to bear. In answer to a reproach about his lack of external epistolary recommendation, Paul has proclaimed himself to be the "new Moses" of God's covenant in Christ.

Conclusion

This study of the exegetical substructure of II Corinthians 3:1-4:6 is now completed, but that does not mean that work on this text is finished, or ever could be. Nevertheless, much has been accomplished. The present work has shown that II Cor. 3:1-4:6 is a unified and integral text containing a single coherent argument in support of Paul's authentic apostleship in conformance to a Mosaic paradigm. In the course of this argument Paul has exegetically defined and explored the key concept of the new covenant, the "Christian covenant." We have seen Paul's mind at work, clarifying in the process both our understanding of an important and exceptionally difficult text and our grasp of Paul's own theological methodology, steeped as it is in the contemporary interpretation of Old Testament scriptures. Yet much remains to be done. This conclusion has called for further investigation of the influence of Moses on Paul's self-identification as apostle. The methodology employed in this study calls for the investigation of other sections of II Corinthians, as well as Paul's other letters, in search of a possible exegetical substructure similar to that discovered here and using a contemporary exegetical methodology similar to that used in this study. Finally, the presuppositions of Paul's own exegesis could profitably be discussed in a future work focused more directly on the terms, rather than the form, of his argument here.

For example, the use of the word "τέλος" in II Corinthians 3:14 has not yet been completely explained. A most serious related question concerns the place of Jesus Christ in Paul's thought in II Corinthians 3-4. From these chapters alone, his role might seem both minimal and mysterious. According to II Cor. 3:14, it is "in Christ" that Moses' glory,

---

[47] Consequently, I do not see the use of the term "γνῶσις" in II Cor. 4:6 and related terminology in II Cor. 3:14 and 4:4 as reflecting a gnostic background. Contra SCHMITHALS, *Gnosticism in Corinth*, pp. 183-184; BARRETT, *Second Epistle*, p. 135.

ministry and covenant is being brought to an end. Even though we might easily accept Paul's statement knowing that it comes from someone firmly committed to [48] Christ, it is still legitimate and necessary to inquire into the intellectual frame of reference out of which it emerges. This inquiry is particularly important in this case, since it is in this detail that Paul's interpretation seems to stand in direct contradiction to the text of Exodus 34 which he is interpreting. Following Exodus 34:29-35 and all later Jewish interpretation of it, one could only conclude that Moses' glory did not end *at all*. Yet Paul says that it ended in Christ. Why? Only an investigation into the understanding of Christ which Paul has presupposed and which has determined his treatment of Exodus 34:29-35 can answer this question.

Furthermore, the fact that his glory was to end in Christ is made, by Paul, to be the motivation for Moses' veiling of that glory. Clearly, Paul has ascribed a motivation to Moses which is not intrinsically related to the story which is thus supplemented, at least not by *modern* standards of biblical interpretation. Therefore, Paul must have supplied this detail out of his own understanding of Christ's relationship to the story of Moses' glorification. Moreover, he very probably · thought it completely legitimate to do so. It is important for us, therefore, to describe for ourselves the total picture of Christ vis-a-vis Moses that could logically give rise to Paul's reading of Exodus.

Finally, Chapter Two of the foregoing analysis of the exegetical substructure of II Cor. 3:7-18 has been preoccupied to a great extent with the word and concept of glory. It was of vital importance to Paul to argue for the presence of "glory" in the new covenant and in its minister. This is what verses 7-11 of II Corinthians 3 so elaborately achieve. Why is this so important for Paul? All sorts of further questions come to mind in reflecting on that one. What is this "glory?" Paul never defines it. He deals with it simply as an element drawn from the Exodus story of Moses' shining face. He must have known what the word "δόξα" meant, but do we? The difficulty of defining the word "glory" even in English reflects a complicated linguistic history.[49] What did Paul understand the

---

[48] Since reading Davies' warning that "the vocabularly of conversion is absent from Paul's epistles" (*Paul and Rabbinic Judaism*, p. xxxvi), I have become reluctant to assert that Paul was "converted to" Christ, lest I be understood to mean that Paul converted *from* Judaism to faith in Christ. Davies is right in pointing out that Paul did not understand himself to be outside of Israel because of his total commitment to preaching Jesus Christ and that his genius was precisely to have attempted to integrate his religious tradition and his new experience.

[49] A.M. Ramsey begins his excellent little book, *The Glory of God and the Transfiguration of Christ* (London: Darton, Longman &Todd, Ltd., 1949) with a quotation from *Alice Through the Looking Glass* by Lewis Carroll which I think it worthwhile to repeat here — "'There's glory for you.' 'I don't know what you mean by glory,' Alice

glowing appearance of Moses' skin to mean? Why is its ending related to Christ so many centuries later? Why should a glory like that of Moses be attached to Paul and to all Christians? Finally, what is the contextual meaning of the exalted phrase which stands in II Corinthians 4:4, "the glory of the Christ, who is the Image of God?" This brief conclusion has presumed answers to these questions especially in its comparison of the vision of Moses in Exodus 33-34 and Paul's "revelation" of the glorious Son of God (cf. Gal 1:16). Yet a further detailed study informed by an appreciation of Paul's exegetical presuppositions, preoccupation and methodology, must continue the present work in order to fully substantiate the parallels drawn in outline here.[50]

Investigation of II Corinthians 3:1-4:6 has proven that it is indeed one of the most fruitful and challenging parts of Paul's literary legacy. We emerge with a renewed appreciation of the genius of Paul the Apostle as exegete and theologian. We take from this study as well a mandate for future research into the exegetical context of Pauline Christology and the Mosaic content of Pauline views of ministry and apostleship. Finally, the effectiveness of analysis of Paul's argument here in II Corinthians 3:1-4:6 in terms of its own exegetical methodology in producing results that clarify the meaning of the passage substantially suggests such a contemporary method of approaching Pauline texts as a most viable and exciting part of Pauline studies in the years to come.

---

said. 'I meant "There's a nice knock-down argument for you." ' 'But glory doesn't mean a nice knock-down argument,' Alice objected. 'When I use a word', Humpty Dumpty said in a rather scornful tone, 'it means just what I choose it to mean — neither more nor less.' " RAMSEY's use of this citation not only illustrates the refreshing combination of literary erudition and whimsy often present in the work of older British scripture scholars, but also very aptly introduces the element of confusion present in our own use of the word "glory." It is a word used frequently in liturgy, for example, and we think we know what it means. Upon examination, however, we probably will find that we do not. An investigation of the Hebrew and Greek roots of this common term helps to sort out this ambiguity.

[50] The 1980 article by A. T. HANSON entitled "The Midrash in II Corinthians 3: A Reconsideration" is an indication of the direction such a future research will take and of the conclusions which will result from a more detailed analysis.

SELECTED BIBLIOGRAPHY

Primary Material

ABERBACH, Moses and GROSSFELD, Bernard, eds. *Targum Onkelos to Genesis.* Denver: KTAV Publishing House, 1982.

BROOKE, A. and McLEAN, N. *The Old Testament in Greek.* Cambridge: University Press, 1909.

BRENTON, C. L. *The Septuagint Version of the Old Testament and Apocrypha with an English Translation.* Grand Rapids, Michigan: Zondervan, 1978.

CHARLES, R. H. *The Apocrypha and Pseudepigrapha of the Old Testament in English*, 2 vols. Oxford: Clarendon Press, 1913.

————. *II Baruch.* Ed. R. H. Charles, pp. 470-526.

————. *III Baruch.* Ed. H. M. Hughes, pp. 527-541.

————. *I Enoch.* Ed. R. H. Charles, pp. 163-281.

————. *II Enoch.* Ed. R. H. Charles and N. Forbes, pp. 425-469.

————. *IV Ezra.* Ed. G. H. Box, pp. 542-624.

————. *Assumption of Moses.* Ed. R. H. Charles, pp. 407-424.

COLSON, F. H. and WHITAKER, C. H., eds. Philo. *The Loeb Classical Library*, 11 vols. *De Vita Moses I and II*, vol. 6. *De Confusione Linguarum*, vol. 4. Cambridge: Harvard University Press, 1949.

ETHERIDGE, J. W., ed. *The Targums of Onkelos and Jonathan Ben Uzziel on the Pentateuch Genesis and Exodus.* New York: KTAV Publishing House, 1968. First published in 1862.

FREEDMAN, H. and SIMON, M., eds. and trans. *Midrash Rabbah I Genesis Rabbah.* London: The Soncino Press, 1938.

JAMES, M. R., ed. *The Biblical Antiquities of Philo.* Prolegomenon by Louis H. Feldman. The Library of Biblical Studies. New York: KTAV Publishing House, 1971. First published in 1917.

RAHLFS, Alfred, ed. *Septuaginta. Psalmi cum Odis.* Göttingen: Vandenhoeck and Ruprecht, 1967.

STENNING, J. F., ed. and trans. *The Targum of Isaiah.* Oxford: Clarendon Press, 1953. First published in 1949.

WEVERS, J. W., ed. *Septuaginta. Vetus Testamentum Graecum. I Genesis*, 1974. *III 2 Deuteronomium.* 1977. Göttingen: Vandenhoeck and Ruprecht.

ZIEGLER, Joseph. *Septuaginta. Vetus Testamentum Graecum. XII, 1. Sapientia Solomonis*, 1962. *XV Jeremiah*, 1957. *XVI Ezekiel*, 1952. *XIV Isaias*, 1967. Göttingen: Vandenhoeck and Ruprecht.

Reference Works

ARNDT, William F. and GINGRICH, F. Wilbur. *A Greek-English Lexicon of the New Testament and Other Early Christian Literature.* Chicago: University of Chicago Press, 1957.

BLASS, F. and DEBRUNNER, A. *A Greek Grammar of the New Testament and Other Early Christian Literature*. Translated and revised by Robert W. Funk. Chicago: University of Chicago Press, 1961.

GINZBERG, Louis. *Legends of the Jews*, 8 vols. Trans. H. Szold. Philadelphia: The Jewish Publication Society of America, 1909.

KITTEL, Gerhard, ed. *Theological Dictionary of the New Testament*. Trans. G. W. Bromiley. Grand Rapids, Michigan: Wm. B. Eerdmans, 1964.

―――. I. Rengstorf, K. "ἀποστέλλω," pp. 398-447.

―――. II. Behm, Johannes, "διαθήκη," pp. 104-134; Beyer, H., "διακονέω," pp. 81-93; Schrenk, G., "δικαιοσύνη," pp. 192-210; Kittel, G., Klinknecht, H. and von Rad, G., "εἰκών," pp. 381-397; Kittel, G., von Rad, G., "δόξα," pp. 232-255.

―――. III. Rengstorf, K., "ἱκανός," pp. 293-296.

―――. IV. Jeremias, J., "Μωυσῆς," pp. 848-873.

―――. VII. Bertram, G., "στρέφω," pp. 714-729; Rengstorf, K., "σημεῖον," pp. 200-269.

LIDDELL, H. G. and SCOTT, R. *A Greek-English Lexicon*. Revised edition with a supplement. Oxford: Clarendon Press, 1968.

MOULE, C. F. D. *An Idiom Book of New Testament Greek*. Cambridge: The University Press, 1953.

MOULTON, James H. *A Grammar of New Testament Greek*. 4 vols. Edinburgh: T. & T. Clark, 1963. v. III.

STRACK, Hermann L. and BILLERBECK, Paul. *Kommentar zum Neuen Testament aus Talmud und Midrasch*, III. Die Briefe des Neuen Testaments und die Offenborung Johannis. Munich: C. H. Beck'sche Verlagsbuchhandlung, 1954.

ZERWICK, M. *Biblical Greek*. English edition, trans. and adapted by Joseph Smith, S.J. Rome: Scripta Pontificii Instituti Biblici, 1963.

ZERWICK, M. and GROSVENOR, M. *A Grammatical Analysis of the Greek New Testament*, II. Rome: Biblical Institute Press, 1979.

Commentaries

ALLO, E.-B. *Saint Paul: Seconde Epître aux Corinthiens*. Etudes Bibliques, second edition. Paris: Librairie Le Coffre, 1956.

BARRETT, C. K. *A Commentary on the Epistle to the Romans*. Harper's New Testament Commentaries 1. New York: Harper and Brothers, Publishers, 1957.

―――. *A Commentary on the Second Epistle to the Corinthians*. Harper's New Testament Commentaries. New York: Harper and Row, Publishers, 1973.

―――. *The Gospel According to St. John*. London: SPCK, 1955.

BROWN, Raymond. *The Gospel According to John* i-xii, vol. I. The Anchor Bible. Garden City, New York: Doubleday and Co., 1966.

BRUCE, F. F. *1 and 2 Corinthians*. New Century Bible 12. London: Oliphants, 1971.

BULTMANN, Rudolf. *The Gospel of John. A Commentary*. Trans. by G. R. Beasley-Murray. Oxford: Basil Blackwell, 1971.

BULTMANN, Rudolf. *Der zweite Brief an die Korinther*. Kritisch-Exegetischer Kommentar über das Neue Testament. Göttingen: Vandenhoeck and Ruprecht, 1976.

CHILDS, Brevard. *The Book of Exodus*. Philadelphia: The Westminster Press, 1974.

COLLANGE, J. F. *Enigmes de la Deuxième Epître de Paul aux Corinthiens. Etude Exegetique de 2 Cor. 2:14-7:4*. Society for New Testament Studies Monograph Series 18. Cambridge: University Press, 1972.

CRANFIELD, C. E. B. *A Commentary on Romans 12-13*. Scottish Journal of Theology Occasional Papers 12. Edinburgh: Oliver and Boyd, 1965.

———. *Romans*, 2 vols. The New International Critical Commentary. Edinburgh: T. & T. Clark, 1979.

FALLON, Francis T. *2 Corinthians*. Wilmington, Delaware: Michael Glazier, 1980.

HANSON, R. P. C. *The Second Epistle to the Corinthians: Christ and Controversy*. New edition. London: SCM Press, 1968.

HÉRING, Jean. *La second Epître de Saint Paul aux Corinthiens*. London: Epworth Press, 1958.

HUGHES, Philip. *Paul's Second Epistle to the Corinthians*. The New International Commentary on the New Testament. Grand Rapids, Michigan: Wm. B. Eerdmans Publishing Co., 1962.

KÄSEMANN, Ernst. *Commentary on Romans*. Trans. and edited by Geoffrey W. Bromiley from the Fourth German Edition of An Die Römer (Tübingen: J. C. B. Mohr [Paul Siebeck], 1980). Grand Rapids, Michigan: Wm. B. Eerdmans Publishing Co., 1980.

LIETZMANN, D. Hans. *An Die Korinther I-II*. Handbuch zum Neuen Testament 9. Tübingen: J. C. B. Mohr (Paul Siebeck), 1949.

LINDARS, Barnabas. *The Gospel of John*. New Century Bible 16. London: Oliphants, 1972.

PLUMMER, Alfred. *A Critical and Exegetical Commentary on the Second Epistle of St. Paul to the Corinthians*. The International Critical Commentary. Edinburgh: T. & T. Clark, 1915.

PRÜMM, Karl, S. J. *Diakonia Pneumatos I*, Theologische Auslegung des Zweiten Korintherbriefes Freiburg: Herder, 1967.

RISSI, Mathias. *Studien zum zweiten Korintherbrief*. Abhandlungen zur Theologie des Alten und Neuen Testaments 56. Zürich: Zwingli Verlag, 1969.

SANDAY, W. and HEADLAM, A. *A Critical and Exegetical Commentary on the Epistle to the Romans*. The International Critical Commentary, fifth edition. Edinburg: T. & T. Clark, 1902.

SCHNACKENBURG, Rudolf. *The Gospel According to St. John*. II. Translated by C. Hastings, F. McDonagle, B. Rigaux, R. Schnackenburg, A. Vögtle. New York: The Seabury Press, 1980. Originally published in 1971.

THRALL, M. *The First and Second Letters of Paul to the Corinthians*. Cambridge. University Press, 1965.

WINDISCH, H. *Die zweite Korintherbrief*. Göttingen: Vandenhoeck and Ruprecht, 1924.

Books

BARRETT, C. K. *From First Adam to Last*, New York: Charles Scribner's Sons, 1962.

BENTZEN, Aage. *King and Messiah*. London: Lutterworth, 1955.

BONSIRVEN, Joseph, S.J. *Exegese Rabbinique et Exegese Paulinienne. Bibliotheque de Theologie Historique*. Paris: Beauchesne et ses fils, 1939.

————. *Palestinian Judaism in the Time of Jesus Christ*. Translated by W. Wolf. New York: Holt, Rinehart and Winston, 1964. First published in 1950.

BOWKER, John, *The Targums and Rabbinic Literature*. Cambridge: University Press, 1969.

BROWNLEE, William H. *The Midrash Pesher of Habakkuk*. SBL Monograph Series 24. Missoula, Montana: Scholar's Press, 1979.

BULTMANN, Rudolf. *Exegetische Probleme des zweiten Korintherbriefes*. Darmstadt: Wissenschaftliche Buchgesellschaft, 1963.

————. *History of the Synoptic Tradition*. Revised ed. Translated by John Marsh. New York: Harper and Row, 1963.

CARREZ, M. *De la souffrance a la gloire*. Paris: Delachaux et Niestle, 1964.

CHARLESWORTH, James H. *The Pseudepigrapha and Modern Research*. Septuagint and Cognate Studies 7S. Chico, California: Scholar's Press, 1981.

CHEVALLIER, M. A. *Esprit de Dieu, paroles d'hommes*. Bibliotheque Theologique. Neuchatel: Editions Delachaux et Niestle, 1966.

CHILDS, Brevard. *Introduction to the Old Testament as Scripture*. Philadelphia: Fortress Press, 1979.

CONZELMANN, Hans. *Jesus*. Translated by J. R. Lord. Edited with Introduction by John Reumann. Philadelphia. Fortress Press, 1973. Originally published as the article "Jesus Christus" in *Die Religion in Geschichte und Gegenwart: Handwörterbuch für Theologie und Religions Wissenschaft*, ed. K. Galling, et al., Vol. 3 (1959) cols. 619-653. Tübingen: J. C. B. Mohr (Paul Siebeck).

CROSS, Frank Moore Jr. *The Ancient Library of Qumran*. London: Gerald Duckworth & Co., 1958.

DAUBE, David. *The New Testament and Rabbinic Judaism*. Jordan Lectures in Comparative Religion II. London: University of the Athlone Press, 1956.

DAVIES, W. D. *Jewish and Pauline Studies*. Philadelphia: Fortress Press, 1984.

————. *Paul and Rabbinic Judaism*. Fourth edition. Philadelphia: Fortress Press, 1980.

DODD, C. H. *According to the Scriptures. The Sub-Structure of New Testament Theology*. London. Nisbet and Co., 1952.

————. *The Apostolic Preaching and its Developments*. New York: Harper and Brothers, Publishers, 1935.

DODDS, E. R. *Pagan and Christian in an Age of Anxiety*. New York: W. W. Norton and Company, 1970.

EISSFELDT, Otto. *The Old Testament, an Introduction*. Translated by P. R. Ackroyd. Oxford: Brasil Blackwell for Harper and Row, 1965.

ELLIS, E. Earle. *Paul's Use of the Old Testament*. London: Oliver and Boyd, 1957.

————. *Prophecy and Hermeneutic in Early Christianity*. Tübingen: J. C. B. Mohr (Paul Siebeck), 1978.

FEUILLET, A. *Le Christ Sagesse de Dieu d'après les Epîtres pauliniennes.* Etudes Bibliques. Paris: Librairie Le Coffre, 1966.

FRIESEN, Isaac I. *The Glory of the Ministry of Jesus Christ.* Illustrated by a Study of 2 Cor. 2:14-3:18. Theologischen Dissertationen VII. Basel: Friedrich Reinhard Kommissionsverlag, 1971.

GEORGI, Dieter. *Die Gegner des Paulus im 2 Korintherbrief: Studien zur Religiösen Propaganda in der Spätantike.* Wissenschaftlich Monographien zum Alten und Neuen Testament 11. Vluyn: Neukirchener Verlag, 1964.

GIBBS, John G. *Creation and Redemption. A Study in Pauline Theology.* Supplements to Novum Testamentum XXVI. Leiden: E.J. Brill, 1971.

GOWAN, Donald E. *Bridge Between the Testaments.* Pittsburgh Theological Monograph Series 14. Pittsburgh: The Pickwick Press, 1976.

GUNTHER, John J. *St. Paul's Opponents and Their Background. A Study of Apocalyptic and Jewish Sectarian Teachings.* Supplements to Novum Testamentum XXXV. Leiden: E.J. Brill, 1973.

HANSON, Anthony Tyrrell. *Jesus Christ in the Old Testament.* London: SPCK, 1965.

———. *Studies in Paul's Technique and Theology.* London: SPCK, 1974.

HANSON, Paul D. *The Dawn of Apocalyptic.* Philadelphia: Fortress Press, 1975.

HENGEL, Martin. *Judaism and Hellenism.* Two vols. Translated by John Bowden. Philadelphia: Fortress Press, 1974.

HERMANN, Ingo. *Kyrios und Pneuma.* Munich: Kösel, 1961.

HILL, David. *Greek Words and Hebrew Meanings: Studies in the Semantics of Soteriological Terms.* Society for New Testament Studies Monograph Series 5. Cambridge: The University Press, 1967.

HOLLADAY, Carl H. *Theios Aner in Hellenistic Judaism. A Critique of the Use of this Category in New Testament Christology.* SBL Dissertation Series 40. Missoula, Montana: Scholar's Press, 1977.

HOOKER, Morna. *A Preface to Paul.* New York: Oxford University Press, 1980.

HORGAN, Maurya. *Pesharim: Qumran Interpretations of Biblical Books.* The Catholic Biblical Quarterly Monograph Series 8. Washington, D.C.: The Catholic Biblical Association of America, 1979.

HUGEDE, N. *La métaphore du miroir dans les épîtres de saint Paul aux Corinthiens.* Neuchâtel-Paris: Delachaux et Niestlé, 1957.

HUNTER, Archibald M. *Paul and His Predecessors.* New Revised edition. Philadelphia: The Westminster Press, 1961. First published in 1940.

JAUBERT, Annie. *La notion d'alliance dans le Judaisme.* Patristica Sorbonensia 6. Paris: Editions du Seuil, 1963.

JERVELL, Jacob. *Imago Dei. Gen. 1, 26f. im spatjudentum, im der Gnosis und in den paulinischen Briefen.* Forschungen zur Religion und Literatur des Alten und Neuen Testaments 76. Göttingen: Vandenhoeck and Ruprecht, 1960.

KIM, Siyoon. *The Origin of Paul's Gospel.* Wissenschaftliche Untersuchungen zum Neuen Testament 4. Tübingen: J.C.B. Mohr (Paul Siebeck), 1981.

KOESTER, Helmut. *Introduction to the New Testament.* Two vols. New York: Walter DeGruyter, 1982.

LE DÉAUT, R. *The Message of the New Testament and the Aramaic Bible (Targum).* Translated by Stephen F. Miletic. Rome: Biblical Institute Press, 1982.

LINDARS, Barnabas. *New Testament Apologetic.* The Doctrinal Significance of the Old Testament Quotations. Philadelphia: The Westminster Press, 1961.

LINDBLOM, J. *Prophecy in Ancient Israel.* Philadelphia: Fortress Press, 1962.

LONGENECKER, Richard. *Biblical Exegesis in the Apostolic Period.* Grand Rapids, Michigan: Wm. B. Eerdmans Publishing Co., 1975.

McNAMARA, Martin. *The New Testament and the Palestinian Targum to the Pentateuch.* Second printing. Analecta Biblica 27-A. Rome: Biblical Institute Press, 1978.

————. *Targum and Testament. Aramaic Paraphrases of the Hebrew Bible: A Light on the New Testament.* Grand Rapids, Michigan: Wm. B. Eerdmans Publishing Co., 1972.

MANN, Jacob. *The Bible as Read and Preached in the Old Sunagogue I The Palestinian Triennial Cycle: Genesis and Exodus.* Prolegomenon by Ben Zion Wacholder. The Library of Biblical Studies. New York: KTAV Publishing House, 1971.

MEEKS, Wayne A. *The Prophet-King. Moses Traditions and the Johannine Christology.* Supplements to Novum Testamentum XIV. Leiden: E. J. Brill, 1967.

MIELZINER, Moses. *Introduction to the Talmud.* Fourth edition. New York: Bloch Publishing Co., 1968.

MOULE, C. F. D. *Birth of the New Testament.* Harper's New Testament Commentaries. New York: Harper and Row, Publishers, 1962.

NEUSNER, Jacob. *Midrash in Context.* Philadelphia: Fortress Press, 1983.

NICKELSBURG, G. W. E. *Jewish Literature Between the Bible and the Mishnah.* Philadelphia: Fortress Press, 1981.

NOTH, Martin. *The History of Israel.* Second edition. New York: Harper and Row, Publishers, 1960.

O'BRIEN, Peter T. *Introductory Thanksgivings in the Letters of Paul.* Supplements to Novum Testamentum 49. Leiden: E. J. Brill, 1977.

OOSTENDORP, D. W. *Another Jesus: A Gospel of Jewish Christian Superiority in II Corinthians.* Kampen: J. H. Kook N.V., 1967.

PATTE, Daniel. *Early Jewish Hermeneutic in Palestine.* SBL Dissertation Series 22. Missoula, Montana: Scholar's Press, 1975.

PEDERSON, Johannes. *Israel. Its Life and Culture.* Four vols. Vols. I-II, translated by A. Moller. Vols. III-IV, translated by A. Fausboll. Copenhagen: Branner Og Korch, 1954, 1959. Vols. I-II first published in 1926; vols. III-IV first published in 1940.

PETERS, F. E. *The Harvest of Hellenism.* New York: Simon and Schuster, 1970.

RAMSEY, A. M. *The Glory of God and the Transfiguration of Christ.* Libra edition. London: Darton, Longman and Todd, 1949. Libra edition, 1967.

RUSSELL, D. S. *Between the Testaments.* Philadelphia: Fortress Press, 1960.

SANDERS, E. P. *Paul, the Law and the Jewish People.* Philadelphia: Fortress Press, 1984.

SCHMITHALS, Walter. *Die Gnosis in Korinth.* Göttingen: Vandenhoeck and Ruprecht, 1965. English translation, Gnosticism in Corinth. Translated by J. Steely. New York: Abingdon Press, 1971.

SCHNEIDER, B. *Dominus autem Spiritus est: II Cor. 3,17a.* Rome: Officium Libri Catholici, 1951.

SCHOEPS, H. J. *Paul. The Theology of the Apostle in the Light of Jewish Religious History.* Translated by H. Knight. London: Lutterworth Press, 1961.

SCHÜRER, Emil. *The Literature of the Jewish People in the Time of Jesus.* Ed. and introduction by N. H. Glatzer. Translated by Peter Christie and Sophia Taylor. New York: Schocken Books, 1972.

SCHWEIZER, Edward. *Lordship and Discipleship. Studies in Biblical Theology.* Naperville, Illinois: Alec R. Allenson, 1960. First published in 1955.

SCROGGS, Robin. *The Last Adam: A Study in Pauline Anthropology.* Philadelphia: Fortress Press, 1966.

STRACK, H. L. *Introduction to the Talmud and Midrash.* New York: The Jewish Publication Society of America, 1959.

TEEPLE, Howard M. *The Mosaic Eschatological Prophet.* SBL Monographs 10. Philadelphia: Society of Biblical Literature, 1957.

TIEDE, David L. *The Charismatic Figure as Miracle Worker.* SBL Dissertation Series 1. Missoula, Montana: Scholar's Press, 1972.

TOWNER, W. S. *The Rabbinic "Enumeration of the Scriptural Examples."* Studia Post-Biblica. Editor, J. C. H. Lebran. Leiden: E. J. Brill, 1973.

VERMES, Geza. *Discovery in the Judean Desert.* New York: Desclee Company, 1956.

———. *Scripture and Tradition in Judaism.* Leiden: E. J. Brill, 1961.

VON RAD, G. *Old Testament Theology,* two vols. New York: Harper and Row, 1965.

WRIGHT, Addison G. *The Literary Genre Midrash.* Staten Island, New York: Alba House, 1967.

ZIESLER, J. A. *The Meaning of Righteousness in Paul.* Cambridge: The University Press, 1972.

Articles

BAIRD, William. "Letters of Recommendation: A Study of II Cor. 3:1-3." *JBL* 80 (1961) pp. 166-172.

BARRETT, C. K. "Paul's Opponents in II Corinthians." *NTS* 17 (1970-1971) pp. 233-254.

BARTH, G. "Die Eignung des Verkündigers im 2 Kor. 2,14-3,6." *Kirche.* Festschrift for Günther Bornkamm. Ed. D. Lührmann and G. Strecker. Tübingen. Mohr (Siebeck), 1980. Pp. 257-270.

BLOCH, Renée. "Midrash." *Dictionnaire de la Bible.* Supplement 5, 1263-1281. English translation in *Approaches to Ancient Judaism: Theory and Practice.* Ed. W. S. Green. Brown Judaic Studies 1. Missoula, Montana: Scholar's Press, 1978. Pp. 29-50.

———. "Note méthodologique pour l'étude de la littérature rabbinique." *RSR* 43 (1955) pp. 194-227. English translation in *Approaches to Ancient Judaism: Theory and Practice.* Ed. W. S. Green. Brown Judaic Studies 1. Missoula, Montana: Scholar's Press, 1978. Pp. 51-76.

———. "Quelques aspects de la figure de Moise dans la tradition rabbinique." *Cahiers Sioniens* 8 (1954) pp. 221-285. Also published as *Moise. L'homme de l'alliance.* Tournai: Desclée and Co., 1955. Pp. 93-167.

BORNKAMM, Günther. "Die Vorgeschichte des sogenannten Zweiten Korinther-briefs." *Sitzungsberichte der Heidelberger Akademie der Wissenschaften.* Phil-Hist Klasse, 1961-62. Heidelberg: Carl Winter, Universitätsverlag, 1965. English translation in *NTS* 8 (1962) pp. 258-264.

BRING, Ragnar. "Paul and the Old Testament." *Studia Theologica* 25 (1971) pp. 21-60.

CALLAN, Terrance. "Pauline Midrash: The Exegetical Background of Gal. 3:19b." *JBL* 99 (1980) pp. 549-567.

CARREZ, M. "Le 'Nous' en 2 Corinthiens." *NTS* 26 (1980) pp. 474-486.

CAZELLES, Henri. "Moise devant l'histoire." *Moise. L'homme de l'alliance.* Tournai: Desclée and Co., 1955. pp. 11-27.

COHEN, Boaz. "Note on Letter and Spirit in the New Testament." *HTR* 47 (1954) pp. 197-203.

COLLINS, John N. "Georgi's 'Envoys' in 2 Cor. 11:23." *JBL* 93 (1974) pp. 88-96.

CORSSEN, P. "Paulus und Porphyrios zur Erklärung von 2 Kor. 3.18." *ZNTW* 19-20 (1919-1921) pp. 2-10.

DAHL, Nils. "Contradictions in Scripture." *Studies in Paul.* Minneapolis, Minnesota: Augsburg Publishing House, 1977. pp. 159-177.

DODD, C. H. "New Testament Translation Problems II." *Bible Translator* 28 (1977) pp. 110-112.

DUNN, J. D. G. "2 Corinthians III, 17 'The Lord is the Spirit.'" *JThSt* 21 (1970) pp. 309-320.

DUPONT, J. "Le Chrétien, miroir de la gloire divine d'apres II Cor. III, 18." *RB* 56 (1949) pp. 392-411.

ELLIS, E. E. "Paul's Opponents: Trends in Research." *Christianity, Judaism and Other Greco-Roman Cults.* Leiden: E. J. Brill, 1975. pp. 264-298.

FEUILLET, A. "The Christ Image of God According to St. Paul (2 Cor. 4:4)." *Bible Today* 21 (1965) pp. 1409-1414.

FITZMYER, J. A. "Glory Reflected in the Face of Christ (2 Cor. 3:7-4:6) and a Palestinian Jewish Motif." *Theo. Stud.* 72 (1981) pp. 630-644.

FRIEDRICH, G. "Die Gegner des Paulus im 2 Korintherbrief." *Abraham unser Vater.* Festschrift for Otto Michel. Ed. O. Betz, M. Hengel, P. Schmidt. Leiden: E. J. Brill, 1963. pp. 181-215.

GELIN, Albert. "Moise dans l'ancien Testament." *Moise. L'homme de l'alliance.* Tournai: Desclée and Co., 1955. pp. 29-52.

GOETTSBERGER, J. "Die Hülle des Mose nach Ex. 34 und II Cor. 3." *BZ* 16 (1924) pp. 1-17.

GRECH, P. "2 Cor. III, 17 and the Pauline Doctrine of Conversion to the Holy Spirit." *CBQ* 17 (1955) pp. 420-437.

GREENWOOD, D. "The Lord is the Spirit: Some Consideration of 2 Cor. 3:17." *CBQ* 34 (1972) pp. 467-472.

HANSON, A. T. "The Midrash in II Corinthians 3: A Reconsideration." *JSNT* (1980) pp. 2-28.

HARRIS, Rendel. "Enoch and 2 Corinthians." *Expository Times* 33 (1921-1922) pp. 423-424.

HICKLING, C. J. A. "Is the Second Epistle to the Corinthians a Source for Early Church History?" *ZNTW* 66 (1975) pp. 284-287.

HICKLING, C. J. A. "The Sequence of Thought in II Corinthians, Chapter Three." *NTS* 21 (1975) pp. 380-395.

HILL, E. "The Construction of Three Passages From St. Paul." *CBQ* 23 (1961) pp. 296-301.

———. "Beyond the Things that are Written? St. Paul's Use of Scripture." *NTS* 27 (1981) pp. 295-309.

JONES, Peter. "L'Apotre Paul: Un second Moise pour la Communauté de la nouvelle Alliance: Une Etude sur l'autorité apostolique paulinienne." *Foi et Vie* 75 (1976) pp. 36-58.

KÄSEMANN, Ernst, "The Spirit and the Letter." *The New Testament Library. Perspectives on Paul.* Translated by M. Kohl. London: SCM Press, 1971. pp. 138-166.

KENT, H. A. "The Glory of Christian Ministry: An Analysis of 2 Corinthians 2:14-4:18." *Grace Theological Journal* 2 (1980) pp. 171-189.

KRAUSS, S. "The Jewish Rite of Covering the Head." *HUCA* 19 (1945-1946) pp. 121-168.

KREMER, Jacob. "'Denn der Buchstabe toetet der Geist aber macht lebending:' Methodologische und Hermeneutische Erwägungen zu 2 Kor. 3,6b." *Begegnung mit dem Wort.* Festschrift for H. Zimmermann. Ed. J. Zmijewski. Bonn: Peter Hanskin Verlag, 1980, pp. 219-246.

———. "Neueste Methoden der Exegese, dargelegt an 2 Kor. 3,6b." *Theol. Prakt Quart.* 128 (1980) pp. 246-259.

LAMBRECHT, J. "Transformation in 2 Cor. 3,18" *Biblica* 64 (1983) pp. 243-254.

———. "Structure and Line of Thought in 2 Cor 2,14-4,6" *Biblica* 64 (1983) pp. 344-380.

LE DÉAUT, R. "A propos a Definition of Midrash." *Int.* 25 (1971) pp. 259-282.

———. "Traditions targumiques dans le corpus paulinien?" *Biblica* 42 (1961) pp. 28-48.

MARROW, Stanley B., S.J. "*Parrhesia* and the New Testament." *CBQ* 44 (1982) pp. 431-446.

MILLER, Merrill. "Targum, Midrash, and the Use of the OT in the NT." *JSJ* 2 (1971) pp. 29-82.

MORGENSTERN, J. "Moses With the Shining Face." *HUCA* 2 (1925) pp. 1-27.

MOULE, C. F. D. "2 Cor. 3:18b, καθάπερ ἀπὸ κυρίου πνεύματος." *Neues Testament und Geschichte.* Festschrift for Oscar Cullmann. Edited by H. Baltensweiler and B. Reicke. Tübingen: J. C. B. Mohr (Paul Siebeck), 1972. pp. 231-237.

NISIUS, J. B. "Zur Erklarung von 2 Kor. 3, 16ff." *ZKT* 40 (1916) pp. 617-675.

PETERSON, David. "The Prophecy of the New Covenant in the Argument of Hebrews." *The Reformed Theological Review* 38 (1979) pp. 74-81.

PROVENCE, Thomas E. "Who is Sufficient for These Things? An Exegesis of 2 Corinthians 2:15-3:18." *Nov. Test.* 24 (1982) pp. 54-81.

PRÜMM, Karl. "Der Abschnitt über die Doxa des Apostolats 2 Kor. 3,1-4,6 in der Deutung des hl. Chrysostomus: Eine Untersuchung zur Auslegungsgeschichte des paulinischen Pneumas." *Biblica* 30 (1949) pp. 161-196, 377-400.

———. "Israels Kehr zum Geist 2 Kor. 3,17a im Vorstandnis der Erstleser." *ZKT* 72 (1950) pp. 385-442.

———. "Rom. I-II und 2 Kor. 3." *Biblica* 31 (1950) pp. 164-203.

RICHARD, Earl. "Polemics, Old Testament and Theology. A Study of II Cor. III, I-IV, 6." *RB* 88 (1981) pp. 340-367.

RICHARDSON, P. "Spirit and Letter: A Foundation for Hermeneutics." *Evang. Quart.* 45 (1973) pp. 208-218.

SCHARLEMANN, Martin H. "Of Surpassing Splendor. An Exegetical Study of 2 Corinthians 3:4-18." *Concordia Journal* 4 (1978) pp. 108-117.

SCHILDENBERGER, J. "'Der Herr aber ist der Geist,' 2 Kor. 3,17a im Zusammenhang des Textes und der Theologie des hl. Paulus." *Studiorum Paulinorum Congressus I.* Rome, 1961. pp. 451-460.

SCHMITHALS, Walter. "Die Korintherbriefe als Briefsammlung." *ZNTW* 64 (1973) pp. 263-288.

―――. "Zwei gnostische Stellen im zweiten Korintherbrief." *EvTh* 18 (1958) pp. 552-573. English translation, "Two Gnostic Glosses in II Corinthians," *Gnosticism in Corinth.* pp. 315-325.

SCHNEIDER, Bernardin. "The Meaning of St. Paul's Thesis 'The Letter and the Spirit.'" *CBQ* 15 (1953) pp. 163-207.

SCHULZ, S. "Die Decke des Moses — Untersuchungen zu einer vorpaulinischen Überlieferung in 2 Cor. iii 7-18." *ZNTW* 49 (1958) pp. 1-30.

SEGAL, A. F. "Ruler of this World: Attitudes About Mediator Figures and the Importance of Sociology for Self-Definition." *Jewish and Christian Self-Definition II.* Edited by E. P. Sanders with A. I. Baumgarten and A. Mendelson. Philadelphia: Fortress Press, 1981. Pp. 245-268.

SMOLAR, L. and ABERBACH, M. "The Golden Calf Episode in Post-biblical Literature." *HUCA* 39 (1968) pp. 91-116.

THRALL, Margaret E. "Christ Crucified or Second Adam? A Christological Debate Between Paul and the Corinthians." *Christ and Spirit in the New Testament.* Festschrift for C. F. D. Moule. Edited by B. Lindars and S. Smalley. Cambridge: University Press, 1973. Pp. 143-156.

―――. "The Origin of Pauline Christology." *Apostolic History and the Gospel.* Festschrift for F. F. Bruce. Edited by W. W. Gasque and R. P. Martin. Grand Rapids, Michigan: Wm. B. Eerdmans Publishing Co., 1970. pp. 304-316.

ULONSKA, H. "Die Doxa des Mose." *EvTh* 26 (1966) pp. 378-388.

VAN UNNIK, W. C. "La conception paulinienne de la nouvelle alliance." *Litterature et theologie pauliniennes.* Recherches Bibliques V. Brussels: Desclée DeBrouwer, 1960. Pp. 109-126.

―――. "Ἡ καινὴ διαθήκη." *Studia Patristica* IV. Ed., F. L. Cross. Texte und Untersuchungen 79. Berlin: Akademie-Verlag, 1961.

―――. "'With Unveiled Face,' An Exegesis of 2 Corinthians iii 12-18." *Nov. Test.* 6 (1963) pp. 153-169.

VANDERHAEGEN, Jean. "2 Corinthiens 3,1-3." *Bible et Terre Sainte* 68 (1964) pp. 21-23.

VERMES, Geza. "La figure de Moise au tournant des deux testaments." *Moise. L'homme de l'alliance.* Tournai: Desclée and Co., 1955. pp. 63-92.

―――. "Jewish Studies and New Testament Interpretation." *JJS* 31 (1980) pp. 1-17.

VORSTER, W. S. "2 Kor. 3:17: Eksegise en Toeligting." *Neotestamentica* 3 (1969) pp. 37-44.

WRIGHT, N. T. "Adam in Pauline Christology." *Society of Biblical Literature 1983 Seminar Papers.* Edited by K. H. Richards. Chico, California: Scholar's Press, 1983.

Unpublished Materials

JONES, Peter. "The Apostle Paul: A Second Moses According to II Corinthians 2:14-4:7." Ph. D. Dissertation, Princeton Theological Seminary, 1973.
LEVISON, Jack. "New Pseudepigraphical Adam Data and Their Relation to Paul's Theology." Paper read at SBL annual meeting, New York, December, 1982.
STEGNER, W. R. "Romans 9:6-29 — A Midrash." Paper presented to the Midwest Regional Meeting of the SBL, February, 1982.
————. "The Self-Understanding of the Qumran Community Compared with the Self-Understanding of the Early Church." Ph. D. Dissertation, Drew University, 1960.

The Works of the Old Testament in the New Testament

Selected Works

BORGEN, P. *Bread From Heaven.* Supplements to Novum Testamentum 10. Leiden: E. J. Brill, 1965.
————. "Observations on the Targumic Character of the Prologue of John." *NTS* 16 (1970) pp. 288-295.
BOWKER, J. W. "Speeches in Acts: A Study in Proem and Yelammedenu Form." *NTS* 14 (1968) pp. 96-111.
BRUCE, F. F. "The Book of Zechariah and the Passion Narrative." *BJRL* 43 (1960-61) pp. 336-353.
CALLAN, Terrance. "Pauline Midrash: The Exegetical Background of Gal. 3:19b." *JBL* 99 (1980) pp. 549-567.
COMBRINK, H. J. B. "Some Thoughts on the Old Testament Citations in the Epistle to the Hebrews." *Neotestamentica* 5 (1971) pp. 22-36.
CROCKETT, L. "The O. T. in Luke with Emphasis on the Interpretation of Isa. 61:1-2." Ph.D. Dissertation, Brown University, 1966.
DAUBE, D. "The Earliest Structure of the Gospels." *NTS* 5 (1958-59) pp. 174-187.
DERRETT, J. D. M. "2 Cor. 6,14ff. A Midrash on Dt. 22,10." *Biblica* 59 (1978) pp. 231-250.
————. "Law in the N.T. Fresh Light on the Parable of the Good Samaritan." *NTS* 11 (1964) pp. 22-37.
DOEVE, J. W. *Jewish Hermeneutics in the Synoptic Gospels and Acts.* Assen: 1953.
————. "Le role de la tradition orale dans la composition des evangiles synoptiques." *La Formation des evangiles.* Ed. J. Cambier and L. Cerfaux. Brussels: 1957. pp. 70-84.
DUPONT, J. "L'utilisation apologetique de l'Ancien Testament dans les discours des Actes." *EphThL* 29 (1953) pp. 289-327.

FREED, Edwin D. *Old Testament Quotations in the Gospel of John.* Supplements to Novum Testamentum XI. Series editor, W. C. van Unnik. Leiden: E. J. Brill, 1965.

GÄRTNER, B. "The Habakkuk Commentary and the Gospel of Matthew." *Studia Theologica* 8 (1954) pp. 1-25.

GERHARDSSON, B. "The Parable of the Sower and its Interpretation." *NTS* 14 (1967-68) pp. 165-193.

GERTNER, M. "Midrashim in the New Testament." *JSS* 7 (1962) pp. 267-292.

GOLDSMITH, D. "Acts 13:33-37: A Pesher on 2 Sam. 7?" *JBL* 87 (1968) pp. 321-324.

GOULDER, M. D. *Midrash and Lection in Matthew.* London: SPCK, 1974.

GUNDRY, R. H. *The Use of the O.T. in St. Matthew's Gospel.* Supplements to Novum Testamentum 18. Leiden: E. J. Brill, 1967.

HANSON, Anthony T. "John I.14-18 and Exodus XXXIV. *NTS* 23 (1976-77) pp. 90-101.

HARTMAN, Lars. *Prophecy Interpreted: The Formation of Some Jewish Apocalyptic Texts and of the Eschatological Discourse. Mark 13 par.* Translated by Neil Tomkinson. Coniectanea Biblica New Testament Series 1. Uppsala: Almquist and Wiksells, 1966.

LE DÉAUT, R. "Acts 7,48 et Matthieu 17,4 (par.) á la lumière du targum palestinien." *RSR* 52 (1964) pp. 85-90.

LINDARS, B. and Borgen, P. "The Place of the Old Testament in the Formation of New Testament Theology: Prolegomena and Response." *NTS* 23 (1976) pp. 59-75.

MALINA, B. "Matt. 2 and Isa. 41:2-3, a Possible Relationship?" *Studium Biblicum Franciscum* 17 (1967) pp. 291-303.

McCULLOUGH, J. C. "The Old Testament Quotations in Hebrews." *NTS* 26 (1980) pp. 363-379.

MILLER, M. "Targum, Midrash and the Use of the O.T. in the N.T." *JSJ* 2 (1971) pp. 29-82.

PERRIN, N. "Mark 14:62: The End Product of a Christian Pesher Tradition?" *NTS* 12 (1965-66) pp. 150-155.

SMITH, D. Moody. "The Use of the Old Testament in the New." *The Use of the Old Testament in the New and Other Essays.* Festschrift for William F. Stinespring. Ed. James M. Efird. Durham, North Carolina: Duke University Press, 1972. pp. 3-65.

STENDAHL, K. *The School of St. Matthew.* Philadelphia: Fortress Press, 1968.

VERMES, G. "Jewish Studies and N.T, Interpretation." *JJS* 31 (1980) pp. 1-17.

WILCOX, M. "The O.T. in Acts 1-15." *Australian Biblical Review* 5 (1956) pp. 1-41.

WILLER, Arnold. *Der Römerbrief — eine dekalogische Komposition.* Stuttgart: Calwer Verlag, 1981.

WUELLNER, W. "Haggadic Homily Genre in 1 Cor. 1-3." *JBL* 89 (1970) pp. 199-204.

APPENDIX

An Outline of the Greek Text of II Corinthians 3:1-4:6

'Αρχόμεθα πάλιν ἑαυτοὺς συνιστάνειν;
ἢ μὴ χρήζομεν ὥς τινες   συστατικῶν ἐπιστολῶν
                   πρὸς ὑμᾶς ἢ ἐξ ὑμῶν;
                     ἡ ἐπιστολὴ ἡμῶν ὑμεῖς ἐστε,
                     ἐγγεγραμμένη
                           ἐν ταῖς καρδίαις ἡμῶν,
                           γινωσκομένη
               καὶ
                           ἀναγινωσκομένη
                               ὑπὸ πάντων ἀνθρώπων.

φανερούμενοι
     ὅτι ἐστὲ ἐπιστολὴ Χριστοῦ
         διακονηθεῖσα ὑφ' ἡμῶν,
         ἐγγεγραμμένη
            οὐ μέλανι
            ἀλλὰ πνεύματι θεοῦ ζῶντος,
            οὐκ ἐν πλαξὶν λιθίναις
            ἀλλ' ἐν πλαξὶν καρδίας σαρκίναις.
Πεποίθησιν δὲ τοιαύτην ἔχομεν διὰ τοῦ Χριστοῦ πρὸς τὸν θεόν.
οὐχ ὅτι ἀφ' ἑαυτῶν ἱκανοί ἐσμεν
         λογίσασθαί τι
               ὡς ἐξ ἑαυτῶν,
ἀλλ' ἡ ἱκανότης ἡμῶν   ἐκ τοῦ θεοῦ,
  ὃς καὶ ἱκάνωσεν ἡμᾶς
         διακόνους καινῆς διαθήκης,
               οὐ γράμματος
               ἀλλὰ πνεύματος.
    (τὸ γὰρ γράμμα ἀποκτέννει,
     τὸ δὲ πνεῦμα ζῳοποιεῖ.)
Εἰ δὲ ἡ διακονία τοῦ θανάτου
     ἐν γράμμασιν ἐντετυπωμένη λίθοις
  ἐγενήθη ἐν δόξῃ,
         ὥστε μὴ δύνασθαι ἀτενίσαι τοὺς υἱοὺς Ἰσραὴλ εἰς τὸ πρόσωπον
                                                Μωϋσέως
            διὰ τὴν δόξαν τοῦ προσώπου αὐτοῦ
            τὴν καταργουμένην,
πῶς οὐχὶ μᾶλλον ἡ διακονία τοῦ πνεύματος
     ἔσται ἐν δόξῃ;
εἰ γὰρ τῇ διακονίᾳ τῆς κατακρίσεως δόξα,
πολλῷ μᾶλλον περισσεύει ἡ διακονία τῆς δικαιοσύνης δόξῃ.

(καὶ γὰρ οὐ δεδόξασται τὸ δεδοξασμένον
ἐν τούτῳ τῷ μέρει
            εἵνεκεν   τῆς ὑπερβαλλούσης δόξης ·)
εἰ γὰρ τὸ καταργούμενον διὰ δόξης,
πολλῷ μᾶλλον τὸ μένον ἐν δόξῃ.
    Ἔχοντες οὖν τοιαύτην ἐλπίδα
    πολλῇ παρρησίᾳ χρώμεθα,
καὶ οὐ καθάπερ Μωϋσῆς
            ἐτίθει κάλυμμα ἐπὶ τὸ πρόσωπον αὐτοῦ,
            πρὸς τὸ μὴ ἀτενίσαι τοὺς υἱοὺς Ἰσραὴλ
                    εἰς τὸ τέλος τοῦ καταργουμένου.
    ἀλλὰ ἐπωρώθη τὰ νοήματα αὐτῶν.
    ἄχρι γὰρ τῆς σήμερον ἡμέρας
        τὸ αὐτὸ κάλυμμα
                ἐπὶ τῇ ἀναγνώσει
                        τῆς παλαιᾶς διαθήκης
    μένει
            μὴ ἀνακαλυπτόμενον,
                    ὅτι ἐν Χριστῷ καταργεῖται ·
    ἀλλ'
            ἕως σήμερον
    ἡνίκα ἂν ἀναγινώσκηται
                        Μωϋσῆς
            κάλυμμα
                ἐπὶ τὴν καρδίαν αὐτῶν
            κεῖται ·
    ἡνίκα δὲ ἐὰν ἐπιστρέψῃ πρὸς κύριον,
    περιαιρεῖται τὸ κάλυμμα.
            ὁ δὲ κύριος τὸ πνεῦμά ἐστιν ·
            οὗ δὲ τὸ πνεῦμα κυρίου,
                    ἐλευθερία.
ἡμεῖς δὲ πάντες
    ἀνακεκαλυμμένῳ προσώπῳ
            τὴν δόξαν κυρίου κατοπτριζόμενοι
            τὴν αὐτὴν εἰκόνα μεταμορφούμεθα
                            ἀπὸ δόξης
                                εἰς δόξαν,
        καθάπερ
            ἀπὸ κυρίου πνεύματος.
Διὰ τοῦτο,
            ἔχοντες τὴν διακονίαν ταύτην,
                    καθὼς ἠλεήθημεν,
    οὐκ ἐγκακοῦμεν,
    ἀλλὰ ἀπειπάμεθα τὰ κρυπτὰ τῆς αἰσχύης,
            μὴ περιπατοῦντες ἐν πανουργίᾳ
            μηδὲ δολοῦντες τὸν λόγον τοῦ θεοῦ,

ἀλλὰ τῇ φανερώσει τῆς ἀληθείας
  συνιστάνοντες ἑαυτοὺς
   πρὸς πᾶσαν συνείδησιν ἀνθρώπων
   ἐνώπιον τοῦ θεοῦ.
εἰ δὲ καὶ ἔστιν κεκαλυμμένον τὸ εὐαγγέλιον ἡμῶν,
  ἐν τοῖς ἀπολλυμένοις
   ἐστὶν κεκαλυμμένον,
  ἐν οἷς
   ὁ θεὸς τοῦ αἰῶνος τούτου
   ἐτύφλωσεν τὰ νοήματα
  τῶν ἀπίστων
   εἰς τὸ μὴ αὐγάσαι τὸν φωτισμὸν
     τοῦ εὐαγγελίου
     τῆς δόξης τοῦ Χριστοῦ,
      ὅς ἐστιν εἰκὼν
       τοῦ θεοῦ.
οὐ γὰρ ἑαυτοὺς κηρύσσομεν
  ἀλλὰ Ἰησοῦν Χριστὸν κύριον,
   ἑαυτοὺς δὲ δούλους ὑμῶν
    διὰ Ἰησοῦν.
ὅτι ὁ θεὸς ὁ εἰπών,
   Ἐκ σκότους
    φῶς λάμψει,
  ὅς ἔλαμψεν ἐν ταῖς καρδίαις ἡμῶν
   πρὸς φωτισμὸν τῆς γνώσεως
    τῆς δόξης τοῦ θεοῦ
     ἐν προσώπῳ Χριστοῦ.

This Greek text is taken from *The Greek New Testament*, Third Edition. Edited by K. Aland, M. Black, C. Martini, B. Metzger and A. Wikgren (New York: American Bible Society, 1975).

INDEX OF BIBLICAL CITATIONS

INDEX OF REFERENCES TO MODERN AUTHORS

TIPOGRAFIA POLIGLOTTA DELLA PONTIFICIA UNIVERSITÀ GREGORIANA
PIAZZA DELLA PILOTTA, 4 - ROMA